Modern Americana

Modern Americana

STUDIO FURNITURE
FROM HIGH CRAFT TO HIGH GLAM

EDITED BY
Todd Merrill
Julie V. Iovine

TEXTS BY
Jeffrey Head
Julie V. Iovine
Erin Johnson
Roberta Maneker
Todd Merrill
Peter Wolf

RIZZOLI
NEW YORK

CONTENTS

INTRODUCTION

There is a tradition in American furniture of individual expression in cabinet-making that dates back to the Colonial period: small shops and itinerant makers creating specially commissioned furniture that defined their era, their region, and their own style. In New York City, there was Duncan Phyfe, a Scottish emigrant who transformed cabinetmaking into a fledgling furniture-making industry, and the Herter brothers, originally from Stuttgart, Germany, whose upholstery warehouse evolved into the most important post–Civil War interior-decorating company in the country. Additionally, there was the Dunlap family of New Hampshire and the Goddard-Townsend furniture dynasty of Newport, Rhode Island, which made the ball-and-claw motif their own. They were all well known as producers of custom designs for wealthy clients who wanted to distinguish their status with styles emulating a refined European sensibility.

In the second half of the twentieth century, the tradition of furniture making was transformed by another explosion of innovation and by an influx of styles, which combined influences from around the world and were created by new Americans—many of them emigrant designers—eager to express their creative visions freely just as their predecessors had in the eighteenth and nineteenth centuries. This new wave of individual design and craftsmanship started with studio artisans who rejected the mass production of the machine age and the art-deco style, as well as the heavy industrial-flavored ornamentation of the Victorian era. Instead they embraced the natural qualities of wood and freely pursued sculptural forms. Even more, they cultivated a pared-down way of living and were devoted to a pure and simple philosophy inspired by early New England Americans, in addition to the Shakers, that ultimately evolved into the beginning of a new movement toward art furniture.

At the same time, small custom factories and shops began to appear producing high-end decorative furniture unlike anything that had been seen before.

OPPOSITE PAGE T. H. Robsjohn-Gibbings designed this dining room in the Davis residence in Palm Springs, California, in 1958.

These innovative designer-makers, whether they were refugees from Europe or from small-town America, migrated to the big cities to express new looks for the twentieth century that were not only influenced by modernism but were also distinctly artistic and decorative, often incorporating disparate new techniques, materials, and cultural influences. This was a specifically American design phenomenon, one that has not been duplicated anywhere else.

Americana is a term that has been used to describe American folk and decorative arts and furniture. It dates back to the earliest days of the pilgrim era and forward to the twentieth century. While modernism in the design sense originated in Europe, the tradition of small-scale production of high-end furniture by artist-craftsmen who designed, built, and controlled the production of their furniture is a particularly strong American paradigm. In the postwar period, there was a flowering fertilized by both European and American movements. It is my belief that the small studios and custom design factories—where individual designer-craftsmen could support careers giving life to their own innovative often technologically advanced visions while finding an appreciative audience of patrons (sometimes extending to a wider public)—are a natural extension of the earlier tradition of small-scale furniture making in America from the eighteenth and nineteenth centuries.

In the early nineties, the revival of interest in midcentury modernism focused primarily on mass-production designers and manufacturers, such as Charles and Ray Eames, George Nelson, Eero Saarinen, Herman Miller, and Knoll. The names of once-famous designers of expensive high-concept furniture—James Mont, Tommi Parzinger, Karl Springer, and others—emerged more slowly toward the end of the nineties, as they attracted the attention of a few dealers

with shops dedicated to the best of decorative custom design, among them Lost City Arts, 280 Modern, Modern One, Liz O'Brien, Alan Moss, and my own Todd Merrill Antiques.

Auction houses were also just starting to take notice of these high-end anomalies: Christie's September 1999 sale on behalf of the Elsie de Wolfe Foundation and the May 2000 sale of the Billy Wilder estate were trigger events and the works of many of the designers and artisans in this book were featured in those sales. Additionally, there were some very important related exhibitions and catalogues produced. In particular, *The Maker's Hand: American Studio Furniture, 1940–1990,* was a seminal exhibition with an accompanying catalogue mounted by the Museum of Fine Arts in Boston that opened in November 2003. It was the first show to comprehensively address and define the modern studio-art movement in America.

Most of the studio artists mentioned in this book were included in that exhibition. *The Maker's Hand* defined studio furniture as work created by an individual who never crossed the line into contract work or mass production. However, both Vladimir Kagan and George Nakashima were included in the exhibition and were located "on the blurry boundary between studio work and contract production." It is easy to see why: both employed a good many craftsmen. Kagan ran a business with his father, a cabinetmaker who emigrated from Germany and started a small factory workshop on the East Side of Manhattan. Nakashima attracted craftsmen who remained loyal to him for decades. According to curator Gerald Ward's essay, both artists still adhered to the basic tenets of the early studio furniture makers, "maintaining individual control over the process of fabrication from beginning to end, from the mind of the creator to the home of the consumer."

ABOVE A Lucite and glass coffee table by Karl Springer, c. 1975.

OPPOSITE PAGE LEFT A welded steel, copper and slate top dining table made for the artist William Katz by Paul Evans, c. 1963. **RIGHT** The Graham residence designed by Vladimir Kagan in the early 1950s.

ABOVE LEFT A Jack Rogers Hopkins Two-piece chair-table, c. 1970. **RIGHT** A sculpted steel wall mounted cabinet by Paul Evans, 1968.

OPPOSITE PAGE LEFT Robsjohn-Gibbings's Madison Avenue showroom in 1938. **RIGHT** A J. B. Blunk stool made of cypress, 1963.

Modern Americana crosses that blurry line even further. It showcases designers and craftsmen of unique individual vision who maintained aesthetic control over their process from start to finish whether an item was hewn by hand or executed by a small staff, or even produced in a small factory. This group of designers has been identified and recognized by the secondary marketplace of auction houses and dealers. Much like art, these craftsmen have been validated by continued interest from collectors—and escalating prices—and their work has been documented and collected by an expanding international audience.

In the early 1990s, the taste for midcentury modern, both studio furniture and decorative modern furnishings, developed rapidly as the economy expanded to include a younger audience with significant discretionary incomes and open-minded stylistic preferences. Not saddled with inherited collections and the acquired tastes of their elders, many of these youthful and wealthy buyers turned away in droves from so-called Brown furniture and heavy Victorian and early American, English, and Continental period pieces. (Plus there were those who gravitated to the secondary market in midcentury modern because it was either what their parents had bought when it was originally produced or they were returning as retirees to the most exciting styles of their own youth.) It seemed that everyone wanted to "freshen" their interior with a modern sensibility. Anything rectilinear and postwar in white lacquer with silver hardware would sell, and dealers were often only too eager to please by painting everything white for the so-called "revival look."

Almost in concert, dealers, auction houses, and journalists began to explore and resurrect many forgotten or retired artists, championing them and researching them on their own to provide the needed background information

and scholarship to satisfy collectors and curious buyers. Among these dealers were Pat Palumbo who started to sell vintage Tommi Parzinger designs, and, in 1999, joined Donald Cameron who had worked with Parzinger for many years to issue reproductions. In March 1997, a solo exhibition, *Edward Wormley: the Other Face of Modernism,* at the Lin-Weinberg Gallery in New York brought Wormley to wider public attention. Liz O'Brien spent a decade researching Chicago architect and designer Samuel Marx and published the first monograph on his work in 2007. On the West Coast, Gerard O'Brien was instrumental in reintroducing the work of J. B. Blunk and other California studio artisans through his Reform Gallery in Los Angeles.

Decorating magazines and newspaper journalists published the first researched articles in years on forgotten designer-craftsmen from T. H. Robsjohn-Gibbings and Paul Evans to Vladimir Kagan and John Dickinson. At the same time the rise of the Internet and, in particular, 1stdibs.com, a Web site that has by now signed on almost every major dealer in America, were able to present the freshest high-end antique and vintage merchandise available to a worldwide audience. This gave tremendous exposure instantly to a new collecting category in midcentury design launching it to the forefront of the antique and vintage furniture marketplace in spite of the limited documentation.

The auction houses have also responded and grown around this new category, particularly Wright Auctions in Chicago and Sollo Rago Auctions in Lambertville, Pennsylvania. They have devoted major sales to mid- and late-twentieth-century modern, selling the very best of the category even as the traditional houses, Sotheby's, Phillips, and Christie's, have caught up quickly to include this new category in their sales as well. As a result, items that ten years ago would have been considered nice used furniture by most experts and passed over are now regularly featured in twentieth-century decorative-art sales.

ABOVE LEFT The Griffin table, c. 1939, is from Robsjohn-Gibbings's most important commission: the Weber residence in Bel Air, California. RIGHT A Wharton Esherick sideboard, 1961.

OPPOSITE PAGE Ellis Orlowitz's Asian-themed bar room design by James Mont in 1963.

PREVIOUS PAGE William Haines designed many of Joan Crawford's homes; the photo was taken in 1949 after Haines updated her Brentwood home, incorporating Haines's pieces like the free-form ottoman and the Elbow chairs. This marks the transition from 1930s colonial revival to 1940s modern.

The audience for modern Americana is international. Collectors from Europe and Asia are competing to purchase the best of these artists' work for the first time. This is a new phenomenon. In the past it was always Americans buying European furniture and importing it to the United States. Never had a European audience seen value in buying Americana. The primary reason for this is that Europeans have traditionally considered American regional furniture derivative of their own European styles and as such provincial. This is not the case, however, with Americana of the mid- to late-twentieth century. Two of the best and earliest exhibitions of American designer furniture took place in Paris in 2004. The first was an exhibition devoted to Paul Evans's work curated by Francois Klein at Galerie Patrick Fourtin; the second was an exhibition with an accompanying catalogue of the work of James Mont at the Eric Philippe Galerie. These two shows were highly successful, garnering press and contributing greatly to the early understanding in Europe of American modern designers.

From the studio furniture makers to the designer-craftsmen with small factories and the decorator-designers who produced custom furniture, the postwar era in America witnessed an awakening in American furniture design that was anything but derivative. Stimulated by an affluent clientele of like-minded individuals who were searching for nontraditional furnishings to celebrate their success, this new wave ranged from imaginative craft to spectacularly designed elegant, artistic, and sculptural furniture. In this book—as in the current collecting market for this period—the featured furniture makers with few exceptions are all men. However, it is worth noting that many of the clients who discovered, commissioned, and encouraged their work were women. Increasingly as we evaluate this era from a new vantage point, the question becomes, what is furniture and what is art?

THE STUDIO ARTISANS

J. B. Blunk

Arthur Espenet Carpenter

Wendell Castle

Michael Coffey

Wharton Esherick

Jack Rogers Hopkins

Sam Maloof

The modern studio-furniture movement began with Wharton Esherick, a woodworker-craftsman, and his America at Home exhibition at the New York World's Fair in 1940. Born in 1887, Esherick began to make furniture in the 1920s coming out of the Arts & Crafts movement and working against the tubular steel modernism of the deco era. For the World's Fair, which was viewed by millions, Esherick produced dramatic high-concept furniture in a cubist style. A staircase reinstalled from his own home was a disjointed abstract rendering in primitive wood with echoes of Duchamp's 1912 painting *Nude Descending a Staircase.* Esherick's asymmetrical forms and free-flowing organic style catapulted studio furniture from the realm of the isolated, regional cabinetmaker to that of the appreciative mass audience, and his work contributed to a post–World War II revival of the Arts & Crafts movement, while it also paved the way for such designer-craftsmen as George Nakashima, Wendell Castle, Sam Maloof, and Arthur Espenet Carpenter.

Early stylistic touchstones in the 1950s came primarily from imported Danish-modern design and from early-American styles and the work of the Shakers. The studio-furniture movement began on the East Coast, but a vibrant and highly artistic group started forming on the West Coast around 1960. In terms of aesthetic sensibility, the two groups have sometimes been played off each other as the East Coast "hard-edge" versus the California "roundover." From the latter group, we showcase the work of Arthur Espenet Carpenter, Sam Maloof, Jack Rogers Hopkins, and J. B. Blunk.

Esherick was one of the first among furniture artisans to make a career and a living from his craft, creating unique work by hand in a small studio essentially by himself. Inspired by a visit to Esherick's home in Paoli, Pennsylvania, Wendell Castle took up woodworking in the late fifties and developed a unique

method of sculpting stacked and laminated wood creating forms that were first inspired by Scandinavian modern but quickly diverged into an organic style all their own. The output of true independent artisans was very limited—during a lifetime of work they would typically produce no more than one thousand pieces.

All of the designers included in this group turned to craft as a way of having an independent life and making a living from art. Michael Coffey did not drop out; he found a meaningful new life in cabinetmaking after a career as a social worker. Jack Rogers Hopkins, whose work can be compared to Castle's, also worked primarily in stacked-laminated wood producing highly sculptural furniture with a fantastic imaginative quality. J. B. Blunk, working in northern California, was a true rebel and a one-man show as well, sculpting giant cuts of wood with a chain saw. Many of his furniture pieces are so monumental in size and dimension that they defy being moved. Working with their hands and creating a personal vision, these were self-taught men who chose an alternative way of life and reached a level of expertise comparable to any artist.

ABOVE LEFT Sam Maloof's cherry and ebony rocking chair, 1997. **RIGHT** Michael Coffey's Satan's Tongue II made of African Mozambique, 1992.

OPPOSITE PAGE LEFT Wharton Esherick's studio stairwell made in the late twenties at his retrospective at the Museum of Contemporary Craft, 1958. **RIGHT** Michael Coffey, c. 1970, using a chainsaw to carve one of his pieces.

THE DESIGNER-CRAFTSMEN

Paul Evans
Vladimir Kagan
George Nakashima
Phillip Lloyd Powell
Silas Seandel

Designer-craftsmen often began work as artisans in the Esherick mold, but along with success they crossed the line to small studios, contract production, and even small factory manufacturing. This transformation came gradually, a natural outcome not only of individual ambitions but also as a result of heady opportunities that presented themselves in the booming postwar years. In every case, however, no matter how close to large-scale production they came, these furniture makers inevitably continued to define themselves as artists or artisans. From George Nakashima—who learned to carve from a traditional Japanese wood-carver while in an American internment camp and ultimately operated a workshop with no more than fifteen assistants, according to his daughter Mira Nakashima-Yarnall—to Vladimir Kagan who considered himself primarily a designer rather than a cabinetmaker like his father, these designer-craftsmen found success pushed them over the line of the simple crafts-person to a more streamlined level of production. This group is distinguished by the way their hands-on work escalated to a level of what might be called a craft factory, employing many hands—in the case of Evans, nearly one hundred workers. At the same time, they never sacrificed their exacting standards of craftsmanship nor their intense personal involvement with each and every individual piece made in their name.

Yet the line between designer and craftsman remains blurry. Any attempt at exact categorization is less important when the secondary market is as enthusiastic about innovative design experiments as it is about single works. Nakashima's furniture can command record-breaking prices at auction (in June 2007, Sotheby's in London sold Nakashima's Minguren II dining table for £150,000), but so can Castle's early experiments in plastic, which have recently been reintroduced as limited-edition collection pieces. Phillip Powell

began as a pure studio furniture maker, but at midcareer he partnered with the ambitious Paul Evans ending up in a place he did not want to be—working for a small factory—so he returned to what he loved, making one piece at a time, at his own pace, for a highly appreciative and select clientele. Silas Seandel did not define himself as an artist or as a craftsman or take a traditional artisan's approach. He just liked to make sculptures by welding metal, and department stores and design venues (he didn't approach museums or galleries) seemed eager to buy them. His move to furniture was almost incidental, a way to thwart copycats, but like most of the designer-craftsmen, private commissions on a piece by piece basis or an installation, which called for several pieces to work in concert, was the common approach to production.

ABOVE LEFT Silas Seandel's Sunspots wall sculpture, 1969. **RIGHT** A carved walnut fireplace by Phillip Lloyd Powell, 1956–58.

OPPOSITE PAGE LEFT A wing armchair by Kagan-Dreyfuss, Inc., c. 1959. **RIGHT** George Nakashima with daughter, Mira, in his New Hope, Pennsylvania, workshop, 1952.

THE CUSTOM DESIGNERS

Charles Hollis Jones
Philip & Kelvin LaVerne
James Mont
Tommi Parzinger
Harvey Probber
T. H. Robsjohn-Gibbings
Karl Springer
Edward Wormley

Custom designers aimed for an even higher level of professionalism. They, too, worked primarily on private commissions, but the distance between themselves and their individual clients began to stretch even farther as they tried new ways to expand their audience. Almost as soon as he arrived from Germany in 1935, Tommi Parzinger was making ceramics for avant-garde shopkeeper Rena Rosenthal's store window on Madison Avenue. Philip and Kelvin LaVerne would at first seem to be a natural fit as designer-craftsmen: Philip trained at the New York City's Art Students League and presented his cast-bronze cabinets, made using a centuries-old casting techniques in collaboration with his son Kelvin, as functional art. But the difference was that rather than make a piece at the request of an individual client—although they did plenty of that—the LaVernes opened a showroom-gallery and had a catalogue from which customers could pick and choose from a series of set designs. Later they even sold through the Baker Furniture Company.

An intense entrepreneurial curiosity characterizes many of the men in this book, especially among the custom designers for whom recognition as innovators more than success making money was the ultimate prize. As a group, however, the custom designers were especially fond of high-style living. It is noteworthy that most of their furnishings were high cost in terms of conceptual effort, labor involved, and materials used and consequently they were never inexpensive to buy. In the fifties, an armoire by Parzinger could easily cost over $2,300, a princely sum for contemporary furniture. While the custom designers Tommi Parzinger, James Mont, Edward Wormley, and T. H. Robsjohn-Gibbings created complete interiors, their emphasis was first and foremost on the individual piece of furniture as a stunning showpiece. This approach to furniture over interiors distinguishes them from the next group of decorator-designers whose focus was on the complete integration of furnishings within a specific interior space.

For the custom designer, the furniture was the star vehicle. Harvey Probber was prolific, designing one hit after another, and after developing the complex design and construction of the Sling chair (1949), he took out a patent for it. Relationships with forward-looking showrooms and small manufacturers, like the Charak Company of Boston, which worked with Parzinger, and Edward J. Wormley's longtime association with Dunbar Furniture, Inc., played significant roles in encouraging entrepreneurial ambition and shaping design direction. The trajectory of these designers often followed the same line: Start out making a singular piece that attracts attention (or catches the eye of a pivotal client; the Duchess of Windsor is said to have discovered Karl Springer), this leads to more demand and wider opportunities for display at a showroom or department store, then as demand for the product increases bring in additional help to complete the orders. And after World War II, especially in New York City, there was a great workforce of available, well-trained artisans to hire.

The more creative the designer, the more tempting to experiment with the new materials—Charles Hollis Jones and his plastics come to mind. Constant curiosity about new opportunities created by new techniques naturally led to enlisting a widening range of talent and technicians. Karl Springer went smoothly from versions of Emile-Jacques Ruhlmann-inspired deco classics to inventing truly original works of carved Lucite. But entrepreneurial zeal could lead to disaster as well: James Mont is the only designer in this book to be a prison habitué, though more than a few skated close to bankruptcy and financial ruin. For all, artistic talent was the commodity at play. And when they died, the production of their work in all but one or two cases (T. H. Robsjohn-Gibbings's exceptionally stringent standards facilitated his original company's ability to rigorously maintain continuous production) came to an end.

ABOVE LEFT Charles Hollis Jones in the workshop, c. 1968. **RIGHT** A Karl Springer coffee table wrapped in python, 1985.

OPPOSITE PAGE The Elrod House in Palm Springs, California, was designed in 1969 and featured many pieces by Charles Hollis Jones. This photo was taken in 2006 for a *Dwell* magazine event celebrating home design in which most of the furniture was replaced with Hollis Jones pieces.

PREVIOUS SPREAD LEFT Charles Hollis Jones's acrylic coffee table, c. 1970. **CENTER** A silver and gold metal leaf console for the Kety residence of Picayune, Mississippi, by James Mont, c. 1950. **RIGHT** Tommi Parzinger's Madison Avenue showroom, c. 1940.

THE DECORATOR-DESIGNERS

John Dickinson
Arthur Elrod
William Haines
Paul Laszlo
Samuel Marx

In the context of design creativity where the intensity of a vision is particularly singular, it is often impossible to isolate the individual piece from its environment. This is the case with the decorator-designers who may at first appear as if they do not share much common ground with the studio artists in this book. But they are, in fact, very much a part of the same impulse to take creative risks in the areas of design and architecture, which were expanding faster in the mid-twentieth century than there was time to define who was being truly artistic and who was not. It is the argument of this book that this period in America represents an unprecedented moment when it was possible to find success being inventive at many different levels.

The decorator-designers approached their work as total environments. Sometimes trained as architects or interior designers, they created spaces and then filled them with objects of their own invention, controlling every detail down to the accessories. While several decorator-designers operated workshops along the lines of the ones run by James Mont or Vladimir Kagan, in his later years, they tended more generally to establish close relationships with outside makers, some were very close. In Chicago, Samuel Marx worked almost exclusively with the distinguished antique-furniture-reproduction company William J. Quigley. For Marx and Quigley, artistic vision was as likely to be expressed through the texture of a wall and the selection of a unique flooring material as it was through the choice of a chair or table—they were composed together. And when clients approached them with commissions for homes, offices, and store interiors, they expected what might be called inhabitable works of art.

A sense of innovation and experimentation separates these decorator-designers from more pedestrian professionals. William Haines invented the Hollywood Regency style; Arthur Elrod laminated fabrics; John Dickinson brought a kind of decorator surrealism to his interiors with his blanched white animal limbs. Though the scale of work was often large—houses, department stores, headquarters—control was not relaxed. For individual furnishings, prototypes would be rigorously inspected to maintain the highest level of execution.

Decorator-designers worked in response to a forward-thinking, nontraditional, and wealthy clientele, many of whom were art collectors, who wanted better quality furnishings and interiors that would distinguish them from the masses. This brought about a reemphasis on "artistic" decorative furniture making and interiors where the aim was always to create a unique, incomparable experience. These interiors and the furnishings designed for them were often less overtly ostentatious than the work of the custom designers. But do not mistake the subtle yet plush designs and neutral palettes for anything other than the highest level of luxury in furnishings attainable at the time.

ABOVE LEFT A living room in a state-of-the-art Los Angles home designed by William Haines in 1950. **RIGHT** A vellum covered cabinet designed by Samuel Marx, c. 1940.

OPPOSITE PAGE LEFT A pair of parchment and painted plaster African table lamps by John Dickinson, c. 1980. **RIGHT** Paul László's Dali console table designed and named after László's friend Salvador Dalí, c. 1950.

These four groups of furniture producers represented a new creative emergence made possible in America at a moment when progressive ideas, prosperity, and talent all converged. The studio artisans and small custom shops that produced furniture for these designers were a direct response to—even a reaction against—the prevalent mass production and factory-produced furniture that became so readily available in the postwar period and furnished the homes of the lower and middle classes. The postwar consumer in America needed to rid himself of the memory of wartime shortages. Affluent emigrants from war-torn Europe felt the need to distance themselves from their traditional pasts and embrace new decorative styles of furniture and interiors that had nothing to do with traditional "Colonial"-derived design or with their own European traditions. They wanted to represent their new and successful American lives. This was the customer of Paul Evans, Karl Springer, the studio artists, and the forward-thinking decorator-designers.

In the early 1990s the initial rage for midcentury modern design that swept the high end of the market gave way to a rediscovery of recently forgotten high-end decorative and craft designers as decorators and their clients became increasingly sophisticated. The names of designers—some that had retired from business only a decade or so before such as George Nakashima, Vladimir Kagan, and John Dickinson—were on the "it" list for trendsetters, high-end interior designers, and taste arbiters of the fashionable world. (Designer Tom Ford, when he was creative director at Gucci, almost single-handedly revived interest in Vladimir Kagan, bringing him out of retirement to produce the Omnibus, when he bought one for each of the 360 Gucci stores worldwide.)

Once these designers were rediscovered as creative makers of a new stripe, a wave of collecting their relatively affordable work followed almost immediately,

paving the way, in part, for the current focus on art furniture. Over the past decade the interest in collecting this period has become increasingly serious and prices at auction for the best and rarest pieces produced by many of the designers in this book have reached into the six figures.

Interest and auction prices notwithstanding, still very little documentation exists to put these designers and their designs in a historical context. There is no overview of the period that takes into account the scope of work produced by studio artisans, custom production shops, and small informal factories. Most of the artists included in this book are not living. Luckily, we still have Vladimir Kagan, Wendell Castle, Michael Coffey, Silas Seandel, Kelvin LaVerne, Charles Hollis Jones, and Sam Maloof. Wherever possible we conducted the most extensive interviews possible about their work, life, and career. Phillip Powell passed away in February 2008 after being interviewed for this book. Some of the designers included have been more extensively documented and exhibited over the years, among them George Nakashima, Wendell Castle, Vladimir Kagan, Sam Maloof, Billy Haines, and Samuel Marx. Recent and forthcoming monographs are only beginning to make them accessible to the general public. Out of the twenty-seven artists discussed herein, only a handful now have books or catalogues devoted to their work. The rest can only be found in contemporaneous periodicals or in museum libraries that hold original archives. In some cases, as with T. H. Robsjohn-Gibbings, Karl Springer, James Mont, and Tommi Parzinger, among many others, the only documentation that remains are traces of their estates and former businesses.

Modern Americana was written in an effort to identify and document the studio, decorative, and custom art furniture of the period from 1940 through the 1990s. In offering a cross section of the best custom-furniture artisans

ABOVE LEFT A drawing of a restaurant by Tommi Parzinger, c. 1955. **RIGHT** A Paul László designed and F. F. Kern executed table made of Lucite embedded with metallic Lurex on a painted and sculpted wood base from the Hudspeth collection of Prineville, Oregon, c. 1950.

OPPOSITE PAGE LEFT From Wendell Castle's Trompe l'oeil series, a Purpleheart wood table with gloves and keys, 1981. **RIGHT** A silver metal leaf and mirrored screen by Phillip Lloyd Powell, c. 2000.

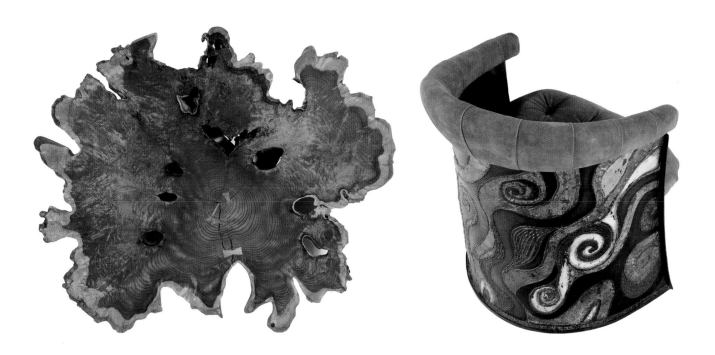

ABOVE LEFT The free-form edge, redwood burl top of the Arlyn table by George Nakashima, 1988. **RIGHT** A unique club chair in patinated steel and colorfully abstract designs by Paul Evans, c. 1965.

OPPOSITE PAGE LEFT An Asian figure lamp in gilded ceramic, wood, paper, and carved plaster with a gold leaf finish by James Mont, c. 1950. **RIGHT** A low Lotus table with a Chinoiserie carved apron on a beautifully carved column pedestal and lotus motif base by James Mont from the Ellis Orlowitz collection, 1963.

and designers—in particular, the ones who have been discovered by the secondary marketplace and are now avidly collected—Modern Americana is not defining a style or a singular moment in time as much as it is identifying an attitude and an approach, a confluence of serendipitous forces and chance opportunities. There is still much to be discovered about this magical period in design when the greatest economic boom of the modern age was concentrated in postwar America, and artistic talent came together with old-world skill, with access to new technology and materials, in order to provide for the exploding population of the baby boom. The resonances go even deeper as old-world craftsmanship and traditional styles melded with the youthful ideologies of the counterculture, rock and roll, Hollywood celebrity, fashion, and even disco influences bringing about a new freedom of expression in design that had not been seen before.

Thanks to their diversity and unexpected forms, these designs are triggering mounting interest in the lesser-known area of a familiar period. Already their influence is inspiring our residential and commercial interiors, art, and custom furniture, as well as the large furniture retailers and catalogues that are the keepers of mass good taste. The full range of the innovative, decorative, and artistic furniture designs of postwar America is only beginning to unfold. But the potential power of these designers and artisans to have a significant and far-reaching influence can already be seen in the growing acceptance and even reverence for the creative impulse of these rare and expressive furnishings and interiors designs as we move deeper into the twenty-first century.

It occurred to me early that the studio and decorative artists of the postwar period constituted a new era in the tradition of Americana and American cabinetmaking. This conclusion was a natural one for me as I had been steeped

in the trade of early-American furniture since childhood and my fascination with this period is rooted personally and professionally in my experience with the evolving history of American design.

In 2000, I opened a small antique, vintage furniture and lighting shop called Todd Merrill Antiques on the Lower East Side of Manhattan. Though artists and musicians had already colonized the area, it was still a marginal, emerging neighborhood and not necessarily a place you would expect to find high-end furniture. I had had it with the corporate world and wanted to break out and establish a small commercial venture, a direction that was hardly unexpected since my family had been in the antiques business with a special interest in Americana for three generations. Growing up in Burlington, Vermont, I had learned the trade at the hands of my grandparents, Nathan and Margaret Merrill, and my auctioneer dad, Duane. Family discussions over dinner often centered on a piece of furniture, vetting its provenance and arguing its authenticity. Such an all-encompassing education had me running my grandparents' shop when I was just fourteen. In my late twenties, I went to work for Christie's in New York as Public Relations Director and got a broad look at the full scope of the high-end antiques trade.

Establishing my own shop was the obvious next step, but my tastes had changed and traditional American furniture was no longer my focus. At the time, the revival of interest in midcentury modern furniture revolved primarily around the manufactured furniture designed by Charles and Ray Eames, George Nelson, and other designers who were dedicated to mass production. But to me, the look remained cold and dated. I was simply not interested in fancy office furniture.

Across the street from my shop was another shop called Los Venus, which
sold a crazy combination of anything pop, cult, or vintage from the fifties to
the eighties. In that mix I began to notice some very high-end, high-concept
furniture by designers with names like James Mont, Paul Evans, and Tommi
Parzinger. Little was known about these designers and their work back then.
In fact, the makers could only be identified if their furniture was signed.

In December 2000, Jean-Yves LeGrand, a flamboyant French dealer and
renowned stylist with vintage shops in Miami and Sag Harbor was closing
his Sag Harbor shop for the winter and offered me his inventory to sell in my
shop. I was just beginning to look for stock so it was a huge and generous
break for me as a new dealer. LeGrand supplemented my space on the corner
of Ludlow and Stanton streets with a fantastic mix of mid- and late-twentieth-century furniture and lighting. At that stage, my dealer instincts kicked
in quickly and whatever the decorators and clients responded to I went out
in search for more. Within months my shop was filled with my own unique
collection. When I went to research these makers, however, I found little or
no published material on them. This book grew out of my need as a dealer to
document the furniture and the makers that I was collecting and selling.
I waited five years for someone to publish a book that would cover this area
and as nothing comprehensive emerged, I decided to produce one myself
based on my own experience.

—TODD MERRILL WITH JULIE V. IOVINE

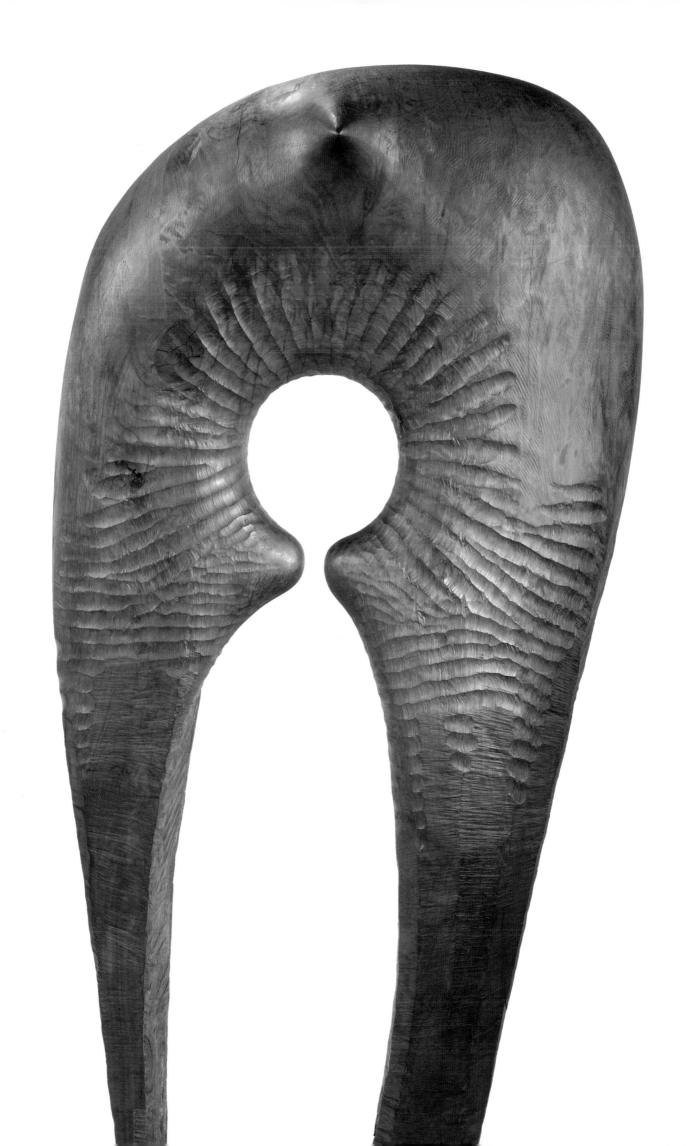

J. B. BLUNK

A product of the Bay Area in the freewheeling sixties, J. B. Blunk (1926–2003) was of a much older American tradition: the independent creative who refused to stay within the confines of any one artistic discipline.

Whether wielding a chainsaw with virtuoso skill or carving into a stone with a carbide grinder, Blunk was able to unleash his expressive energies in whatever way seemed to make sense to him at the moment. He joined other California woodworkers, such as Gary Knox Bennett and Arthur Espenet Carpenter, in a school of the unschooled that flourished on the West Coast, and especially around the Bay Area, in the 1950s and '60s. Rather than strive for recognition or fame as an artist, James Blain Blunk, who always went by J. B., seemed interested first and foremost in following a self-sustaining creative life. Many of his most ambitious works were created as gifts for friends. But now a wider audience is beginning to recognize his works as compelling and original touchstones in the history of American craft-art.

From the beginning, Blunk followed his own instincts, eschewing an orthodox approach. Somehow he used his early training in Japan—in the refined art of making Mingei pottery—to prepare for a vigorous approach to woodworking on a massive scale. "I just do it, that's all," he liked to say.

His one-of-a-kind wood furniture and sculpture, using primarily a chainsaw, was created with a pragmatic and expressive technique of removing material to reveal a new form while maintaining the natural characteristics of the tree. Rather than designing a finely milled table and chair, Blunk explored the sublime qualities of shape and color in an abstract way, avoiding the generic and reductive methods of carpentry.

The result was an organic and independent aesthetic with little relationship to traditional furniture design. Blunk's benches, chairs, tables, and stools are both sculptural and functional. They often convey a sense of vitality and growth, and in many instances the tree or stump from which they were carved retains the essence of its appearance, honoring what Blunk called the "soul of the piece." In his large-scale work, the effect is particularly dynamic. It hardly seems appropriate to call such massive creations "furniture," when they seem more like multidimensional environments or interactive tactile abstractions of space and depth.

To achieve such immediacy in his furniture, Blunk spent days and weeks studying a wood's burl and grain, its bent and twisted shape, visualizing the final form before making a cut with one

OPPOSITE PAGE Arch 1 is also referred to as Hawk Arch and was made in 1975 from an ancient cypress tree that Blunk salvaged from Point Reyes, California, near his studio. Here chainsaw techniques are combined with a chiseled surface texture. The piece was exhibited at the Blunk retrospective at the Los Angeles Craft & Folk Museum in 1978.

ABOVE LEFT J. B. Blunk, 1970, in Inverness, California.
RIGHT "Blunk's Hunk" is a free-form seating area for
the Stevenson College plaza at the University
of California in Santa Cruz. The 15' × 10' × 5' piece
was made in 1968 from a single redwood trunk. This
is an early example of Blunk's sculpted monumental
environments.

OPPOSITE PAGE Entrance to the Blunk house and
studio in Inverness, with a Zenlike stone arrangement
of carved and polished sensual forms. During the
1990s Blunk expanded perceptions of surface texture
by using stone carving as a contrast to his larger wood
pieces while retaining his organic and tactile aesthetic.
In some instances he combined wood and stone.

of his chainsaws. He did not make plans or sketches of his ideas; nor did he chalk or outline the
wood. Instead he contemplated, masked, and measured lines in his mind. When it came time
to carve, Blunk executed his design with absolute confidence, saying, "since I principally use a
chainsaw to do this, it is a process that moves quickly."

"At times the cutting away and forming happen so fast it is almost unconscious," he added.
With his swift cuts sometimes requiring as many as nine different chainsaws, Blunk per-
formed the three-dimensional equivalent of action painting. For the plaza of Stevenson College
at the University of California at Santa Cruz, Blunk carved an immense free-form seating area
and slab bench from a redwood trunk. Affectionately known as "Blunk's Hunk," the fifteen-
foot-by-ten-foot-by-five-foot sculpture has a tactile resonance, surrounding people as well as
seating them.

Though born and raised in Kansas, Blunk had an early interest in handmade objects that led
him to UCLA, where he studied with the well-known ceramist Laura Andersen. After seeing
an international exhibition of ceramics that included traditional Japanese Mingei pottery, he
decided he had to go to Japan "someway, someday" to meet and study with the artist who had
made the pieces, Shoji Hamada.

In 1951 Blunk found a fortuitous way to travel to Japan, serving in the army during the Korean
War and being stationed in Tokyo. As an officer, Blunk had off-base privileges and used a
military jeep to seek out Japanese pottery. During a visit to a traditional Japanese folk art
shop he was unexpectedly introduced to sculptor Isamu Noguchi, who became a mentor and
lifelong friend. As Noguchi recalls, "we happened to meet in Tokyo in 1952. It was in Takumi,
the Mingei store, that I overheard the young soldier asking about ceramists, and I said why not
come to Kamakura where I could introduce him to Rosanjin Kitaoji, the great potter of whom
I was then a guest."

After Blunk completed his military service in 1952, he made the unusual arrangement to be
discharged in Japan, instead of the United States. While there he worked for two different
ceramic masters, Kitaoji and Kaneshige Toyo, whose Bizen stoneware technique in some ways
foreshadowed Blunk's approach to wood. Toyo had developed a method of leaving organic
clay surfaces natural, unglazed, and rough, establishing a clear connection to the earth and
making each piece unique without being precious. Toyo's hand-operated potter's wheel and
his molding and sculpting may also have inspired Blunk's later interest in sensual forms.

In 1954 Noguchi assisted Blunk again. Seeing that Blunk had accumulated a sizeable collection of pots, Noguchi arranged for him to have a show in a gallery, where he could sell
enough to cover his return trip to the States. It was Blunk's first one-man show and featured
his ceramics as well as his drawings. Once Blunk returned to the United States he became
an artist-in-residence at Palos Verdes College in Rolling Hills, California, where he taught many
of the Japanese pottery techniques he had learned. He moved to Northern California a short
time later, initially working at a rural camp for children, at a sheep farm, and as a carpenter.
In another well-timed gesture, Noguchi introduced him to surrealist painter Gordon Onslow

Ford, who immediately recognized Blunk's artistic approach and skills. At the time, Onslow Ford was building a house in the forested hills of Inverness, California, north of San Francisco in Marin County. Blunk was already living in the area, working on ceramics and jewelry, when his friendship with Onslow Ford began in 1957.

The Onslow Ford house was designed by Bay Area architect Warren Callister. Blunk got involved as a craftsman when no one else could figure out how to make the curved roof in Callister's design. According to an interview with a Smithsonian documentation project for craft in America, Blunk first used a chainsaw for woodworking during the construction of Onslow Ford's roof.

His solution involved fifteen thin layers of laminated wood to create a dramatic arch in the beams, which Noguchi described as "huge rafters that curve like the ribs of some Egyptian ship." (Onslow Ford harbored a lifelong attachment to the sea.) A lasting friendship resulted from the house project, and Onslow Ford offered Blunk an acre of his land to live and work on. As a gift to Onslow Ford for his friendship, Blunk made a sculptural chair of cypress in 1964.

Over a three-year period Blunk built a home for his family, a studio, and a wood-burning kiln. The house is considered one of his most creative masterpieces, combining the raw energy and spiritual resonance that became the artist's hallmarks. Blunk's daughter, Mariah Nielson, remembers hearing stories about the building of the house and how "he would drive down to Drake's beach in a pick-up truck with friends and load it with driftwood found on the beach for us to build the house." He also retrieved pine beams from a defunct World War II shipyard. Windows cast off from a schoolhouse and telephone poles were also incorporated. Blunk built wood features into the interior as well, including a redwood kitchen table and a carved cypress bathroom sink.

From 1962 to 1995 Blunk completed about three to five wood pieces a year, ranging from epic-sized commissions to fourteen-inch stools. Some of the wood he acquired for free because it was not conventionally usable. Much of it was salvaged, like the Bishop pine trees indigenous to the Pacific Coast and readily available on Blunk's property. Collected and found wood were part of his process, but as Blunk's daughter explains, "most of his material came from loggers in Northern California, in Eureka and Mendocino, where they would be logging or excavating the burls for export to Japan. If they found a piece they thought he would like, they would call him."

It was common for Blunk to work in a field because of the size of the tree stumps—some larger than twenty feet in diameter. He preferred working with redwood and cypress but occasionally made pieces from oak, myrtle, eucalyptus, fir, and laurel.

Though he rarely sought attention for his work, he was generous about making furniture for friends and other artists in the area, and word spread to collectors. Blunk's first major commission—a cypress table, chair, and benches—was for his friend, landscape architect Lawrence Halprin, in 1965. The strong, naturalistic quality of the pieces produced a functional, aesthetic environment that would reoccur in Blunk's furniture installations. The first of his many public art commissions, "Blunk's Hunk" formalized the artist's ability to integrate functionality and unconventional aesthetics. In this early piece the influence of Noguchi was evident. Like Noguchi, Blunk left some surfaces natural and rough and others smooth or textured. Both artists used contrasting surfaces to symbolize the connection between art and nature. Neither one pursued the type of perfection that made a piece too precious for use. Blunk deliberately designed his furniture for exploration and utility.

Blunk's organic approach is especially visible in one of his favorite pieces, *The Planet*, completed in 1969 for the entrance to the Oakland Art Museum. The twelve-foot circular bench made from a single redwood burl embodies Blunk's signature curvy, twisted, and knobby forms. Work on the two-ton sculpture took about six months and many different chainsaws. With his assistant, a young Bruce Mitchell, who later became a successful woodworker himself, Blunk created a large-scale seating environment with room enough to engage ten people. The scalloped and varied textured patterns that Mitchell created on the surface with a chisel enhanced the playful, interactive feeling of *The Planet*.

The tactile combination of rough and graceful forms in Blunk's sculptural environments was carried even further when he created the *Magic Boat* in 1979 for the California Orientation Center for the Blind in Albany, California. A bench made from a redwood tree trunk, it was nine feet by nine feet by five feet, with curved ridges and different textures, giving people the

ABOVE Home of Surrealist painter Gordon Onslow Ford, Inverness, late 1950s. The curved roof beams, constructed by Blunk are one of the home's most distinguishing features. Blunk's friendship with Onslow Ford began in 1957 through an introduction from the architect Isamu Noguchi. At the time, Blunk was doing various types of carpentry for Noguchi when the architect of the house, Warren Callister, asked him to find a solution for bending and forming the timbers for the roof. Blunk recalled later, that "nobody wanted to take it on. It was considered some sort of a freak or whatever." The project gave Blunk the opportunity to learn to use a chainsaw for the development of the fifteen layers of laminated wood used in the truss.

OPPOSITE PAGE Front door of architect Sim Van Der Ryn's house in Inverness, California, 1980. The door is made of carved cypress with suggestive, sensual forms that occasionally appeared in Blunk's sculptured pieces. Van Der Ryn, a friend and neighbor, was a leader in the development of responsible environmental design in California during the 1970s. For Van Der Ryn's house, Blunk also created a free-form cypress sink.

ABOVE LEFT The table on the left, made of buckeye burl, c. 1985, was from the J. B. Blunk estate and was commissioned by a Japanese businessman as a low dining table; however, Blunk was asked to create a new table because the client was worried about food collecting in the openings of the burls. This piece sold at Sotheby's in 2007 for $28,000. **RIGHT** The low table on the right exemplifies Blunk's ingenious designs in functional art by incorporating a bowl into the table's top.

OPPOSITE PAGE *The Planet*, 1969, is a 12' × 12' × 3' sitting environment made from a single redwood burl. It was created for the Oakland Museum of California and completed in time for the museum's opening. Blunk considered the two-ton sculpture one of his favorite pieces. The piece is especially inviting for children to climb over and under. Blunk created the curvy, twisted, and knobby forms with a combination of chainsaws. The extensive sanding and texturing was done by Blunk's assistant Bruce Mitchell.

experience of climbing into an open, boatlike space. Another communal furniture setting was the unparalleled three-ton group of connected tables and stools all cut from a twenty-two-foot redwood stump for Greens restaurant in San Francisco, completed with Mitchell's assistance in 1977.

Many of Blunk's public art commissions are still in place, such as the redwood bench he created with assistant Rick Yoshimoto for the CalTrans Station on the Lunny Ranch in Marin County, California. When he was not working on huge projects, Blunk was making comparatively smaller yet full-scale furniture, including a conference table for his friend Paul Hawken of Smith and Hawken, or a cypress sink and front door for his neighbor, architect Sim Van der Ryn.

Although Blunk's work influenced many Bay Area woodworkers, he did not consider himself part of any movement. While friendly, he was independent and focused on his work. He did not participate in the nearby Bolinas open studio visits, finding discussions about art unproductive. But his daughter Mariah recalls the days when she was a young child: "We did host informal family shows. I had drawings, which I would sell for fifty cents, my mother [textile designer Christine Nielson] had her weaving and tapestries, my brothers had their paintings and sculptures, and my father had his work to show. We'd open up the house and invite friends."

Blunk's work was included in several traditional exhibitions, including *Objects: USA* at the Los Angeles Municipal Art Gallery in 1970 and *California Design* at the Pasadena Art Museum in 1976. The Craft and Folk Art Museum in Los Angeles held a retrospective of Blunk's career in 1978, featuring more than 120 examples of his furniture, sculpture, ceramics, and jewelry from 1952 to 1977. In 2007 the Reform Gallery of Los Angeles included a table and a sculptural arch in a sale-exhibit at Design Miami/Art Basel, and both sold for $250,000 each.

The renewed appreciation for Blunk's contributions as an artist and craftsman are making it possible for Blunk's heirs to realize one of his dreams: establishing an artist-in-residence program. With the assistance of the Decorative Arts Council for the Los Angeles County Museum of Art, Blunk's house and studios offer an inspiring and productive setting for woodworkers, ceramists, painters, and other artists to create new work within the nurturing environment of Blunk's singular vision. **J.H.**

WENDELL CASTLE

There is a long tradition in America of the itinerant craftsman traveling far and wide to share an artistic talent developed without the benefit of apprenticeship or master training but still resonating with the impulses of the age. Though Wendell Castle (b. 1932) has stayed close to Rochester, New York, his explorations have included various schools of thought and different aesthetic approaches. His work combines a spirit of constant creativity with a style that is entirely original, quintessentially American, and definitively of its time.

Castle's vigorously three-dimensional woodworks—some sensuously organic, others precise and architectural—transcend easy categorization, and the artist himself has strived over the years to confound definitions. Is it sculpture? Is it furniture? "I would just prefer it be accepted as a beautiful thing," he said in an interview conducted for the Smithsonian's Archive of American Art in 1981.

Though his name can be found on lists that also include Wharton Esherick, George Nakashima, Sam Maloof, and Arthur Espenet Carpenter, Castle remains something of an anomaly: first in his desire to be viewed as a sculptor rather than as a craftsman, woodworker, or furniture designer; and also by his refusal to settle into any one creative groove. From polymorphic forms made of laminated wood, to trompe l'oeil carvings (with a segue into electric-acid-colored molded plastics), to Ruhlmann-esque master cabinetry and postmodern monumental pop, Castle has constantly reinvented his approach to art and furniture. "My creative urge is to be at risk. Without that, it's just not very interesting," he said in a 2006 interview, shortly after he returned to making limited editions of plastic shapes he first envisioned in the sixties.

There are echoes of different influences on his work: Scandinavian furniture designers Finn Juhl and Hans Wegner; sculptors Henry Moore and Jean Arp; art nouveau; art deco; and Italian postmodernism. Through all of his work, however, there runs a common thread: creating furniture that is equal in resonance to sculpture and painting.

Wendell Castle was born in 1932 in Emporia, Kansas. His parents objected to his desire at a young age to become an artist, and so instead he studied industrial design at the University of Kansas. But his interest in experimentation and working alone persisted, so he switched to sculpture, earning his Masters of Fine Arts in 1961. Castle described a 1958 road trip to rural Pennsylvania as the real turning point in his early life. Many years later he told Robert Brown of the Smithsonian that a school friend suggested they drop in on the famed, and famously

OPPOSITE PAGE A detail of *Victory*, a desk in walnut and walnut plywood that debuted in 1980 at a Washington, D.C., exhibit called *Furniture as Art II*. It is a fine example of Castle confounding the differences between sculpture and furniture, decoration and function.

ABOVE LEFT Portrait of Castle, 2006. **RIGHT** Blanket chest (1963, cherry) resembles a stylized pomegranate and exemplifies Castle's efforts to escape from the historical and stylistic assumptions of traditional American furniture.

OPPOSITE PAGE TOP The Desk and Chair (1965) further Castle's ongoing efforts to transform the functional into the sculptural. **BOTTOM LEFT** The Cabinet (1966) is a refined example of the stacked-laminated process he focused on in the sixties. **BOTTOM CENTER** The Music Stand is one of Castle's most iconic works as well as one of the earliest pieces he made in a limited edition. First designed in 1964, this example in oak is from 1980. Castle described the legs as roots that support the saplinglike body. **BOTTOM RIGHT** The Stool Sculpture (1959) is an early experiment reflecting Castle's early interest in Scandinavian- and Italian-modern design.

eccentric, Wharton Esherick at home. The seventy-year-old furniture designer was none too pleased at being interrupted by young students, but Castle was struck immediately at the original environment that the painter-turned-woodworker had created. It was then that he realized it was possible to create a life out of self-expression. Esherick was "the first person I'd seen who worked in wood, whom I'd think of as an artist who approached it like an art form," he told Brown.

Back in Kansas, Castle started to make furniture that he has since called strictly derivative of the Scandinavian designs then dominating the American design front. And while his first few pieces never attracted the attention he sought (nor sold, he claimed, because he priced them so high at about $300), there was one that had a different look. The Scribe's Stool, designed in 1961–62, was a chair so high it needed a foot rest with an arm that swung out into a table. Sinuous, almost quivering like a sapling, it seemed to grow up from the ground, taking the shape of a stool as if only by chance. Castle made only two Scribe's Stools, both walnut pieces laminated around a solid form. One is now in the design collection of the Metropolitan Museum of Art.

Castle exhibited the Scribe's Stool at the Young Americans, a seminal 1962 exhibition held at New York's American Craft Museum, where it attracted considerable attention. Castle's laminated woodworks stressed creativity over practicality, something unheard of at the time. "I don't start with function. I take that for granted," he wrote in the 1980 *Wendell Castle Book of Wood Lamination.*

Castle took a different approach to organic forms than other prominent woodworkers of the time, such as Esherick and Nakashima. He ignored grain, had little concern for cost, and often intentionally used cheap woods to prevent his pieces from feeling too precious. He wanted to create a floating surface that appeared to rise from the floor, with the base acting as an anchor or stem. As a result, his work had more of a connection to art nouveau than to the biomorphic organic look associated with the sixties. One of his early stack-laminated pieces, the Music Stand of 1964, had a treelike form made of eight sections that reached up to a slated rack in walnut and rosewood. It was Castle's first attempt at a limited edition, and after finishing the protoype, he made twelve more, numbering them like prints. In the 1980s, he made two more: one went to his gallerist Evan Snyderman; the other was priced at $200,000, as Castle recalled in an interview. And finally, in the 1990s, he made one for himself.

After the early success of his laminated pieces, Castle was working in what he came to call "the space between sculpture and furniture." He moved to New York to join the art scene, but once there, he found that most galleries did not know what to do with a sculptor inspired by furniture. Lee Nordness, who became his dealer and most active champion, started out by commissioning Castle to design furnishings for his home, including a sofa with one leg extending from floor to ceiling, a bookcase, and a coffee table. (The entire collection, except for a chest of drawers with twelve legs, is now at the Art Institute of Chicago.) Determined to remain as independent as possible, Castle began teaching furniture classes at the School of American Craftsmen, which was part of the Rochester Institute of Technology but had close ties to the American Craft Museum in New York. A very early commission came from the

ABOVE LEFT The three seater with carved base (1968) and a matching cantilevered table in cherry is anchored by four dramatic rootlike corners. RIGHT Wall Table No. 16 from the late sixties demonstrates Castle moving toward purer sculptural forms and away from practical use. (Notice how little space is given to the tabletop.) This direction may have been driven in part by his determination to be considered an artist rather than a craftsman.

OPPOSITE PAGE A stylized palm tree is fused with the top banister of a curvaceous wood staircase created in 1976 for the Gannett headquarters in Rochester, New York. By the mid-seventies Castle was attracting large, private commissions as well as creating pieces for the corporate collections of Forbes, Steinway, American Express, Bausch & Lomb, and DuPont, to mention a few.

Gleason Works, a local manufactory in Rochester for whom Castle created furnishings for two presidential suites. Castle later dismissed the collection as far too traditional for his aims as an artist.

With a studio in Rochester (and plenty of students to lend a hand), Castle was able to refine a process of wood laminating that he had begun as a student in Kansas. Stack lamination appealed to Castle for its flexibility, malleability, and strength. It meant that he was "not dealing with solid logs that are going to crack and split unpredictably," he later said. Castle glued together layers of wood (the thinner they were, the quicker they dried—a key consideration) until he achieved the desired thickness. He used regular white glue, which, unlike epoxy, absorbed more easily into the wood and did not leave a visible seam. Castle then carved it with a chainsaw, finishing with a power chisel, body grinder, router, and increasingly smaller refining tools. The final step, and one he soon turned over to assistants, was a full week of sanding.

By the mid-sixties, Castle had exhibited his work throughout New England and was selling coffee tables for $2,000. A few years later, his studio required three assistants to help him produce about seventy-five pieces a year.

Among his early laminated pieces were the three-part settee (1960) made of stack-laminated cherry, with cupped seats that would have been impossible to make with traditional joinery methods. The Alpha Chair (1964), a fairly straightforward piece with four legs, was "not wild," as Castle put it, but conveyed a subtle dynamic fragility. The Crescent Rocker (1972) was his most popular laminated piece, but as far as Castle was concerned, according to Michael A. Stone in *Contemporary American Woodworkers*, it didn't "push back the limits of design" and was too much like real furniture.

Determined to position himself as an artist, Castle was often frustrated that, even as his pieces were finding a wider audience at such exhibitions as the *Fantasy Furniture* show at the Smithsonian in Washington, D.C. in 1969–70, he was not described as a sculptor, but somewhat dismissively as working, as one reviewer put it, in "the sculpture role."

Castle started to lose interest in laminated wood just as it was taking off. Ever the artist, he seemed to associate wider acceptance with creative bankruptcy. So it is not entirely surprising that in 1968, Castle exclaimed that he was sick of brown—the color of wood—and started to work in bright-colored plastic. The molded pieces took the organic shapes of his stack-laminated wood pieces and expanded them to surreal extremes. There were slug-shaped lamps, tables with legs like melting wax, and, famously, the Molar chairs that looked distinctly dental. Though he later said he enjoyed the freewheeling experimental nature of working in plastic, the production costs to make reusable molds were prohibitive and the type of people who had come to value his wood sculptures did not appreciate psychedelic-colored synthetics. In 1973 Castle abandoned his foray into mass production, having made less than four hundred pieces in about fifteen shapes.

Intellectually restless but still determined to be more artist than artisan, Castle started to study more classical forms in the mid-seventies. During a trip to England, he visited John

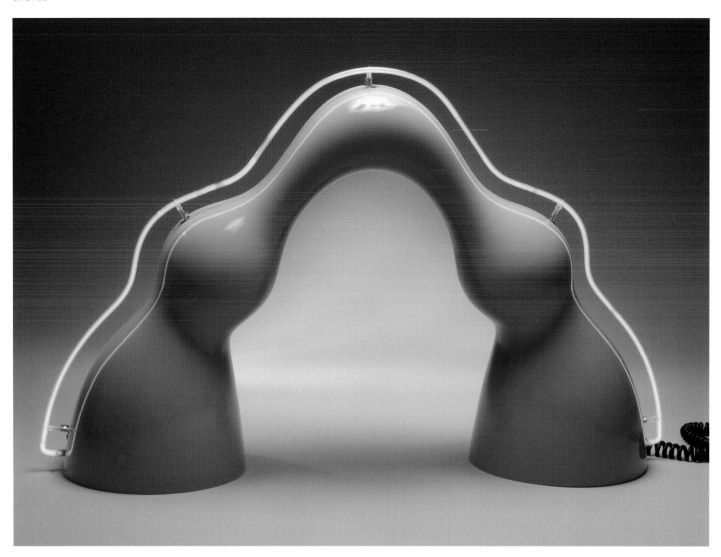

Makepeace, a craftsman also working in a contemporary vein and the founder of Dorset's School for Crafts in Wood, later known as Parnham College. Makepeace opened Castle's eyes to the highest level of workmanship. Castle's career entered a new phase, characterized by trompe l'oeil pieces—exquisitely wrought everyday still lifes in wood. One distinctly historical table had a pair of gloves and keys tossed on top, all carved from wood. Ghost Clock (1985), a grandfather clock shrouded in a sheet, was made entirely of bleached and laminated Honduras mahogany. Castle's trompe l'oeil pieces brought him immediate national attention, though not a huge following in the art world. And while Castle continued to seek inspiration in art and history rather than from the crafts, it is clear that his work gained increasing recognition, in part because it was buoyed by the mainstream crafts movement sweeping across the country.

The trompe l'oeil work, though successful, was equally important for leading Castle to examine the long history of furniture making. He was drawn to the strong profiles of deco, but it was the work of Emile-Jacques Ruhlmann that impressed him most for its exquisite detailing and sculptural coherence. (Other historic pieces had disappointed him once he looked behind the ornate facades to find unfinished backs and joinery that favored expediency over care.) The influence of Ruhlmann is especially evident in the massive but refined Ladies Desk (1981), with its 8,500 ebony dots inlaid in a surface of curly English sycamore and drawers made of amaranth. Where once Castle deemed exotic woods too precious and distracting, he now embraced them, adding inlays of ivory and sterling silver to add to the luster. In an interview, he called his trompe l'oeil period "a transitional phase." "It was exciting for a moment, but it was not really rewarding," he said. "I like inventing things."

Castle's work became increasingly architectural, even monumental. Pieces were conceived in the round like sculpture, not pushed against the wall like furniture. In the eighties, the influence of postmodernism was everywhere. Italians such as Ettore Sottsass and Andrea Branzi were pronouncing the need to inject passion, emotion, and a sense of the past into architecture and design. A similar way of thinking could be detected in such late Castle pieces as *Late Proposal for the Rochester Convention Center* (1982), a lacquered jewel box with bagel feet supporting Howard Johnson–colored pilasters.

From 1980 to 1988 Castle established the Wendell Castle Workshop in Scottsville, a two-year program in contemporary studio furniture making, possibly inspired by John Makepeace's school for modern crafts in England. The best students were invited to begin their careers in Castle's own studio, which had grown to employ ten cabinetmakers, each with a particular technical expertise, working under his close supervision. The workshop operated much in the same manner as the finest furniture makers in the seventeenth and eighteenth centuries, quite a shift from Castle's intuitive, almost naive approach of the early sixties. He still started as he always did, with a drawing in a sketchbook, but now pieces might take five hundred to one thousand hours of labor, as well as the involvement of many workers, to guarantee that every detail and finish was perfect.

Edward S. Cooke, a professor of the American decorative arts at Yale University, has written that studio furniture is characterized by intense conceptualization, independent

ABOVE LEFT Nirvana, in molded fiberglass and **RIGHT** Night on Earth, an inventive spot-welded stainless-steel collage, are both limited editions from 2007 representing Castle's most recent creative direction toward bulbous, almost totemic forms. In 2007 the Brooklyn Museum honored Castle with a Lifetime Achievement Award at the annual modernism show, recognizing him as "the father of the art-furniture movement."

OPPOSITE PAGE TOP The semifunctional Benny lamp (1969) was the result of Castle's experiments with plastic in the sixties. Its super glossy moss-green color was achieved by using paints and enamels normally used for cars; it was made in an old mill building that Castle converted to his work studio around 1968. **BOTTOM LEFT** The most iconic piece from his experiments in the sixties is the Molar chair (1969–70) made of glass-reinforced polyester. In 2003, Castle resumed production of pieces in molded plastics. **BOTTOM RIGHT** The large and modular dining table (2003) was originally made in 1970 for an office in Rochester but was later destroyed. Castle reissued it in a series of eight.

professionalism, and custom production. Castle doesn't quite fit the mold, combining the idea-driven and custom-making aspects of studio art with the centuries-established perfectionism of guild cabinetmaking.

The collectors of Castle's woodworks have tended to be ardent, but none more so than Peter Joseph, who operated a craft gallery dedicated to studio art furniture in Manhattan's Fuller Building from 1991 to 1997. The eponymous gallery was Castle's home base during those years. Joseph hosted six one-man shows dedicated to Castle's work in as many years. The first was Angel Chairs, a series of patinated bronze and wood chairs that some consider his finest work. He made ten chairs in combinations of bronze and mahogany. All, he said, were inspired by the idea of making a wingback chair more literal. (In 2005 an Angel chair from Joseph's estate sold for $59,000 at Sollo Rago Auctions.) Privately, Joseph commissioned many individual pieces, as well as an entire library installation for his home. Castle was inspired by the German expressionist film *The Cabinet of Dr. Caligari* and featured Castle's experiments in integrating form and surface. There, everything from bookshelves to a Steinway piano was treated in faceted wood painted with black-and-white, abstract expressionist, Franz Kline–inspired strokes.

By the nineties, Castle's work was in museum collections across the country, from the Metropolitan Museum of Art and the Art Institute of Chicago to the Museum of Decorative Arts in Montreal and the White House. In a 2001 interview with Edward Cooke at the Furniture Society, Castle said that he didn't document his work, but that his slide library contained some 3,800 images of individual pieces. Auction estimates for Castle's pieces are consistent whether for pieces made early or late in his career. At a 2004 Christie's twentieth-century decorative arts sale, a stacked laminated swivel chair in walnut (1973) sold for $14,340.

In recent years, Castle has dabbled in different modes of production, establishing the Wendell Castle Collection. Manufactured by a separate company, the collection produces streamlined versions of the artist's studio works, with a slight Asian and African inflection to the upholstered seating collection. Since launching in 2003, the collection has grown to about seventy-five pieces. In 2006 Castle returned to plastic, reissuing a handful of the originals, including a Molar chair and a table with parabola-shaped legs as limited editions.

Castle's most recent works fuse the muscular quality of his early laminated pieces with the bulbous forms of the plastics. Made primarily of polychrome fiberglass—some gilded, some coated in slick auto paint—they possess a totemic energy that is part tribal, part alien. Night on Earth is a stainless-steel chaise lounge composed of many amoeba-shaped pieces welded together, creating a skin of lacelike complexity. Castle's new works offer apt testament to this artist–furniture maker's ongoing quest for personal and artistic resonance. **J.I.**

ABOVE Ghost (1985), in carved mahogany, represents Castle's trompe l'oeil experiments, or as he called them "illusions." It was conceived for the Clocks series of 1983. Completely nonfunctional, Ghost is the most daring example from the group, which otherwise consisted of working clocks. Clocks appeared in two major traveling shows and several of the pieces commanded six-figure sums. In 1987 Castle received a major public commission in Toronto and Full Moon was installed at one of the city's busiest intersections.

OPPOSITE PAGE The stacked-laminated Library sculpture was made for an exhibition at the Memorial Art Gallery of Rochester in 1965. Although the piece is composed of a desk and double settee, it has an impressive sculptural presence. It also demonstrates Castle's growing expertise with stacked-wood lamination, a technique using layers of wood glued together to create shapes that would be otherwise impossible to carve. Once dried, the piece is carved, sanded, or sculpted by the artist to the desired shape.

MICHAEL COFFEY

A product of the burgeoning self-taught craft movement of the 1960s that extended from the East Coast to the West Coast, Michael Coffey (b. 1928) engineers masterpieces of sculptural furniture. His pieces blend the organic styles of art nouveau, the radical spirit of the 1960s counterculture, and the calculations of an engineer. A man driven by idealistic dreams of helping the needy, Coffey turned a disenchantment with the world into a passion for woodworking. His sculptures are functional, strong, and fluid; they defy gravity with their cantilevered forms and swimming motions; but, most important, they're durably useful, tactile objects that give Coffey status as a master woodworker.

Born and raised in New York City, with a six-year childhood stint in New Hope, Pennsylvania, Coffey, like so many self-taught artists, thought of woodworking only as a hobby. As a kid he loved wood carving, but he majored in psychology in college, and from 1953 to 1972 he worked as a community organizer helping low-income groups fight for basic needs. This excited the idealist in him but also provided the income to nurture his woodworking. As his frustrations with bureaucracy rose and his hobby flourished, Coffey bought a house in Staten Island where he worked in his basement from 6:00 a.m. to noon as a woodworker and from noon into the evenings as a community organizer.

Coffey was influenced by his East Coast contemporaries, such as George Nakashima, Wendell Castle, Wharton Esherick, and Walker Reed, and was also aware of West Coast woodworker Sam Maloof. He was captivated by Jack Rogers Hopkins because, Coffey stated, "he had no limits." While his contemporaries inspired him, he resolved not to copy them and carved new paths using his innate ability to engineer the most structurally solid, uniquely sculptured furniture with flare and wit.

Early on, Coffey produced pieces with slabs of wood, similar to Nakashima, but as his skills evolved his pieces took on a spirit of their own. Coffey's independent streak drove him away from conventional furniture and traditional styles. "I objected to the way many pieces of furniture had different parts," Coffey stated. "I wanted one part to flow into another without separation, and that was the principal."

In 1971 Michael Coffey, at the urging of his wife, brought some pieces to Directional Furniture in Manhattan, a company that was interested in innovative furnishings and was representing Paul Evans. The president, Bud Mesberg, liked the pieces and asked Coffey to "go big,"

OPPOSITE PAGE Coffey made this giant rocker Aphrodite (c. 1975), which was exhibited at the American Craft Museum around 1978. Like all of Coffey's work, it was designed to be functional, and in spite of its monumental proportions, it was both ergonomic and comfortable. After the first sold, another was quickly commissioned. For the second version (only two were ever made), Coffey left a hollow space in the head and foot and used sacks filled with metal pellets to get the correct weight distribution. Without telling the client, Coffey also added a letter to the hollowed part at the base as if it were a time capsule.

ABOVE This cabinet, completed in 1990, is typical of Coffey's work with its carved ridges that in some places are 3½ inches deep. Coffey enjoyed working with the existing quirks of the wood he selected, including its color, grain, growth rings, and even odor, which he considered one of the most enjoyable parts of the creative process. The Mozambique wood used here is one of Coffey's signature materials.

OPPOSITE PAGE TOP The hand-carved and laminated American walnut stools borrow their form from a nun's habit. **BOTTOM** For this Mozambique table called Riptide, Coffey expertly produced the effect of the phenomenon in nature where countercurrents run against each other in water. Coffey creations were often inspired by nature and the world around him.

giving him some guidelines to follow. Coffey created his Swahili cabinet, a piece carved on three sides with swirling, sweeping motions. Coffey utilized the wood's grain to create the perfect pattern.

Coffey never met Paul Evans but was aware of his Sculpted Bronze line for Directional and felt his woodwork would complement it. So did Directional, as some of the company's advertisements featured Evans's and Coffey's work together. Coffey developed several pieces for Directional, which helped his business and repertoire grow. Throughout the 1970s he also exhibited at such places as Artists & Craftsmen of New York, American Craft Council, and American Craft Enterprises. He felt that gallery shows and exhibitions better suited him, so around 1980 Coffey stopped filling orders for Directional and focused his energy on individual client orders.

In 1973, inspired by Wharton Esherick's home in Paoli, Pennsylvania, and his woodworking friends' lifestyles, Coffey took the ultimate plunge. He bought a house in Poultney, Vermont, with seventeen acres and a barn he converted into a workshop. He loved living in a total work of art and being surrounded by the sights, sounds, and smells of nature. Vermont provided different inspirations for him. At exhibitions, admirers compared his work to art nouveau, and once Coffey studied the turn-of-the-century movement, he saw the correlation. He became enthralled and inspired with nature: streams that carved stone, trees with meandering branches, or waves of a trickling brook.

Another recurring statement he heard was, "you must be very romantic," which caught Coffey off guard, but he said that "it helped me realize a part of myself I was not entirely comfortable with; it helped me to be more expressive." His whimsical, sensual pieces show how his emotions guide his forms more than function and purpose. No piece is the same, and every turn and detail reflect his spontaneity and instinct. Coffey reasons that furniture, versus sculpture, uses the fourth dimension (time and space) and tactility to invoke interaction. With his idealism finally fulfilled, he has produced furniture that yearns to be seen, touched, and used.

To create his sculptured furniture, Coffey begins with a free-association sketch. Once he finds the right form, a model is made in clay or wax to create a 360-degree view. Once Coffey is satisfied with the sculpted model, a wood model is created to work out the hard-edged details. Finally, a working drawing is done to scale, showing every dimension and joinery detail.

Wood is his medium of choice, and Coffey studied tree anatomy in order to select wisely. Clients come to him with specific wood choices in mind, but Coffey favors African Mozambique. It is similar to walnut but has less sap and features slight color variations in a wider range of colors. Coffey handpicks the wood for every piece of furniture and carefully matches the color and grain of the boards.

After wood selection, Coffey places each board on the floor to visually plan out the piece. By moving the boards around and cutting them to size he is able to design the appropriate scale, determine bolt placement, and, most important, determine which boards to carve and where. His carvings usually go through multiple layers of laminated wood, and Coffey wants a congruous color throughout the carved surface. A metal bolt hidden inside a piece is a distinct feature in Coffey's furniture that allows unified functions and gravity-defying forms.

Once satisfied with placement, Coffey begins the lamination process. Layers are built to a point where bolts are needed, usually at a joint or major curve in the structure. A hole is drilled, then the next section of laminated layers gets a hole and is joined with the bottom section. Butterfly joints, or miter joints for thicker pieces, are used at right angles, and, when necessary, metal bolts are inserted—all of which help in the durability and longevity of the piece.

Coffey's El Morro desk exemplifies his ability to gracefully combine functions. A sweeping motion is created using steps of pivoting drawers spiraling up to form the pedestal base. Instead of an abrupt corner transition to the desktop, Coffey made a wide, round corner that leads to a cantilevered desktop with built-in drawers. The smooth lines and soft edges emanate fluidity, but its clever functionality and strong curve hugging the pedestal base adds austerity.

The Matador chair, one of Coffey's earliest pieces, is designed with only one arm. As he said, "the issue was integrating the piece...instead of having a backseat and pedestal...[I] start at a point in the pedestal [that] winds up in that arm." He felt a second arm would break the organic flow of the chair, so in one motion its base zigzags up, then swirls around the back and ends at the armrest. The piece is extremely comfortable, since Coffey was concerned with back support, which the Matador graciously provides, allowing the sitter to melt into the chair. A large metal bolt is placed at the pedestal seat juncture but is hidden deep inside.

Many of Coffey's forms play off negative space. His Riptide double-leaf coffee table has two surfaces that fold into one another, leaving slices of space in between. A bulbous curve opposite a short, slender curve provides visual asymmetry, and two thin surfaces sweeping toward each other create movement. Again integrating the piece's base and surface, Coffey plays with ebbs and flows of form, and balances visual weight with negative space to further the illusions of motion and lightness.

Blurring the lines of function and form is his Aphrodite lounger, a generously proportioned piece that embraces the body with its sensual, flowing form. Another creation using negative space and sweeping motions, the lounger illustrates Coffey's ability to produce light and fluid forms in a large, heavy piece. It is built as one unit that appears to be carved out of one solid piece of wood, rocking the sitter with its curved base. Coffey redefined the traditional rocking chair by making the form come full circle. His overly concave seat molds to the sitter's body then turns down with a wide, rounded corner to complete the circle at the base.

Coffey's organic and enigmatic forms assist in the naming of his pieces. "When I developed that carving motif it looked to be...sort of mysterious, enigmatic, and Swahili as a language is so far from our language and our culture that I named the cabinet Swahili." Satin's Tongue, Serpent's Tongue, Lily Pad table, and Whale of a Bar are just some of the whimsical yet appropriately named pieces. Unique forms and soft edges speak of Coffey's ability to blend the human senses and emotions with art. When asked how he categorizes himself, he states, "I wandered accidentally into sculpture because by going in a direction away from things [conventional furniture] I feel more like a sculptor. I'm playing with forms that I like and I'm expressing feelings—and so it's from within and it's not just furniture."

Early in his career he founded a couple of woodworking schools: Michael Coffey's School of Fine Woodworking and One Cottage Street School of Fine Woodworking. He eventually sold his schools but never abandoned his basic principles of designing organically formed and well-structured pieces, and he continues to produce one-of-a-kind sculptural furniture. The artist's signature can be found on each piece—an incised M Coffey. He still works against the traditional grain and always wants his clients to use his furniture to its sturdy potential and not to treat it as sculpture to merely admire from afar.

Coffey's pieces command high prices at auction, such as a glass and Bubinga wood Serpent coffee table that sold in 2006 for more than $10,000 at Chicago's Wright auction house, and an African Mozambique Satan's Tongue II that sold for more than $14,000 at Sotheby's New York in 2007. As a furniture designer in the twenty-first century, Michael Coffey encompasses aspects of handicraft and art by blending honest construction with unrestrained creativity. His pieces rival other contemporary art furniture with their sensual designs and whimsical names. **E.J.**

ABOVE Michael Coffey in 2007 sitting in his walnut stool. Coffey almost always made small maquettes, along with many sketches, to experiment with shaping the fluid lines of his pieces. Even with the help of these small maquettes, Coffey created only about ten full-scale pieces, even for such iconic designs as Riptide or Satan's Tongue, because he considered that by then the idea was played out and he was ready to "move on."

OPPOSITE PAGE TOP LEFT The large jewelry box, made of Mozambique wood, was commissioned by the Signature Gallery in Boston around 1987. **TOP RIGHT** The Lectern (1988) is also made of Mozambique and is part of a series, which includes music stands. Both forms allude to nature found on Coffey's Vermont land, such as trees, rocks, and streams as shown in the image below. **BOTTOM** From 1973 to 1983 Coffey lived alongside the river in Poultney, Vermont. When he arrived there, he was finally able to be a full-time artist after seven years living throughout New York state. Poultney was an ideal place to have a studio; the Poultney River had gradually worn away an ancient rock bed that fascinated and inspired Coffey.

WHARTON ESHERICK

With expressionistic verve and decided wit, Wharton Esherick (1887–1970) defied traditional furniture forms and established a new benchmark in the history of American art furniture. His striking forms bridged a wide range of genres, including Arts & Crafts, cubism, and abstract expressionism, while his intuitive approach and working methods anticipated such artist-woodworkers of the 1960s and '70s as Sam Maloof and Wendell Castle. And while he created functional pieces of striking originality, Esherick was equally determined to express his whimsical side. His ingenious forms led the American Institute of Architects to award him the Craftsmanship Medal, thus designating him (posthumously) the Dean of American Craftsmen in 1971.

Born in 1887 in Philadelphia, Wharton Esherick was drawn to art early in life. Upon graduating from high school, he attended the Philadelphia School of Industrial Arts (now the University of the Arts) to study drawing and printmaking. After studying painting for nearly two years at the traditional Pennsylvania Academy of Fine Arts (then a leading American school for impressionists), Esherick left, eager to begin his career. His first jobs were as an illustrator for two Philadelphia newspapers and as a poster illustrator for Victor Talking Machine Company. But when he was laid off in 1912, due to advancements in photo reproductions, he moved with his wife to Paoli, Pennsylvania, a small town twenty-five miles outside of Philadelphia, where he focused solely on his painting. The Eshericks' new home was an 1839 farmhouse with a huge cherry tree out front. He never moved again.

Though skilled at drawing, Esherick was not a natural painter and felt the medium did not allow him the freedom of expression he sought. "I was a good draftsman who didn't know how to think," he later stated in an interview with *Craft Horizon*. And ever the iconoclast, he was happy to bite the hand that fed him, telling students visiting his studio, "You're never going to get anyplace in this world unless you get away from those people over there—your teachers."

When his wife went to Fairhope, Alabama, in 1919 to study progressive education techniques at the School for Organic Education, Esherick went with her; he would paint anywhere. Through the school Esherick acquired his first set of carving tools and proceeded to carve representational designs on the handmade frames for his paintings. He found this medium challenged and excited him creatively. Esherick returned to Paoli in 1920 and began creating woodcuts for illustrations in books. While his frames are impossible to find today, his illustration woodcuts can be found at auction with prices ranging from $1,500 to $9,000.

OPPOSITE PAGE This sideboard made in 1961 for the Armstrong Cork Company is representative of Esherick's ability to create movement using abstract forms. This piece is part of the permanent collection of the Philadelphia Museum of Art and is a good example of Esherick's blending of 1930s German Expressionism with sixties minimalism.

ABOVE LEFT Wharton Esherick, pictured here in his Captain's chair. **RIGHT** Esherick drawing a design on boards, was profiled in 1954 in the *New York Times* as a designer and craftsman. Although he appreciated craft and design in furniture making he always said he was an artist, not a craftsman, stating that "it takes a sculptor to sculpt."

OPPOSITE PAGE Esherick's woodblock prints dating from 1923 to 1938 are great examples of his ability to create the finest of details in an almost lost art. They also illustrate the influence nature had on the reclusive artist who ventured into the city only to feed his artistic hunger. These particular woodblock prints were from the collection of York Fischer, grandson of Esherick's longtime patron Helene Fischer, and allow the public to see the strong connection between client and artist. Esherick loved all forms of art, including medieval mythology.

From the woodblocks, he started to explore sculpture, and then, out of necessity, furniture. When the newly formed Whitney Museum of American Art in New York began acquiring Esherick's sculpture, he dropped painting and began construction of a studio atop the hill of his twelve-acre property.

Like Frank Lloyd Wright, whom he admired, and as a follower of the Arts & Crafts movement, Esherick believed a building should conform to its surroundings. He built his studio with stones and wood that he found near his property and, for the next forty years, he remodeled and added on as needed. The result, now the Wharton Esherick Museum, is a compelling vision of his belief in organic expressionism as well as his most impressive masterpiece.

The first phase of the structure was built over one long summer in 1926, with the help of just four men (to show his appreciation, Esherick carved caricature coat hooks of each man near the front door). He carefully chose each stone for its color and shape, and every night after the stonemason filled the gaps between them with mortar, he would deeply rake the joints so that the walls would not be flat but three-dimensionally organic to emphasize the individuality of each stone.

The interior of the studio is a visual utopia, demonstrating the master craftman at his best. Esherick hated waste, and every space is utilized: curved drawers that pull out at angles fit snugly in corners; above a free-form sink hangs a matching shaped cutting board and alongside it Esherick's handmade wooden bowls and spoons. He built a sofa that curves with the room, an alcove bed with drawers that fit discreetly underneath, and a dining table and bench that tuck into the corner overlooking the wooded valley. The dining room floor is a random but cleverly conceived pattern of applewood and walnut salvaged from Esherick's supplier's discard pile.

The centerpiece is the spiral staircase constructed in 1930 and carved from heavy timbers of red oak. Esherick twisted the shaft so that all of the treads cantilevered from the same face, their deep tenons pulled into the shaft by long bolts. He placed the treads all the way up to the second-floor loft; they veer to the left halfway up for access to the kitchen and dining area on an intermediate floor. The metal bolts allowed the piece to be easily dismantled on two occasions: first for his collaborative work with the architect George Howe in their room "Pennsylvania Hill House" for the 1940 New York World's Fair, and again for a 1958 retrospective of the artist at the Museum of Contemporary Craft. Above the dining room is a small room built for his son, Peter. With his ever-playful mind, Esherick carved a handrail for the stair to the room in dogwood that looks like a bone.

In 1928 he built a garage exploring his interest in German expressionism. He ran the roof's ridge diagonally so that each rafter is on a progressively steeper slope, resulting in concave and convex surfaces. His third structure, completed in the mid-1950s, became his workshop and is now the home of his daughter, Ruth, and her husband, Bob Bascom. To design it, Esherick enlisted the help of his friend, Philadelphia architect Louis Kahn. The seemingly

unlikely pair—Kahn, lover of straight lines; Esherick, enamored of curves—was intensely interested in the materiality of things and created a building of three connecting hexagons set on a crescent curve. It was made with cinder blocks, but Esherick disliked the hard edges, so he angled the blocks with 120-degree corners, producing a dovetail effect, and staggered the blocks on the sidewalls to create a slight curve.

His decision to focus on sculpted furniture came in the late 1920s. Clients had come looking to purchase a painting but ended up buying Esherick's kitchen table. His friends urged him to sell more pieces, and eventually he saw this as a more fruitful endeavor than painting. According to a docent at the Wharton Esherick Museum, Esherick constantly gave away pieces he had made for himself. Clients often requested pieces similar to those they saw in his studio, however, as the docent mentioned, Esherick knew he could not duplicate a piece because the intricacies of wood never show until cut into, so he would send them that very piece.

He worked as a sculptor, not a cabinetmaker, and his first pieces were simple in form, with low-relief carvings as the only decoration. Many were modeled on pieces he had seen at Rose Valley. Esherick explored many styles, from Arts & Crafts to a more cubist feel with jutting angles and asymmetrical forms, to finally experimenting with the forms of abstract expressionism. Yet Esherick was always original. "I begin to shape as I go along. The piece just grows beneath my hands," he often said. Or as he once told a reporter for the *Christian Science Monitor:* "I dig up what I do out of my own soul."

As personal as Esherick's approach was, he found inspiration in the changing art scene in Philadelphia (where he often made trips) and through his involvement with the Rose Valley Arts & Crafts community near Paoli. Esherick also enjoyed the theater and helped with the design and carpentry of the Hedgerow Theater repertory, established in 1923 by Jasper Deeter. He even built the theater chairs, using hammer handles that he had bought at an auction. Those chairs, born out of Esherick's determined thrift and ingenuity, now command high prices at auction. He used the theater as a kind of gallery to display his sculpted pieces in the hopes, he told Bascom, that "somebody who liked modern theater would like modern sculpture."

Commissions came mainly by word of mouth. One of his first clients, Helene Koerting Fischer of Philadelphia, bought *Finale*, a wistful sculpture of a dancer reclining after her dance, the fanning pleats of her gown forming an expressionistic pattern. Hooked on this iconoclastic artist, Fischer commissioned several other pieces, including a prismatic cubist corner desk. Esherick found other patrons who also became addicted to his art forms. One such patron was Curtis Bok, a Pennsylvania Common Pleas Court justice who was looking for someone to make interesting bookshelves.

The Bok commission (1935–38) was the largest Esherick ever accepted. Once Bok saw the types of pieces Esherick had made for others, he found more things in his house that needed work. In the end, Esherick created a harmonious and ingenious work of interior art,

ABOVE LEFT The Captain's chairs here are well-known forms, but Esherick found a way to smooth out the stiffness usually associated with this chair without sacrificing its sense of importance. **RIGHT** The sensual multifunctional dining table is a testament to Esherick's ingenuity in creating functional art, not to mention his determination. Furniture, he once said, "must be non-tippable, so a fool like myself won't break it if he leans back."

OPPOSITE PAGE The studio at the Wharton Esherick Museum is a masterpiece in form, function, beauty, and resourcefulness. Many pieces found there were made by him, or his artist friends, from salvaged wood. The handrail for the spiral staircase was found by a friend. The sofa in the main work space follows the exact curvature that Esherick used for his sculpture pitone floor below. The studio abounds in surprising details, from an asymmetrical hand-carved light switch to the organically-shaped kitchen utensils. In a simple wooden desk chair, Esherick inlaid the leather straps rather than simply wrap them around the wood. A cabinet (seen in the photo of Esherick drawing on wood) opens to reveal a desk with thin drawers fitting snugly inside; the small light was wired by Esherick himself.

ABOVE The Bok commission is another residence where Esherick proved his ability to create a total work of art. The prismatic archway and fireplace seen here are very much of the period. Started in 1936, the rooms flowed harmoniously one into the other. The massive spiral staircase (seen on the following page) fanned out as if inviting the guests to venture further into the home. The library offered shelving for all shapes and sizes; a built-in sofa with concealed drawers sat below the sculpted wooden-framed window. Geometric forms were featured throughout adding a lightness to the massive amounts of hardwood. The Bok fireplace and door are now part of the permanent collection of the Philadelphia Museum of Art.

including a library, a music room, a spiral staircase, three fireplaces, and portals with furniture and sculpture that fit perfectly for each space. Esherick, who lacked business savvy and preferred to work alone, soon learned about running a business. He had eleven people assisting him on the Bok job. The harmony began at the spiral staircase in the foyer, constructed in white pine that came from a 150-year-old bridge in Frenchtown, New Jersey. Esherick painted the wall behind the stair black to accentuate the wide, bulbous first step. The treads melt into each other as they rise, providing a soft ascendance accented with a silvery-toned, sinewy metal handrail.

Esherick used archways, wall and ceiling panels, and furniture to create an angular, sleek unit that visually joined the library and music room. Esherick built bookshelves into the corner of the music room to house Bok's albums. Partitions were tucked into a corner that fanned out, so all the albums could fit but were still easy to reach. A radio-phonograph cabinet was built on casters to slide under the shelves when not in use. For the nearby window, Esherick, in his characteristic playfulness, sculpted wooden curtains blowing open.

In the judge's library, Esherick designed a desk with extensions for large reference books. He made a library ladder of hickory and oak that had two opposing finials—one in the form of a donkey, the other in the form of an elephant—to remind the justice to be unbiased politically.

As a woodworker, Esherick had an intimate relationship with the material. In a tribute article that appeared in *Fine Woodworking* magazine after Esherick died, Louis Kahn said, "Trees were the very life of Wharton….He had a love affair with them; a sense of oneness with the wood itself." He worked mainly in local Pennsylvania hardwoods, including oak, cherry, hickory, walnut, birch, maple, apple, tropical woods, tulipwood, and cottonwood. "If you can't make something out of the woodpile then you might as well quit," he used to say. A local woodman, Ed Ray, would set aside the best, most unique, even oddly shaped wood specifically for Esherick.

Though it later became a standard approach of woodworker artists from Nakashima to Maloof, Esherick was the first to make a point of following the wood's grain, choosing free-flowing

forms and protruding angles. He often used twisted wood or crotch wood, the discarded piece from the juncture where a tree branches out. He was the consummate sculptor of wood, saying in a 1969 interview with the *Christian Science Monitor* that he saw wood as "intimate, alive…. The wood has an influence on you…. You can't fool with wood."

The Whitney Design Studio, forerunner of the Whitney Museum of American Art, began exhibiting his wood sculptures in 1929. By 1932 Esherick's furniture and sculptures began showing up in galleries, like the Art Alliance in Philadelphia, and in museums, such as at the 1933 Whitney Biennial. His pieces gained notoriety from the 1940 New York World's Fair and 1958 Brussels World's Fair, and his designs can be found today in several iconic institutions. His Music Stand of 1962 is in the collection of the Metropolitan Museum of Art, and the Philadelphia Museum of Art holds the impressive Bok library fireplace and library steps.

Function and comfort were very important to Esherick. Ruth told the *Washington Post* that her father "always wanted to know how people moved through a room before he made a piece of furniture for it." When one client wanted a dining table to seat a certain number of people, Esherick told her to bring him that many dinner plates. Once he could see how the client wanted the plates arranged, he spread newspapers on the floor and drew his ideas directly on the paper. While Esherick became close to his clients, almost like family, they knew better than to tell Esherick what they wanted a piece to look like. The result always looked different from what they expected, "and always much better and more interesting," recalled Bascom.

Esherick employed a few workshop assistants, among them John Schmidt, Bill McIntyre (who worked for him for more than forty years), and Horace Hartshaw. They were there for construction and jointing, but Esherick did the designing and shaping for every piece. He used typical woodworking machines, but his favorite was a bandsaw built by John Schmidt, who incorporated bicycle wheels into the design. As Esherick stated in the *Christian Science Monitor*, "this business of hand-done stuff is a lot of nonsense. It's made by the hand, of course. But more, it's made by heart and head." He used whatever tools he needed to help speed the process. "Handcraft has nothing to do with it. I'll use my teeth if I have to," he exclaimed in *Craft Horizons*. His cabinetmakers worked on the polishing and the construction details, since Esherick wasn't trained to do so and since he wanted to be an originator and creator more than a cabinetmaker.

Esherick drew directly on the board, while his assistants cut out the shapes that he then finished by hand. Esherick "always handled with great sensitivity and had a regard for the natural qualities of the wood," said Wendell Castle in a eulogy to the artist, describing how he "had many shaping techniques which were uniquely his, including a special way of handling checks and knots. Cracks would be carefully sanded, emphasizing their shapes. Knots would be allowed to project above the surface, adding a tactile quality."

Tactility was a quality Esherick always appreciated in wood. In the Wharton Esherick Museum the kitchen table is flat on the top surface but Esherick shaped the underside to remove

ABOVE LEFT Esherick's desk from 1929 represents his first forays into furniture making. The simple form is accentuated with reliefs from nature: a tree changing with the seasons. **CENTER** The corner desk was made for Helene Fischer in 1931 and reflects his experiments with cubism. Standing at almost four feet high this desk is an exercise in space saving. Esherick often made corner units for his clients to utilize every inch of their home. In this desk he not only made it fit in the corner, but he also turned every nook and cranny into a useful drawer. Esherick never wasted materials. **RIGHT** His hammer-handle chairs are a great example of the artist creating simple and supple forms out of something that was strictly utilitarian and near at hand. Esherick made thirty-six hammer-handle chairs for the Hedgerow Theater's rehearsal room.

termite damage, keeping it natural rather than flattening it. He was quoted in the *New York Times* in 1954: "It must be beautiful in all positions, even upside down." Sometimes his recipes for a finish sounded as simple as a salad dressing: "Take a table top. Throw oil all over it, add salt and pepper, rub them in carefully, then scrub them off with an abrasive cleaner."

His original joy in creating still echoes through every piece. Esherick's ability to transform an old-world vernacular form into a work of art is conveyed in stools that are simple in form but each with a different organically shaped seat. He applied his aesthetic to everything he touched—even such workaday creations as wooden trays and spoons (which now sell for between $3,000 and $7,000 at auction). The larger pieces exemplify the same pervasively artistic but economical attitude about design. In a large bench Esherick designed for Ms. Fischer's home, which sold at Sollo Rago Antiques for $132,000 in April 2007, he constructed pivoting drawers under the seat that illuminated when opened. He usually did not apply hardware to his case goods, perhaps because it would have introduced an artificial element to his organic expressions.

Expressing his joy as purely as possible through the shaping of wood was always Esherick's focus. He once told Sam Maloof matter-of-factly that he signed pieces as Chippendale had, in the hopes that they would become valuable. Making money was always an issue, but Esherick kept his eye on a different prize: "If you don't have joy, are not enthusiastic with what you're doing, no matter how much dough you've got, you're no good." **E.J.**

ABOVE This bench for Helene Fischer showcases Esherick's skill in creating movement using prismatic, space-saving forms. Not only do the lines allow the eye to move smoothly along the sleek form, but they also conceal the drawers that light from within as they are pivoted open. Over seven feet wide, the bench is bold and statuesque but not overbearing.

OPPOSITE PAGE A photo of the Bok staircase shows the contrasting effect Esherick strove to achieve when he chose to use a dark paint for the wall. A 1939 sculpture made from the crotch wood of a cherry tree was named *Actress*. Esherick made this sculpture after seeing a photograph of his daughter preparing for a play at the Hedgerow Theater; it is now housed at the Wharton Esherick Museum.

ARTHUR ESPENET CARPENTER

With bulldog independence, shrewd experimentation, and an appreciation for beautiful utilitarian objects, Arthur Espenet Carpenter (1920–2006) was a woodworker whose pieces resonated with simplicity, functionality, and ingenuity.

While many a soldier returning from World War II chased jobs and success at the big corporations fueling America's growth as an industrial superpower, Arthur Espenet Carpenter chose instead to root himself in the world of design and craft, forsaking the security of a stable income for his own definition of success and happiness. A furniture maker whose pieces were sensually smooth and functional but never mass-produced, Espenet Carpenter (professionally known as Espenet) had an appreciation for utilitarian beauty. His success as a self-taught woodworker creating sculptural, functional pieces using innovative, time-saving techniques set him apart from woodworkers who used traditional techniques and simple forms, making him a fixture and a major influence in the field of American woodworking.

Born in 1920 in New York City, Espenet became one of the many self-taught craftspeople who moved to and flourished in California, which, unbeknownst to him, would become a haven for corporate-rejecting, nature-loving artists a decade after the war. After a childhood spent in Oregon, followed by studying economics at Dartmouth College and serving as a lieutenant in the Navy, Espenet returned to New York to work for an Asian art import/export firm. This job, as he told an interviewer with *American Craft* in 1982, provided an early exposure to the strong tradition of Asian crafts. He also regularly visited the Good Design shows at the Museum of Modern Art, where he found inspiration in the organic, functional designs of Charles Eames and the sleek bowls of woodworker James Prestini.

This early appreciation of streamlined, organic shapes (he also admired the technical genius of the Swiss engineer Robert Maillart's bridges) gave Espenet a singular vision that became his main tenet when making furniture: function plus simplicity created beauty. He felt the simplest form, with the simplest line, made with a minimal amount of material— not for financial economy but for visual and aesthetic economy—created the most beautiful and useful pieces.

Visiting MoMA's Good Design shows inspired Espenet to make a new path for himself in a new home in San Francisco. With a $100-a-month stipend from the GI Bill of Rights, Espenet started a business in the Mission District in 1947, selling lumber, woodworking supplies,

OPPOSITE PAGE This 1961 carved-walnut lounge chair fitted with wide leather straps has bold, accentuated curves but a diminutive presence. Espenet produced functional pieces that were influenced by clean lines and organic forms; this chair exemplifies his originality in finding beauty in the simplest forms.

ABOVE A portrait of Arthur Espenet Carpenter in his workshop in 1999. According to friends, Espenet was a quiet but strong man who enjoyed his work to the fullest.

and do-it-yourself items. He also began experimenting with making "small utilities"—mostly bowls. Espenet first planned to design while others produced; so his first mediums were Formica and aluminum. And since his influences in craft stemmed from Eames's lamination process for producing compound curves, his forms imitated those of Eames and Alexander Calder. He designed fish shapes, boomerang shapes, and even emulated a Bertoia wire sculpture.

Espenet then realized that design and construction went hand in hand, and as a voracious reader—*Scientific American* being one of his favorites according to his former apprentice Robert Brown—he studied woodwork, learning about the tools of the trade. He bought his first lathe in 1948 and started learning how to turn bowls. For about six years Espenet turned out bowl after bowl, among other small utilities, to sell in his shop, getting the bowls to about a quarter-inch thick, something no one else was doing with that level of refined detailing. The bowls sold at shops in Los Angeles, then at the Merchandise Mart in Chicago. It was in Chicago that MoMA's Industrial Design Department director, Edgar Kaufmann, Jr., first saw Espenet's bowls and asked him to exhibit in the *Good Design* shows, where they were featured from 1950 to 1954.

After eight years in the Mission, Espenet was steeped in the San Francisco craft scene. As a savvy marketer, he entered every local craft fair and art festival in the area and exhibited at museums on both the West Coast and East Coast to advertise his business. He then changed locations to have a storefront and accommodate his machinery, and opened another shop where he and four other craftspeople sold their pieces. However, he never considered himself a craftsman, stating, "I didn't care how I made it, provided it came out right." So self-taught Espenet solicited local cabinetmakers for advice on basic construction techniques, and he gradually experimented, making simple stools and coffee tables with turned legs or wrought-iron bases and slabs of wood. His craftsmanship became refined enough to make a solid structure in the quickest amount of time, and allowed him to exist solely on private commissions rather than retail (most clients came to him by word of mouth). Seeing the smooth, sculptural edges and asymmetrical forms of Wharton Esherick encouraged Espenet to pursue his dream of a career as a woodworker. And in 1957, with savings from the Navy, Espenet bought ten acres of land in Bolinas Beach, California, of which he sold off five acres to afford the construction of his home and workshop, which he and one employee took eight years to build. By late 1957, he had six employees prefabricating his bowls (which he personally hand finished). At his Bolinas workshop he perfected his skills in furniture making and then sold everything at his Geary shop—a success to which few woodworkers can relate.

One of Espenet's bigger commissions was for the Mill Valley Library (1966), for which he designed more than one hundred pieces, including chairs, tables, and reading carrels with soft curves and simple forms. Espenet once explained that he developed the tables' form—an inverted U shape with three flat planes meeting at right angles using dovetail joinery—from an ancient Chinese style of furniture he called Lu Pan. With this simple yet durable structure, he was able to build more than one hundred pieces in twelve months with only one assistant.

In 1991 he designed the dais for the Mountain View Council Chamber. It is a half-moon shape lined with varying widths of vertical slats in natural wood color accentuated with dark wooden grooves. The top rail appears to float and has soft, rounded edges stained dark to contrast with the light-colored vertical slats.

A true innovator, Espenet liked to experiment with form based on the necessities of the piece. "I never listened to my clients," he stated in 2001, because "once you did that you lost your reputation; you're just another cabinet shop." Although wood was his medium of choice—California black walnut being his favorite—he also experimented with color in his pieces, such as using colored felt under poured resin and enamels. Function, however, was his true mantra. In a 1983 article he wrote for *Fine Woodworking*, titled "The Rise of Artiture, Woodworking Comes to Age," he objected to designers making furniture that is "arty" or "artiture" and described some pieces as "people traps" that are not only nonfunctional but are harmful as well.

When designing a piece, he started with sketches on plywood. "In one gesture, one movement, he'd outline the piece, study it for a while, then sand it down, and start again until he found what he liked," stated Brown. Finally, he would cut out the form to use as a template. Models at one-eighth scale were used to experiment with form, and he sometimes mailed them to clients. Again, Robert Brown: "Everything was low-tech [in his studio].... Art loved the intellectual side of design [and] was interested in and open to learning from people."

As necessary, Espenet invented the tools and techniques required to expedite his visions, resulting in the use of pigeonholes or devices that burned wood to make the interiors of bowls. He created a jig that made several dovetails at once (a tool widely used by craftsmen today). With these time-saving tools, he explored new forms and could produce durable, beautiful pieces faster; although, according to his son, Tripp, "he spent hours on each piece" until it was perfect. The development of his innovative, free-form band-saw boxes was the result of experimenting with new forms and ridding himself from the doldrums of cutting joints. He used the band saw to cut out drawers in organic shapes and to hollow them out, then he simply placed the drawer back inside the box. This reduced the process into two simple tasks. He used the lathe to make "mushroom cap" handles on drawers, placing them randomly (but functionally) on the surface, as if they sprouted there on their own.

While faster production resulted in faster profit, Espenet's frustration with ease of production also fueled his ingenuity. From the development of the band-saw box came the use of pigeon-holes in his iconic Roll-Top desk designed in 1970. In this piece, Espenet gave new meaning to the phrase "form follows function" by adding production. Economy of production was important to him as the means by which the small furniture maker could survive. His use of the pigeonhole for a slot not only eased production—it gave an added sensuality to a form that was often characterless.

Espenet thought of himself as "an experimenter and originator, " according to an interview in *American Craft,* and his pieces offered individuality and personality in even the most basic forms that he duplicated. Some have spinal-looking slots and asymmetrical forms; others offer more drawers and more symmetry. But with each desk, he always returns to the same principles of utility, economy, and curvaceous sensuality—traits found in every Espenet piece.

Espenet also once described his craft as an "engineered art; because no craftsman in their right mind would make a sloppy joint." With another iconic piece, the Wishbone chair designed in 1965, one so-called "sloppy joint" took two years for Espenet to figure out how to combine the concave back with the legs without using mortise and tenons, and how to prevent the legs from twisting with the back. "I didn't know how to put two pieces of wood together…literally. … I didn't know how to make a good mortise and tenons. So it occurred to me, skeletons: how did bones hold together? So the first Wishbone chair was bony; I had a fist going into a socket. How do you hold a fist in the socket? I ended up using bolts."

ABOVE This bureau and music rack show Espenet's use of nature in his furniture. Rather than alluding to nature with sinuous shapes and bulbous forms, he made his references literal in these pieces. For the bureau he created clusters of mushroom-cap knobs scattered about as if in a field, and in the music rack he used the form of a snake to make the rack hold the sheets of music. As an "experimenter and originator" Espenet was able to create novel forms for otherwise banal pieces by exploring his ideas through the use of his band saw. Even though these pieces are quite common, Espenet found a way to make them involving and fun for the user.

Although Espenet exhibited at many venues throughout his long career—and was the recipient of countless awards—his humility and sincerity never faltered. The 1972 *Woodenworks* exhibition at the Renwick Gallery in Washington, D.C., was eye-opening for Espenet, who realized that he was recognized nationally alongside such influential peers as Wharton Esherick, Sam Maloof, George Nakashima, and Wendell Castle.

As a teacher, Espenet taught by example, allowing his apprentices to watch him make pieces rather than telling them how it was done. In 1970 his own apprentice, Tom D'Onofrio, approached Espenet to cofound the Baulines Craftmen's Guild, a group that offered aspiring craftspeople the opportunity to learn from professionals and that still exists today. Even Espenet's son, Tripp, continues the legacy of producing finely crafted objects and furniture of his own design, and he also aspires to publish his father's autobiography.

Today, Espenet's pieces are slowly showing up at auction and commanding good prices, ranging from $6,000 for a black-walnut box to $42,000 for a trestle table. His sensuous one-of-a-kind pieces can be identified not only by their ingenious construction and sexy curves, but by his simple carved signature: Espenet, then the last two digits of the year the piece was made and, if necessary, an edition number. While as a craftsman he wanted to "keep prices at a consumer's, not collector's level," Espenet pieces can now rightfully command collector prices. In "Reflections on the Chairs of Charles Eames," an article Espenet wrote on his hero for *Craft Horizons* in 1973, he wrote that vision and experimentation are "two of the sine qua nons of every good craftsman." But Espenet, who died in 2006, never considered himself a craftsman. He thought of himself instead as just a man who wanted to earn a living making things no one else had done before him. **E.J.**

ABOVE The pieces above represent Espenet's innovative use of tools and time management. The Wishbone chair was the result of Espenet engineering the construction of a chair without using the typical mortise and tenons that most woodworkers employ. The chair's laminated legs have a slight flare at the bottom, and the gentle upward curve allows the front legs to meet the back legs at the seat back. Shaped by hand, the seat back's concave shape hugs the sitter, and Espenet's "fist-in-socket" joinery—filled with walnut plugs and beeswax—provides a beautiful detail to the structure. The base of the desk is a primitive shape that uses a trestle to support two planks that split in two at the floor. A slender roll-top shape forms the case with three simple drawers placed at its apron. The band saw allowed Espenet to shape each slot in one fell swoop, allowing him to produce the piece faster but without losing its appealing sensuality. In his long career, Espenet was much more than a studio designer. The band-saw boxes, for which Espenet was so well known, allowed him to experiment with details he later used in his roll-top desk. Each drawer leads to another in one motion, and he even fit a drawer within a drawer proving his mastery of this technique.

OPPOSITE PAGE In 1966 *Life* magazine included Espenet's Bolinas circular home in its article on domestic architecture. Centered around the circular kitchen, the uniquely functional home radiates into an array of separate, circular rooms that were built almost entirely by Espenet with the aid of one assistant. The sunken living room is an iconic gesture for this period in California design. Espenet's large round fireplace also offered warmth and security from the outside elements, but the floor-to-ceiling windows allowed the residents to still feel a part of nature.

Above left: Photograph © 2008 Museum of Fine Arts, Boston.

SAM MALOOF

Sam Maloof (b. 1916) has spent his very long career deeply committed to hand craftsmanship. He has, and wants, no factory, no advertising, no marketing program. Self-taught, he is guided by an innate understanding of the interrelation among material, form, and function—and an underlying reverence for beautiful wood. Maloof furniture is simple, sophisticated, and strong. Each piece has clean lines, graceful and balanced curves, figured wood, and the tactile pleasures of a labor-intensive rubbed finish. Determined to control all of the creative process, he limits his output by the pieces he can produce with his own hands, to his exacting standards of excellence. Still, over a span of sixty years, he has produced more than five thousand clearly Maloof pieces and has had a very personal relationship with every single one of them. His work occupies the intersection of craft and design, although he disavows the term "craftsman," preferring all his life the plainer label, "woodworker."

Maloof has been remarkably consistent in his aesthetic vision. "Fashion comes and goes, but my pieces have to have the integrity of my vision," he says. Ninety-five percent of Maloof's pieces have been made of black walnut, which he values for both its lovely grain and its forgiving nature; he also uses figured woods such as fiddleback, or curly maple, treasured by many for its strong grain and warm color; and he has less frequently worked in oak, Brazilian rosewood, and ebony. He never mixes woods in a piece. He always exposes his artful joints, considering them a design element not to be hidden but to be appreciated for their beauty and resourcefulness. He doesn't use metal or other man-made substances. His typical finish is a painstaking process involving several applications of a turpentine-boiled linseed-oil mixture, pure linseed, and then a careful rubbing with pumice or rottenstone and an oil-soaked leather pad. He does much of it himself, even these days, aided by the elbow grease of three other master woodworkers (he has never had more than three assistants).

A second-generation American of Lebanese descent, Maloof was born in Chino, California, in 1916, and, over parental objections, went directly to work upon finishing high school, first as a self-taught graphic artist at Claremont-based Vortox Manufacturing Company, and then for Harold E. Graham, an industrial designer. At Graham he picked up the basic skills he would later use to great success, learning to handle wood power tools and mastering the intricacies of wood joints. After an army stint during World War II, he took a job with the Los Angles–based commercial art firm Angelus-Pacific and rented a one-bedroom apartment that he furnished with pieces he made from plywood and red-oak packing crates.

OPPOSITE PAGE The rocking chair is one of Maloof's most iconic forms. Instead of using his preferred material, walnut, here he used cherry and ebony, a combination that he worked with successfully beginning in the late eighties.

  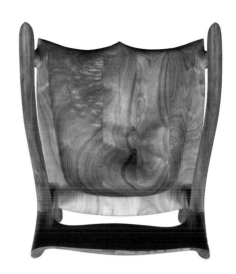

ABOVE Maloof's chairs range from sinuous to geometric with allusions to different historical genres. This trio best captures the range of his artistic expression. **LEFT** A prototype dining chair in maple and walnut with leather upholstery from 1952. **CENTER** A prototype horn-back chair with carved arms in walnut (c. 1960). **RIGHT** A Low-back side chair in walnut and ebony signed "No. 5 1987 Sam Maloof f.A.C.C."

OPPOSITE PAGE TOP Maloof married Alfreda Ward in 1948. With not enough money to buy furniture, Maloof set out to design and construct an interior for their new home. Using borrowed tools and found or reclaimed materials—including fir plywood that had been used for containing wet cement—Maloof created a full interior that astonished friends and acquaintances with its ad hoc bravura beauty. With Alfreda's encouragement, Maloof quit his day job (working in the studio of Millard Sheets, a high-profile California artist) and dedicated himself to private commissions. In 1951, the home was featured in *Better Homes & Gardens*. **BOTTOM** In 1981 the first piece of studio furniture entered the White House's collection. Presidents Carter, Reagan, and Clinton have collected and enjoyed Maloof's pieces.

In late 1946 Maloof made a life-altering decision, taking the job of studio assistant/printmaker/jack of all trades for Millard Sheets, then head of the art department at Scripps College (and a leading painter in the California watercolorist school). This was a very good move. It was Maloof's first exposure to the world of fine art, and it enabled him most happily to return to his beloved Pomona Valley, from whence he never again wandered. But most important, at Scripps Maloof met and in 1948 married Alfreda Ward, with whom he had an adoring relationship for fifty-two years. Freda was remarkably supportive, initially encouraging him to start his own business, keeping meticulous (extant) records, and serving always as his beloved inspiration. (Imagine writing "To Freda with all my love" on the underside of furniture.)

Maloof caught a lucky break in 1951 when *Better Homes and Gardens* published "Handsome Furniture You Can Build," an illustrated spread on the Maloofs' modest tract home, along with working drawings of his plywood furniture, offering the plans for twenty-five cents each to amateur woodworkers. He earned a lordly $150 for the plans, according to a 2002 interview. Not long after, renowned industrial designer Henry Dreyfuss gave him his first solo commission: Maloof designed and made almost all the furniture for Dreyfuss's new, modern Pasadena home—twenty-five pieces, his total output for 1952—for $1,880.

Although a one-man furniture design manufactory was as unusual then as it is now, Sam, urged on by Freda, decided to take a shot as an independent furniture maker. Maloof quit his day jobs, and the couple happily moved to the bucolic community of Alta Loma, forty miles east of Los Angeles, acquiring what was essentially a one-room shack—all they could afford. Over the decades, as he could, Maloof built new rooms, until the home had eight thousand square feet of what he calls "add-ons"—twenty-six rooms filled with increasingly sophisticated and beautiful pieces made in his adjacent workshop. His home always was his showroom. This extraordinary structure eventually landed on the National Register of Historic Places.

Maloof 's reputation was rising just as the modernist school of Southern California architecture was gaining traction and press, and literally changing the landscape. His aesthetic vision was completely congruent with it—sleek, clean-lined houses cried out for those qualities in furnishings—and he received commissions from the movement's leading architects and designers. With the help of good coverage in the *Los Angeles Times Sunday Home Magazine, House Beautiful, Arts & Architecture,* and *Craft Horizon*, his name spread in the 1950s and '60s, and he has never since wanted for work. As Maloof's star was rising, the Scandinavian furniture juggernaut swept the land, captivating the cognoscenti as well as the Scarsdale housewife. Georg Jensen was a raging retail success, and MoMA lent its imprimatur in the 1952 exhibit, "New Design Trends." Although Maloof's work shares some qualities with what was commonly called "Scandinavian modern," he maintains that his style was firmly in place well before the teak invasion. In any case, modern was in the zeitgeist, and Maloof was in the right place. He was busy and happy.

Maloof has done commissioned projects for churches; businesses such as Kaiser Industries, Lawry's Foods, and SAS (the now defunct Scandinavian airline); and major department stores like Saks Fifth Avenue and Goldwater's. But about 85 percent of his commissions are for private homes, and he is most renowned for his clean-lined, graceful chairs, unadorned save for the wood grain and those wonderful joints. He has said that chairs should welcome, not dare, people to sit in them, that they should be embracing and comfortable. "It doesn't matter how beautiful the workmanship is on a chair. If it doesn't sit well, it's a lousy chair," he said in *Woodworker's Journal* (2000). His chairs are unusually comfortable (especially unexpected in slat backs) for people of all sizes, shapes, and weights—attributable to the support they provide to the lumbar region. Maloof's signature rocking chairs first appeared in 1958, to little demand, but they have become his best-known design and now sell for around $40,000 (each takes nearly four weeks to make). They have been owned by presidents Reagan, Clinton, and Carter—Maloof counts amateur woodworker Jimmy Carter as a friend—and are represented in the official White House collection.

Maloof's furniture is distinctive and recognizable because of his fidelity to his vision of function and simplicity. In six decades of continuous work and more than five hundred different designs, he has never made a change or redirect that could in any sense be called radical. Each new design evolves directly from its predecessor. His earliest pieces were characterized by angular, geometric lines—square legs, right angles, and the like. In iterations over the years, his style softened: the legs became round (the first turned legs appeared on Maloof's string chairs in the 1950s), ninety-degree edges were smoothed and rounded, and angular straight lines gave way to undulating and increasingly complex curves. Stretchers disappeared as innovative joints obviated them. He introduced a detail he called a "hard line"—an integral sculptured crest or ridge, like an attenuated curl, that visually strengthened the vertical members. And in more recent years, he has dialed up the details—the "hard-line" ridges now sometimes run twice as deep, edges are sharpened, legs are more angular, lines are strengthened by ebony stringing. The pieces look more forceful, yet a Maloof piece is, clearly, a Maloof piece.

It is a measure of Maloof's achievements that in 1985 he was awarded a five-year, $500,000 MacArthur Fellowship—the so-called "genius" award—the only craftsperson so honored to date. Soon after, *People* magazine ran a feature on him, and in 1986 he shipped a record twenty-six rocking chairs. Equally prestigious, in 2001 the Renwick Gallery of the Smithsonian American Art Museum held a major retrospective of his work, "The Furniture of Sam Maloof," which was accompanied by a hardcover exhibition catalogue by senior curator Dr. Jeremy Adamson. Over his long career Maloof has accumulated many honors, including an honorary degree from the Rhode Island School of Design (1992) and a Gold Medal from the American Craftsmen's Council (1988), of which he was a longtime trustee. His work is represented in major museums across the country.

ABOVE LEFT Maloof's low-back chair, a diminutive sculptural chair made in walnut with ebony details. **RIGHT** Maloof, c. 1965, on his property in Alta Loma, California.

OPPOSITE PAGE The national recognition and financial stability that arrived in the mid-eighties, courtesy of a generous MacArthur "Genius" fellowship, inspired further artistic evolution. Maloof began working with variations of maple and this handsome two-drawer desk possesses an almost iridescent shine. Regardless of the wood, Maloof perfected the convergence of functionality and artistry so evident in this fiddleback maple and ebony piece from 1992.

ABOVE LEFT Like the rocking chair, the music stand is another icon of American studio art. Maloof occasionally experimented in making it with exotic woods like the Brazilian rosewood used in this example from 1972. **RIGHT** During the late sixties Maloof's reputation and output grew considerably as tastes in interior decoration and design tended to the more organic, especially in California. Maloof's work shares some characteristics with Scandinavian design, most specifically an affinity for wood, and function before ornamentation. Yet Maloof is distinct from the Europeans in his willingness to play with proportions and create graceful, and occasionally elongated, lines. Most importantly his pieces posses an inimitably idiosyncratic personality and confidence. The walnut desk hutch (c. 1970) features carved "J" hook latches that close the upper and lower doors.

OPPOSITE PAGE Some of Maloof's most adventurous and impressive pieces, like this spiral staircase (1981), were made for his sprawling 8,000-square-foot compound in Alta Loma, California. What started out as a modest cabin had expanded over the years to include an impressive cluster of workshops, guesthouses, and living quarters all surrounded by a lush citrus grove. After a lengthy procedure, the compound was designated as a historic property even as the government spent over $12 million to relocate the majority of the buildings to another grove in the area in order to accommodate a freeway. During the nineties, some 3,000 visitors toured the compound to see Maloof's inspiring extended studio and over one hundred of his pieces on display.

Above left and right: © 2008, Jonathan Pollock.

Times change. When Sam Maloof opened his shop, the world was a simpler place. He was esteemed for his artistry and his craft, for making beautiful and functional objects, and for a profound commitment to the personal, almost spiritual process of production by hand. In any discussion of "craft" today, utility is disdained, displaced by self-expressive art that almost by definition is unconcerned with useful application. Craft has come to look a lot more like modern art and a lot less like a skill, however inspired, that produces useful pieces from a reproduceable design. Jeremy Adamson described the rift that divided the craft world when emphasis shifted from the nobility of the process to the intellectual challenge of making one-off studio pieces. "In the 1980s," he said, "as crafts became increasingly 'artified' and the market for unique forms boomed, Maloof's practical designs and traditional techniques found a more appreciative audience among amateur cabinetmakers. Instead of critical acceptance in *American Craft*, his work was now celebrated in the pages of *Fine Woodworking*. During the 1980s and 1990s, the number of woodworking demonstrations he conducted exceeded the number of museum exhibitions in which his work appeared."

Although the craft community may view Maloof today as an early achiever, as a designer/craftsman rather than an artist/craftsman, he was an important member of the "first generation" of postwar studio furniture makers and retains a loyal audience. At age ninety-one he has enough commissions to keep him busy for many years. Chairs that sold for $35 when he was young sell at auction today for tens of thousands of dollars. Maloof's record auction price was set by a conference table and chairs from the 1960s that sold in 2006 for close to $200,000.

Maloof has summed up his lifelong philosophy: "For me it is not enough to be a designer only. I want to be able to work a piece of wood into an object that contributes something beautiful and useful to our everyday living. To be able to live and work without subsidy, to be able to work with materials without destroying their natural beauty and warmth, to be able to work as we want—that is a God-given privilege." **R.M.**

JACK ROGERS HOPKINS

The furniture of Jack Rogers Hopkins (1920–2006) was initially inspired by the sensual forms created on a potter's wheel. Its thought-provoking style invites people to spend time contemplating its highly unusual shapes and construction from across the room, rather than simply enjoying its physical comfort and functionality. Hopkins, whose work contains few straight lines, sharp angles, or even edges, was a leading figure on the California design scene during the late 1960s, as American furniture everywhere was becoming more sculptural and free-form.

As a studio craftsman and university professor, Hopkins considered himself primarily "a sculptor-designer," finding the term "artist" too generic for his Renaissance approach to drawing, painting, ceramics, and jewelry. He saw "art as an expression of problem solving," as he once said, and he sought aesthetic and technical challenges to discover how he could apply what he learned from pottery or sculpture to other creative mediums, such as furniture design.

Hopkins grew up in Bakersfield, California, and as a young boy learned to make toys for his friends in his father's wood shop, the Sierra Furniture Manufacturing Co. While the shop provided access and exposure to materials, it did not appeal to Hopkins. Instead he and his brother, who had both been exposed to photography in high school, enlisted in the Navy as photographers. Serving as a Photographer's Mate First Class, Hopkins was stationed in Pearl Harbor for two years, shortly after the 1941 attack. During a visit to Washington, D.C., Hopkins met his future wife, Esther, at a dance. After the war Hopkins returned to California with Esther and attended the California College of Arts and Crafts, where he studied painting and drawing on the GI Bill of Rights and a scholarship from the State of California. After graduating in 1950, Hopkins earned his Master of Fine Arts from the Claremont Colleges. In 1960 he began teaching in the art department at San Diego State University, where he remained an influential teacher until his retirement in 1991. Esther remembered, "his first creative form was painting, working on a flat surface. He became tired of working within the limits of two-dimensional work and wanted to get into three-dimensional pieces." Hopkins did not start working in wood until later, around 1965, after he was already experimenting with jewelry and ceramics. His creative process, said his wife, was on "a continuum, progressing forward but not in a linear way, since he continued to work in other mediums concurrently."

OPPOSITE PAGE The walnut rocking chair is one of Jack Rogers Hopkins signature pieces. He made the first of two known examples in 1977 for his daughter, Ann, in anticipation of the birth of her child.

ABOVE LEFT In September 1970, Hopkins and his wife Esther attended the juried craft show at the Los Angeles County Fair. Hopkins showed completed work and demonstrated his stack-lamination, gluing, and shaping techniques. Hopkins's son David, a college student at the time, remembers assisting with the demonstrations having "seen the process a million times while growing up in the house." RIGHT Hopkins first sculptural furniture piece from 1966 is made of Honduras mahogany and birch veneer. The construction and design of it helped Hopkins to define his creative approach. The chair is particularly unique for the large unshaped piece of wood integrated with the seat. Hopkins experimented with veneers in the chair using stack lamination, a process he used throughout his career.

In 1966 Hopkins completed his first furniture piece, a combination chair and coffee table made with Honduras mahogany and birch veneer, using the stacked-lamination process. While the technique was generations-old at the time, Hopkins's sculptural approach was not derivative of past or contemporary furniture styles. Other woodworkers such as Wendell Castle, Bob Falwell, and James Nash used the same technique, but Hopkins brought a vision and commitment to working exclusively with stacked lamination for his furniture designs.

Traditional lamination, in which two to three thin layers of wood are stacked on top of each other, required clamps to set the glue, which was placed on the wider flat side of each layer, known as the face. This was a slow, labor-intensive method to build up a flat, smooth stack so that the wood could be carved, sculpted with a shaper, then polished and eventually sanded, until Hopkins felt by intuition that a piece had been perfected.

A vital aspect of his artistic process was the extensive use of sketchbooks, which contained ideas, notes, figurative drawings, free-form shapes, and designs, and were primarily a means for him to work through problems to advance his perspective. Collectively the sketchbooks illustrate the artful and intellectual evolution of his work. Using a sketchbook, Hopkins would document the details of a piece before starting construction. He then developed a prototype of the piece before designing the cut patterns, which were very similar to conventional dress patterns. He drew the patterns on paper, cut and laid them on top of wood boards, then cut the boards to match the pattern. The cutting was time-consuming, since it had to be repeated for each layer.

Hopkins automated part of the painstaking lamination effort by using a high-frequency wood welder, operated like a hand-held microwave device, transmitting heat rays to cure the glue in minutes. The welder was one of the mainstays of his studio, a converted five-car garage fully equipped to be a self-contained wood shop.

Hopkins handpicked his woods and spoke of "letting the material speak for itself, to let the material come out based on its grain." He usually worked with hardwoods such as black walnut, cherry, Honduras mahogany, maple, rosewood, and teak. He also used Finnish-birch plywood and veneers, and occasionally oak. Instead of using the more common half-inch boards, he always worked with three-quarter-inch stock, a subtlety that added to his aesthetic and improved the strength of the laminated boards. Hopkins often combined various woods into a single piece so the different grains created a dynamic color pattern and form. His command of the lamination technique also reduced, or in many instances eliminated, conventional wood joinery.

Hopkins was also an exception among his peers when it came to studio help. He worked alone and did everything himself, without assistance, because he felt the act of creating was ultimately an independent experience and should not be imposed on another person. While he enjoyed talking and found conversation an essential part of his creative thinking, he was a loner, listening to classical music on the radio while he worked in the studio.

His first chair is particularly distinctive, because it is the only known example to integrate a single, nonlaminated solid board into the form of a chair. While the piece is functional and

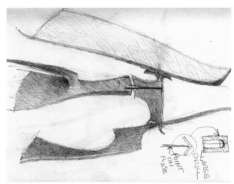

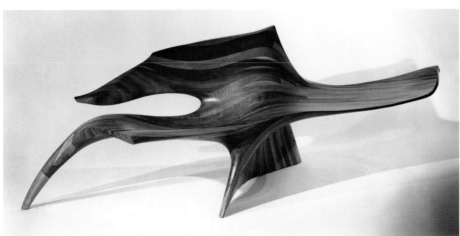

attractive, it lacks the flowing sculptural essence of later pieces, and the board has a dis-jointed quality that may have discouraged Hopkins from repeating it in future work. However, the piece does mark his entry into the field of furniture design. While pursuing his ongoing interests in others arts, he continued to produce furniture pieces, all of which were one of a kind, with the exception of the Edition chair, first created in 1969 as a wedding gift for his daughter Ann. A total of seven black walnut Edition chairs were made, featuring an arm tray that extended from the right side (for his daughter's version of the chair he placed the arm tray on the left side). The last Edition chair, completed in 1973 for his son David, was included in the 2003 exhibition *The Maker's Hand: American Studio Furniture, 1940–1990* at the Museum of Fine Arts in Boston. The retrospective featured well-known woodcrafters, including Wharton Esherick, George Nakashima, and fellow Californian Sam Maloof. Speaking at the exhibition, Hopkins described how "the Edition chair was made of two pieces of furniture and I wanted to bring them into one sculpture so I made a jig…and filled it with wet clay and then I covered it with plastic and sat in it and designed it with my derriere." The chair, which was also exhibited in the *California Design Eleven* (1971) show at the Pacific Art Center in Pasadena, is now in the permanent collection of the Museum of Fine Arts in Boston. For Hopkins, participating in the Boston exhibition was "the one most salient achievement in my art pursuits throughout my career."

During the late 1960s Hopkins started to address "explorations of sculptural forms uniting several human needs in a single unit, such as a chair-table-lamp idea." The most visible manifestation of this concept, and the largest piece Hopkins made, was his 1972 Womb Room made mostly of Honduras mahogany. The name was an allusion to its warm, cocoonlike spatial environment. Hopkins created the piece while on a six-month teaching sabbatical from San Diego State University. The Womb Room was thirteen feet long, six feet deep, and about seven feet high, and was made in four pieces containing a radio, speaker, bookshelf, and foot-rest (Hopkins also fabricated the brass lamp cover). The Womb Room attracted considerable public attention when it was first seen at the Pasadena Museum of Arts' Triennial California Design Show in 1971 as part of the *California Design Eleven* exhibition and at the Los Angeles

ABOVE LEFT Hopkins collected driftwood, dried bone shapes, and different natural forms and studied them for inspiration. In the construction of this chair, Hopkins explored engineering and balance as the chair pitched to the left under the weight of any items placed on the shelf, or when a person got up from sitting in it.
RIGHT Hopkins's family recalls how he "never left the house without a sketchbook and always seemed to be drawing." In addition to the chair sketch shown here, his sketchbooks also contain various notes about tools, types of glues and woods, dimensions of planned work, and philosophical thoughts.

County Fair in 1973. The space requirements for the Womb Room made it a difficult purchase, and the piece went unsold. Several years later, Hopkins burned some of the Womb Room wood and chopped it into pieces for different projects. He would often cut up or burn work if there was no room or storage for it. For him the creative process was more important than the final product. When people reacted to what he did to the Womb Room, he would say, "I created it and I can destroy it. If you can't destroy your own work, you shouldn't be an artist." It was one of his most strongly held convictions, one that he both practiced and taught.

Of the several hundred pieces of furniture Hopkins designed, about one-third were commissions he received through word of mouth, while others resulted from his work being exhibited in numerous galleries and museums. Among the clients who responded immediately to his work was the economist, scholar, and Nobel laureate Milton Friedman and his wife, Rose, who bought a coffee table for their home. Hopkins saw each commission as a challenge that gave him purpose: to take the client's needs and artistically realize that vision with functionality and usefulness. One of his more elaborate commissions was a black walnut executive desk made in 1973 for Dr. Carl Djerassi, a chemist and writer known internationally for developing the formula that led to the birth control pill. Djerassi was also a leading collector of Paul Klee, Hopkins's favorite artist. Instead of using a traditional kneehole design, Hopkins kept the front of the desk open, arranging features on the sides because Djerassi had a fused knee and required ease of movement at the desk, as well as the ability to sit unencumbered, without struggling with a chair. Hopkins laid out the preliminary design with shipping boxes from a washing machine to help conceptualize his idea. He did not typically make full-scale models but found it necessary to prototype the desk because of its complexity. The final desk included an ergonomic solution for Djerassi's filing cabinet, phone, and work space, and incorporated a feature to enable the doctor to keep his leg elevated while sitting at the desk in a specially built-in chair. Another unusual commission for Hopkins was a wood organ with a water fountain completed in 1977 for filmmaker Joseph Waxler. When played, water and colored lights came out of the pipes to create a fountain. Hopkins also made a dining table and chairs for Waxler.

When Hopkins finished a piece, whether for a client or a gallery, he signed it using a hot metal stamp with his full name, branding the wood where it was not visible. He did not varnish his work but developed a special formula for sealing the wood that included boiled linseed oil rubbed in with fine steel wool.

Toward the end of his life Hopkins did not work on large pieces because of the physical demands, although he did continue to work with wood, sculpting freestanding pieces. He also painted more, experimenting with acrylics and motor oil to find a viscosity for his abstract, sculptural expressions. Pottery was the last medium he tried, exploring the effects of mixing paper with clay and embracing his lifelong creed that the experience of creating is more important than the result. Hopkins wrote in one of his last sketchbooks, "If creative, it is born and dies in resolution, all in an instance of time and space. I am merely searching for my rock: hoping to identify Me in this desolate scape of everyone." **J.H.**

ABOVE LEFT As Hopkins grew older he was unable to manage lifting and carrying larger pieces, so he began to work with smaller forms. These works were generally pure sculpture. During this time he also combined wood sculpture with his paintings. More functional pieces still were his sculptural clocks. From the 1960s through the '80s, Hopkins designed jewelry with the same organic sculptural forms. **CENTER** For Hopkins even the workaday functional world of the office provided an opportunity to make sculpture as this desk and chair attest, c. 1975. **RIGHT** Exhibited at the Los Angeles County Fair Arts and Crafts Building in 1973, this grandfather clock, which stands almost eight feet tall, is comprised of two wood pieces of contrasting size and color. The weights for the clock mechanism were left open to view, unlike traditionally enclosed grandfather clocks. In the background, Hopkins's chairs and a two-person dining table with a glass top.

OPPOSITE PAGE TOP The first Edition chair (1969) was a wedding gift for Hopkins's daughter Ann and was made in a lighter color Finnish plywood than the black-walnut plywood Hopkins used for the remaining six chairs. Her chair is unique among the group for the placement of the table on the left side to accommodate her left-handed husband. All other editions of the chair have the table on the right side. In 1973 Hopkins made the last Edition chair for his son David, which is now in the permanent collection of the Museum of Fine Arts, Bostons. **BOTTOM** Completed after the Womb Room, this chair was a commissioned by a San Diego client who requested a reading environment with a lamp, bookcase, ottoman, and armrests to hold a book in a resting position.

PREVIOUS SPREAD The Womb Room (1972) made mostly of Honduras mahogany was an opportunity for Hopkins to pursue questions about aesthetics and technique. At 13' wide × 6' deep × 7' high, it offered a sculptural experience plus a radio, speaker, bookshelf, and footrest. Although widely exhibited, the Womb Room was never purchased and, with the experiment in creative discovery complete, Hopkins destroyed the work.

PAUL EVANS
& PHILLIP LLOYD
POWELL

At a singular moment in midcentury American history in a relatively brief burst of creative output, two inimitable craft artists collaborated and flourished in the unlikely setting of New Hope, Pennsylvania. Paul Evans (1931–1987) and Phillip Lloyd Powell (1919–2008) functioned anomalously as outsider producers working in rural isolation and generally spurning interaction with other artists and influences. And yet their work—Evans in sculpted metals and Powell in sinuous molded wood—was entirely attuned to the freewheeling exploratory mood of the sixties and seventies, their creative heyday.

Powell and Evans, whether working together or apart, defy easy categorization. While Powell, who died in early 2008, enjoyed living life as a carefree artist, Evans, who died in 1987, was a natural sculptor thwarted by a contradictory drive to be a deal-making entrepreneur. In fact, his best pieces exhibit the tension between his personal visions as a sculptor and his honed instinct for new looks and techniques.

Powell and Evans's intensely crafted studio works were made at the same time as Evans busily fulfilled manufacturer's orders for an expanding array of set pieces. While all were handmade, the creating hands were sometimes many as the studio evolved into a sort of craft factory. This combination of artistry and entrepreneurship had a uniquely American flavor, made possible at a time when the furniture industry itself seemed to be guided more by intuitive gambles than calculated business growth.

Powell, the older and ultimately more traditionally artistic of the two, was born in Germantown, Pennsylvania, in 1919. He studied engineering at the Drexel University of Technology, but after World War II he moved to New Hope and started refurbishing antiques and making furniture, while building his own house by hand. (A stint fulfilling an order for one thousand handmade children's step stools for Macy's one Christmas soured him permanently on the idea of production in quantities.)

At a time when Scandinavian minimalism was popular, Powell opted for a more naturalistic approach, not unlike the work of neighboring artist and architect George Nakashima. Fond of travel and of people with a knack for salesmanship, Powell opened a showroom on the Lambertville–New Hope road (that soon moved to Main Street), selling modern furniture by Knoll and Herman Miller, and lamps by Isamu Noguchi, alongside slate-topped pieces of his own. The store was an unusual success, affording Powell the chance to explore his own furniture making, using rejected wood that he bought for half-price from a salesman making deliveries to the Nakashima Workshop.

OPPOSITE PAGE Paul Evans made this whimsical, patchwork steel sculpture layered with patinated gray and white paint—his largest known metal sculpture—as a gift for Phillip Lloyd Powell in 1964. The two had been collaborators and friends for almost a decade at that point. Evans was busy producing furniture for Directional, but still found time for both the purely and nearly sculptural, such as this rare sofa. Although Evans did not usually sign his sculptural works, this one is signed "Paul Evans 64."

ABOVE LEFT Paul Evans (c. 1962) always had a sketch pad close at hand. It was used more to convey to clients a vision than an actual drawing of the piece he would be making for them. RIGHT Phillip Lloyd Powell in the early sixties at the shop and showroom that he opened in New Hope, Pennsylvania, in 1951. Through his creative eye and his infectious excitement about design, he was soon able to attract an avid following of clients coming from New York and well beyond.

OPPOSITE PAGE TOP The showroom Phillip Lloyd Powell and Paul Evans shared on Bridge Street in New Hope, Pennsylvania, in the early 1960s. Powell maintained a store in town until 1976. BOTTOM The shop interior had a domestic feeling, apart from the pebbles on the floor to offset any potential damage from frequent floods. Powell designed the wall unit made of walnut with pewter inlays in the mid-fifties.

Around 1951 Paul Evans dropped by the shop en route from his home in Newton, Pennsylvania, to the School for American Craftsmen in Rochester, New York, where he was studying to be a silversmith. Evans, twelve years younger than Powell, was already producing notable works that had attracted the attention of Aileen Vanderbilt Webb, an art patron and a founder of the American Craft Council. Webb secured a scholarship for Evans at Cranbrook Academy of Art, one of the country's premier training grounds for artists and artisans. Instead of completing his degree, Evans became a silversmith at the working history museum Sturbridge Village near Springfield, Massachusetts, which was also funded by Webb. Evans was hired to be a living craftsman demonstrating how silver bowls, tea pots, and the like were once made. (A silver coffeepot with a rosewood handle that he made in Sturbridge won first prize in an American Craftsmen's Educational Council competition.)

It's no wonder that the bold modern furnishings at Powell's shop caught the young man's eye, and he asked Powell if he could put a few of his own pieces on display. But it wasn't until 1955 that Evans moved permanently to New Hope and his acquaintance with Powell turned into a business and creative partnership.

The scene in New Hope was vibrant in the fifties, a magnet for artists, among them a group known as the Bucks County Impressionists, as well as theater people surrounding the Bucks County Playhouse, a popular summer stock and tryout stage since 1938 that attracted the likes of Moss Hart, George Kaufman, and Gene Kelly. Powell kept his store open from 8:00 p.m. until midnight to draw in couples after the show. "It worked incredibly well, since you had both the women who like the furniture and the men with the checkbook there together," recalled Powell at a July 2007 interview at the home he had built himself in the heart of the town.

It was Powell who encouraged Evans to venture into making larger pieces. Their early work together was small in scale. Powell was living off the Noguchi lamps that were selling briskly in the shop, and Evans fashioned menorahs out of metal and walnut that were very popular. Together they also made decorative screens with a loopy fish-scale pattern of welded iron. Around 1958 Evans started making copper chests with decorative doors, followed by sculpted steel-front cabinets that revealed Evans's unique way with welding. Much like Powell's woodworks, in which he let the contour of grain reveal itself and even dictate the shape and flow of the piece, Evans let the tough energy of the welding show through in what journalists—but never Evans—sometimes called a "brutalist" style, an easy tag that did not really suit the artist's intentions.

Those early metal cabinets were truly unique, and in later years, as production pieces for manufacturers were copied, these sculpted front consoles and cabinets defied imitation. Each piece started out as a wood "carcass" on a frame, on which Evans sketched with chalk. Details—sunbursts, spiderwebs, pipes, buttons, and stalagmites—were welded on according to a verbal code that Evans worked out with Dorsey Reading, a young machinist from Lambertville.

Reading came to work for Evans in 1959 as an apprentice but stayed on to become Evans's most relied-upon right hand, in an almost literal sense. For a sculptor, Evans was oddly

squeamish about working with his hands—he found the touch of sand, for instance, unbearable. His working method with Reading was symbiotic: he would scrawl an idea on a piece of paper with the coded symbols that only the two of them really understood. Dorsey would build up the base structure, and Evans would direct all the additions and alterations. For Evans, Reading was an essential sounding board as well, and when the artist was thinking about new techniques, Reading would flesh out the research.

Most of Evans's ideas, with the usual artist's rhythm of some good days and some bad, just dawned on him as he doodled in his studio, but many had a lot to do with the materials themselves. Despite the naturalistic names, the shapes of the details on ornate cabinets had more to do with the properties of the metals themselves, whether steel, braised brass, or ingots of iron pounded into "buttons" or drizzled into stalagmites. Different colors were achieved by using solid heavy pigments that were treated with alternating applications of heat and acid and then lacquered with an acrylic finish. Gold leaf, a favorite way to treat the edges, was applied last; however, textured edges, even though they tended to warp, were more common. According to Reading in a 2007 interview, Evans made roughly seventy-five such cabinets but in many variations—with rough edges outnumbering gold-leafed ones four to one—each one taking about three weeks to complete, and only ten of them in the monumental vertical shape.

Powell and Evans's work caught the attention of Bud Mesberg of Directional Furniture (a New York showroom tied to the High Point, North Carolina, manufacturer Sedgefield), who had avant-garde tastes and an interest in new talent. In addition to signing on Evans, Directional was also known for working with Vladimir Kagan, Paul McCobb, and Kip Stewart. The company ordered six steel coffee tables that Evans and Reading, driving all night, delivered to a showroom in High Point. They all sold in less than a week. Thus began Evans's relationship with Directional, the most important, though in the long run limiting, professional and creative connection in his career.

The big breaks, however, started coming in 1961, when Powell and Evans had a two-man show at the America House, another Webb operation, and Evans started working on a collection for Directional that debuted in 1964. Contemporaneous reviews of the America House show describe a thirty-piece exhibition of one-of-a-kind pieces, including a room-height oxidized-steel screen with an abstract checkerboard pattern; a travertine topped table trimmed in walnut on a base of gold-leafed iron ribs; and contoured burled-wood chairs. In 2007 Powell compared the excitement of the show to winning an Academy Award but recalled most vividly that Aileen Vanderbilt Webb invited them to stay overnight at her East Side penthouse.

At this time, the two started to be featured in *Interior Design* and other magazines and were attracting a discerning audience of collectors, among them Paddy Chayefsky, the writer and playwright, and Shari Lewis, the television star and creator of Lamb Chop, the chatty puppet. Powell and Evans made more than thirty pieces for Lewis. The two installed complete interiors at her Upper West Side apartment, covering the walls in silk velvet with gold-leaf trim. The Lewis commission represented a true sampling of their earliest collaborations, mostly in walnut and steel, including a loop-screen room divider and a wire coffee table with gold-leaf edges and a slate top. Evans even made a sculpted-steel front door.

ABOVE LEFT Paul Evans originally studied to be a silversmith and made this silver coffee set when he was a "living craftsman" at the Sturbridge Village history museum near Springfield, Massachusetts. It was included in a 1954 exhibition at America House in New York City. **RIGHT** Paul Evans made this wall-mounted cabinet in verdigris copper with steel and brass detailing in 1962. The metal loop form, in a larger scale, was a shape Evans used often in the design of table bases and decorative screens. The cabinet has two accordion doors that conceal adjustable shelves. This piece represents the first case piece employing a sculpted metal front.

OPPOSITE PAGE TOP This early collaboration piece and Evans wall sculpture from a photo taken around 1965 show the harmonious spirit of two artists working in tune with their admiration for each other's art. The wall sculpture has elements that can be seen in many Evans and Powell works, such as the fishscale motif, abstract shapes, and even the bulbous form of the sculpture shown at the beginning of the chapter. **BOTTOM LEFT** A small vignette showing the New Hope showroom in 1959. **RIGHT** Paul Evans and his foreman Dorsey Reading in 1962 working in the vertigre loop cabinet that is seen in color on the opposite page.

ABOVE For Evans, making sculpture was an ongoing exercise to maintain his creative edge. These three pieces were made in the sixties as part of the series, Sculpture in the Fields, and were photographed near his home in New Hope. They were made using experimental metalwork that Evans called "Argente," a treated aluminum that was highly toxic to produce. Argente was also briefly applied to one of his furniture lines. From left, an inverted pyramid on a black-enameled pedestal base; a room-divider screen in a solid rectilinear block is suspended by two metal supports; a "pinwheel" sculpture, made with three circular pieces cut from a single sheet of aluminum.

OPPOSITE PAGE In the early sixties, Evans often combined slate with metal bases as in this dining table with a slate top and Argente pedestal base made of treated aluminum.

Rina and Norman Indictor also met Evans and Powell in the early days and went on to work with them both, then with just Powell, for more than thirty years. In a 2007 interview, the couple described the details of their relationship, revealing how the pair worked, both together and separately. It was 1960, and the young couple was just starting out—Norman was a post-doctorate in chemistry at Princeton—and in need of furniture. By chance one wintry afternoon, they parked in front of Powell's showroom, and Rina, seeing a set of his carved walnut chairs in the window, decided that all their furnishing problems had been solved. Evans met them at the shop: "He just sailed out, so handsome and tall," Rina recalled, and they arranged for him to see their apartment in Princeton. "They were working at that time like decorators," said Norman, "doing all the furniture for entire places." As always Evans showed up with a yellow doodling pad in hand and asked bluntly how much money the couple had to spend. If they returned a stack of oriental rugs to B. Altman's, they told him, they had $2,500.

Powell and Evans set to work with a $100 retainer, and about three months later, the two of them delivered more than a half-dozen pieces, a perfect sampling of highlights from their earliest days of collaboration. There was a room divider framed in burnished and oiled walnut with an iron loop-pattern scrim; a coffee table with a metal base and cleft slate top; two of the chairs that first caught Rina's eye; and a display case with textured triangular-shaped bronze stanchions and sveltely carved walnut shelves with velvet backs. There was a small slate-topped dining table on a bronze pyramid base that, when a red-lacquered top—that could be affixed as a screen hinged to the wall—was lowered, became a table for six. There was even a planter that came with plants, and a pile of beat-up but beautifully designed antique oriental rugs to replace the new ones that had been returned to Altman's.

The Indictors had never seen more than a single sketch—"Paul made these doodles that showed you absolutely nothing," Norman said—and never got a bill, simply paying the pair the agreed-upon amount as they went along. Over the years there would be many more pieces, and when the couple moved, Powell and Evans would show up as movers to reinstall them in their new home and sometimes even repurpose a piece to better fit the new surroundings. At one point they took the loop screen and reframed it into two parts on a track that they made into sliding doors to separate the bedrooms at the couple's Upper West Side apartment.

At another apartment for libertarian Karl Hess undertaken in the mid-seventies, they lined all the walls in champagne-colored raw silk and installed beige reverse-painted acrylic ceilings

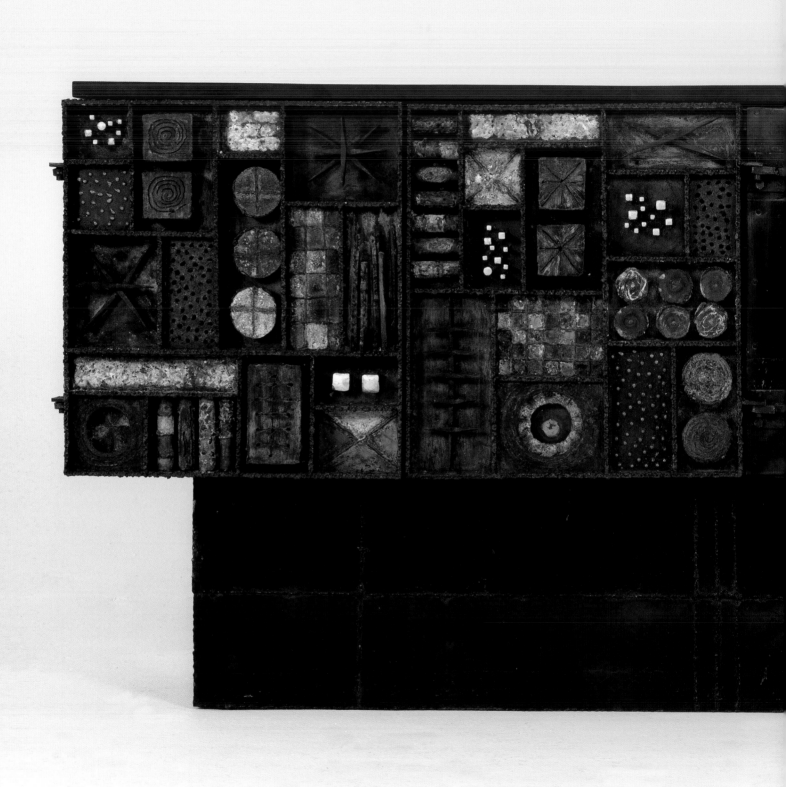

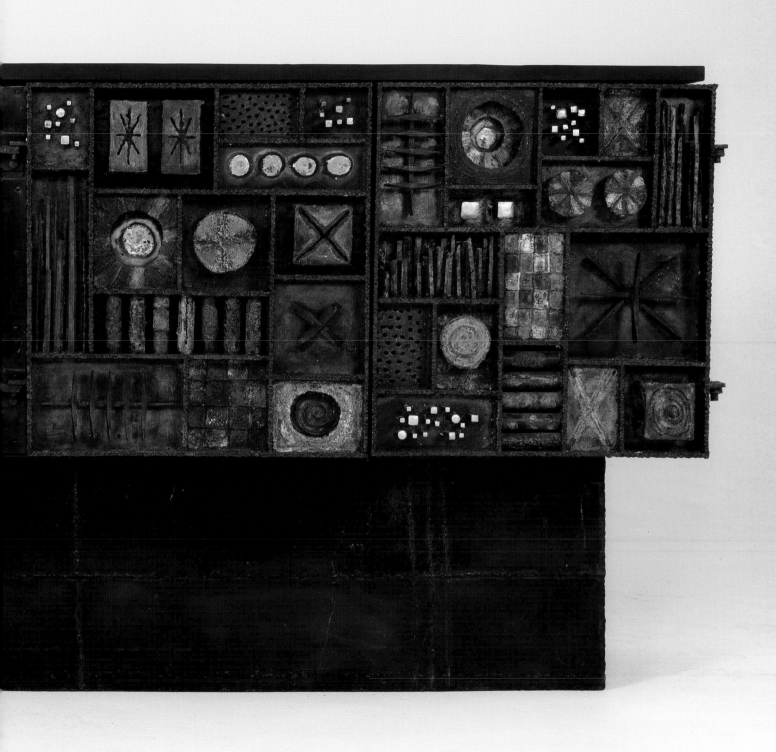

ABOVE Directional touted Evans as "craftsman extraordinaire in metal," and produced catalogues featuring solely his work. The showroom shot on the right features Evans's sculpted bronze work in "stalagmite" forms as well as a heavily sculpted front console and classically inspired chairs interpreted by Evans in his signature look.

OPPOSITE PAGE This Phillip Lloyd Powell walnut armoire with silver-leaf sides conveys his fluid style on a nearly monumental scale. Most often carving with a spoke shave tool with side handles, he worked wood as if it was as malleable as draping. In fact, he considered an uncle who was a clothing designer, Michael Demay, to be an important influence on his work.

PREVIOUS SPREAD While each sculpted front piece was unique, collectively they represent Evans's most distinctive and sought-after art furniture. This console from 1966 has a slate top on a steel base and decorative steel doors. Cabinets could be ordered to specification as hanging cabinets, separate panels for room dividers, or wall reliefs. The array of hand-sculpted abstract details, such as sunbursts, buttons, and stalagmites, painted in yellows, reds, and blues or in various patina finishes, was typically executed by Evans's foreman Dorsey Reading.

and acrylic cabinetry for a modish elegant look well before transparent plastics were in vogue. Evans also added a pair of mirror-polished stainless-steel cylinders with hinged doors for storing dishes.

Powell and Evans were in their heyday. When working with clients and customers, Reading recalled, the two artists never provided much detail. "They basically sold an idea on a piece of paper," he said. What they got in the end was often a surprise. In particular, Evans's way of working was intuitive. A roll of onionskin sketch paper was always on hand to capture an idea and pass it onto Reading for a first try followed by a longer process of trial and error.

In the early days of the New Hope showroom, Powell and Evans showed furniture side by side, each artist contributing elements to the work of the other. Reading described them both working over the customers with irresistible charm: Powell with his curly hair and piercing blue eyes, and Evans in an Oxford shirt and khakis finished off with sockless sneakers. ("Once they fixed on someone, he or she was not going to get out of there without writing a check," recalled Reading.)

The first Directional collections included wood pieces by Powell as well as metal ones by Evans, but gradually Powell, who had always insisted on top billing, began to withdraw from the equation. His way of operating, according to the Indictors, who made a considerable effort to stay in touch and commission more pieces, was to work intensely to produce enough pieces and make enough money to allow him to travel abroad for a while. While Evans largely ceased to deal with individual clients after finding more widespread success at Directional, Powell would always eventually return to clients when he needed money or they craved more of his furniture. Thus, between the mid-sixties and the late eighties, the Indictors acquired from Powell an ongoing stream of unique pieces, among them a bed, a pyramid-inspired chest incorporating seventeenth-century Indian artifacts as hand pulls from their own collection, a "roll-top" desk with mirrored screens that lowered on pulleys from the ceiling, numerous display bookshelves, a lectern, and a library ladder.

Meanwhile, as Evans became more focused on the business of making furniture collections, Powell decided to concentrate on being an artist, and around 1964 he left for an extended world tour.

Directional was a forward-looking company at a time when the American furniture industry was dominated by the market interest in traditional reproductions. Herman Miller and Knoll were beginning their ascent with a stable of modernist designers dedicated to new methods of mass production. Under Bud Mesberg, Directional boldly focused more on artistic innovation than on new production methods.

In 1964 Evans introduced the bronze series at Directional. Production was equal parts old-fashioned craft, random artistry, and experimental technology. Reading prepared the plywood base shape, to which epoxy was applied, and then, using a spray-on technique adapted from shipbuilding, the bronze that solidified on contact. With some pieces, Evans, with the help of Reading, applied more bronze mixed with epoxy, and sandblasted (using sterilized

play-box sand) it onto a frame. Or sometimes chunks of steel "rock," leftover from the day before and hammered into pieces, were stuck to the epoxy for sculptural effect. The technique worked with any case-goods shape, but the most distinctive form was the Disc bar, a large, wall-mounted circle (fewer than two hundred were produced) suggesting an abstract ancient Aztec calendar whose doors opened to reveal an amber-lacquered or black laminate wet bar. Produced with the help of eight workers in a 1,500-square-foot studio off Aquetong Road, the first series for Directional (numbered PE11 and up, and starting with six steel tables) sold out in one week. However, it was the bronze series, PE100-200, that became the longest and best-selling series by Evans for Directional.

Each year, Evans was required to come up with a new line, preferably involving some new technique. The artist had always imagined himself a savvy entrepreneur and enjoyed the expanding business, setting up larger production facilities, first in Lambertville and finally in a thirty-thousand-square-foot factory in Plumsteadville, while also maintaining an artist's studio for experimentation and research.

The Argente line of welded aluminum, named for its shiny silver look, including freestanding coils and three-dimensional swirls, was really more art than furniture. Evans had already been making studio pieces out of aluminum in the early sixties and then started mixing them with the Directional PE100 series in 1968. But they remained a rarity, as the process of welding the aluminum exuded billowing clouds of toxic fumes. "We'd stand beside these huge fans and suck Hull's cough drops, but nothing made it easier to breathe," recalled Reading. Today some of those aluminum pieces, notably from the "Series in a Field," are commanding prices in the six figures.

By the early seventies, Evans had developed one of his signature looks—the hugely popular, sleek modeling of Cityscape in brass and chrome (PE200) that so perfectly captured the glitz of the disco era. Subsequent lines ran the gamut of materials and techniques—whatever could be imagined that used a wood foundation and a strong adhesive, moving from burled woods (PE400 series) to patchwork chromes and metal stripes (PE600). The PE700 line was made primarily of suede-covered tables and desks with steel handles.

In the late seventies, Evans was an early proponent of motorized furnishings: shelves that rotated, cabinets that elevated, remote-controlled columns that opened to reveal a bar.

At the height of production in the mid-seventies, the factory was dispatching a twenty-four-foot truck containing 150 to 200 pieces to New York twice a week. It was a demanding schedule that put too much pressure on Evans, diminishing his ability to develop new ideas as he raced to fill orders. He told an audience at an American Society of Interior Designers conference in 1975 that he spent less than 3 percent of his time on design. The factory—if it could be called that, as it was a series of shops where workmen labored to complete each stage of production by hand, whether it was building a wood base or applying the final layer of acrylic lacquer—at one point employed eighty-eight people.

Each season, Evans would assemble a new line and put it on display in the barn; the salesmen from Directional would come along and take their pick. In the early years, Directional took everything Evans had to offer, but according to Reading, the salesmen became increasingly selective and in the last two years signed up fewer pieces. (The relationship had ended by 1980, and in 1994, the Mesberg family sold Directional.)

In 1981 Evans started producing a few designs for Selig, a contemporary upholstery maker in Leominster, Massachusetts. That same year Evans decided to open his own showroom at 306 East Sixty-first Street in New York, outfitted with a Qwip computer and paintings by the New Hope School of Artists. Evans stocked eight thousand square feet with prototypes of motorized concept furniture, and, in spite of a positive reaction in the press and a substantial order from a Saudi Arabian princess, running a showroom, according to Reading, was "the kiss of death."

Sculptor, entrepreneur, and charmer, Evans had never been especially materialistic, though in a peculiar twist on the American dream, he was obsessed with using labor-intensive art to turn a faster buck and seemed unable to accept himself as the true artist that he was. The Plumsteadville craft factory kept him in debt, and when he was unable to fill orders for the concept pieces in the showroom, he retired in 1987. He was fifty-six years old and, borrowing his son's car, he headed with his second wife, Bunny, for their vacation home in Nantucket. The next morning, while enjoying a cup of coffee on the lawn, he had a heart attack and died.

OPPOSITE PAGE This monumental wall-mounted cabinet, known as the Disc bar, was made for Directional by Paul Evans in the seventies. Its semicircular sculpted-bronze doors conceal a single drawer and storage areas.

PREVIOUS SPREAD Powell and Evans appear here at their shop in the early sixties looking as effortlessly fashionable as their designs, including this wall unit by Powell with metal loops by Evans.

ABOVE The Cityscape series evolved into an even more three-dimensional style, called Faceted. This rare 1970 Directional cabinet has a lacquered wood top and hinged doors concealing an adjustable shelf and storage area. Each piece from this series was made by hand—each section was placed and polished one at a time.

OPPOSITE PAGE This L-shaped cantilever desk belongs to Evans's popular Cityscape series of the early 1970s satin bronze plates. The Cityscape line also included bedroom, living, and dining room pieces in either polished or brushed chrome with golden brass and exotic wood veneers.

PREVIOUS SPREAD Rina and Norman Indicator met Evans and Powell at their New Hope shop in 1960 and commissioned the artists to design dozens of pieces for their Manhattan apartment, continuing to work with Powell through the late eighties. In the living room, the chairs, tables, bookcase, and metal-loop room divider (not shown) were all made by Powell and Evans. The slate-topped coffee table was a collaborative effort with an iron base.

An avid market in collecting Evans furniture developed almost immediately, and since 2005 his pieces have regularly achieved six-figure prices at auction and private dealer sales have advanced. Copies of the Directional series also abounded, while the steel consoles of the early sixties have always proved too complex and labor intensive to fake. Clumsy imitations of the Disc bar and other pieces in the bronze series, along with the laminated patchwork chrome and brass series, are more common. Fake bronze pieces usually are stamped with a repeating pattern like wallpaper rather than clearly sculpted by hand; even the resin is of a different density. Copies of the brass and chrome chests tend to show much simpler strip patterns that are laminated on fiberboard rather than built up on one of Dorsey Reading's sturdy, handmade wooden frames.

Paul Evans took a unique approach to furniture making, a combination of handcraft wedded to technology that anticipated the limited edition art furniture of today, such as the work of Ron Arad. More particularly, the artist's relationship with Directional set a unique standard for creative manufacture, as described so poignantly in a brochure of 1975: "Every piece is made by hand. One piece at a time. Every piece is finished by hand. One piece at a time. And every piece is supervised every step of the way by the artist who conceived it—Paul Evans."

While ever a close friend to Evans, Powell always followed more of the artist's way, traveling for inspiration. In the late seventies, he even lived in Spain for three years. Back in New Hope, Powell resumed working on intensely crafted wood pieces, sometimes more fantastical than functional, as in the mobile library ladder (1990), which featured muscular tenons of attenuated wood—walnut, bubinga, wenge, and padouk—stretched around a Duchampian bicycle wheel, or a tea cart of walnut, ebony, and inlaid red wenge with handles made of deer antlers.

After the Directional venture, Powell never again worked on anything resembling a production scale, telling a local reporter at one time, "I do not want to be in the business of making furniture. When I had eight employees, I realized I was in business. As a drop out, I did not want to be just a designer." Perhaps more to the point, he also noted that "my imagination runs over itself" and meeting deadlines rather than following an inner muse was never going to work for him.

Until his death at age eighty-eight, Powell was as spry as he was in his youth, sporting a silver charm in the shape of a saw dangling from one ear. In recent years, he watched with wry amusement at auction, sometimes sitting right in the audience, as the selling prices of his pieces started to soar. In October 2007 a relatively simple walnut floor lamp with a grass shade sold for $13,000. Overall prices that year at the auction house Sollo Rago Antiques ranged between $4,000 and $60,000 but concentrated at the high end for Powell's signature sculpted cabinets with silver-leafed and enameled interiors. When a spindle-backed walnut bench with a presale low estimate of $6,000 sold for $19,200, Powell was delighted to tell how he had originally sold it for $500.

While Powell continued to work on select commissions and revisit the homes of patrons whose complete installations are lovingly maintained, his real attention was always focused on his own home in what he called his studio tower, a thoroughly crafted environment. And it remains a single-handed work of artistic expression, from the carved swirl of the front door to the cerulean-blue dome with gold stars above his hand-carved platform bed at the top. **J.I.**

Evans's foreman and chief designer, Dorsey Reading, describes how Evans, as a creative release from workaday pressures, often balanced his demanding output for Directional with experiments in sculpture, as seen in this monumental sculpted bronze hanging cabinet. This custom commission represents Evans's sculpted bronze work in its most innovative form.

VLADIMIR KAGAN

Vladimir Kagan (b. 1927) has always said that his mission was to "interpret my century," and only a few contemporary furniture designers have been as successful at capturing—even defining—the look of a cultural moment. Sleek but organic, definitively modern yet often made by traditional methods, Kagan's furniture represents the adaptive spirit of American creativity. His natural impulses have always been in tune with the zeitgeist: when curves were popular in the fifties, no one's furniture turned them faster; when cubism and multifunctionalism caught on in the seventies, he designed the Omnibus, a rectilinear platform couch-bed-table-light-chair that could be reconfigured to fit any lifestyle.

Kagan used the materials and technologies of his time, from foam rubber to CNC (computer numerical control) milling, to advance his expressive ends. While he dabbled in different approaches to production—after all, the American spirit is entrepreneurial to its core—his concerns always focused most on how to adapt furniture to a more modern way of living. In fact, his constant experimentation with different approaches only emphasizes how completely Kagan is a furniture artist, one of a particularly American stripe.

In fact, Vladimir Kagan was born in Worms am Rhein, Germany, in 1927. His father, Illi, was a Russian cabinetmaker who learned his trade in a prison camp during World War I; his maternal grandfather owned a fashionable folk art and furnishings shop in Dachau, near Munich. In Worms and in Heidelberg, Illi Kagan sold art at Kunsthause Kagan by the likes of Kathe Kollwitz, Oskar Kokoschka, and other members of the German-speaking avant-garde. The family lived a prosperous middle-class Jewish life in an apartment above his father's workshop. But by the time "Vladi" was ten years old, the family was preparing to flee the Nazis, and by 1938, the Kagans were living with cousins in New Jersey.

Kagan adapted quickly to American life. Tapping into an established group of German émigré craftsmen, his father started out by repairing furniture but soon had his own cabinetmaking shop on East Fifty-fifth Street in New York. One early client was the flamboyant decorator/furniture designer/con man James Mont, who paid Kagan's father $12 a week but ended up trying to bilk him for much more. At school, young Kagan showed a natural flair for drawing. But at home he was expected to help out as a traditional apprentice by cleaning tools. His father also encouraged his son's creative tendencies. "He was amazingly supportive. He gave me all the leeway. No matter how impractical he thought my designs, he let me play with them,"

ABOVE LEFT Portrait of Vladimir Kagan, 2001. **RIGHT** Vladimir Kagan and his father Illi at their factory, c. 1955. Illi Kagan admired Bauhaus modernism and passed on his enthusiasm to his son. Grandfather Julius's collection of folk furniture would also be an influence on Vladimir. Ultimately, however, Kagan developed his own approach synthesizing past design movements and contemporary impulses into a distinct style all his own.

OPPOSITE PAGE Kagan produced some of his most iconic designs, like the Tri-symmetric dining table (1953) pictured here in the Kagan-Dreyfuss showroom in the fifties. He invented the term "tri-symmetric" inspired by the branching pattern of tree roots and used the shape both as chair legs and, flipped over, as supports for biomorphic-shaped glass tops.

Kagan said in an interview at his Manhattan home in October 2007. "I had an opportunity to come up with a creative idea and see it to fruition within the factory in an incredibly short time. I considered the factory my laboratory for creativity."

With playboy good looks—a 1950s photograph of him in a Thunderbird smoking a cigarette and wearing a white bathing cap is the very image of insouciance—Kagan was befriended by socialites and moved in circles that would later ensure him a clientele for his furniture. After studying abroad and taking architecture courses at Columbia University, Kagan joined the family furniture-making business, although his real interest was still in sculpture and painting.

Kagan Designs supplied furniture for both private clients and expanding businesses. The small factory had moved to Forty-fourth Street and First Avenue. When the contract department at Wanamaker's department store needed someone quickly to fill a large furniture order for the delegates' Cocktail Lounge at the first United Nations headquarters in Lake Success in 1947, father and son jumped at the chance. Kagan said that he knows of no drawings or photos of the installation that he described as "not earthshaking," but acknowledged that it was his first big break.

Kagan quickly discovered, however, that he did not share his father's temperament for exacting hands-on craftsmanship. Designing was his forte, not measuring. Nor did he particularly admire the mass-production methods that characterized the work of such other young American designers as Charles and Ray Eames and George Nelson. Instead, he continued to approach each piece as an individual expression of an idea, composed and recomposed from elements that had worked before. Starting with a sketch on onionskin paper, he would work closely with his father's trusted craftsmen, constantly pushing them to try new things. "I scoured every woodworking machinery show for the latest technologies," he recalled in an interview.

For inspiration, Kagan turned to Europe, where he was attracted to the sophisticated organicism of Danish modern. In a wonderfully detailed monograph, *The Complete Kagan: A Lifetime of Avant-Garde Design*, he wrote that another important influence on his developing aesthetic was the primitive folk furniture collected by his grandfather. "The three-legged milking stool was a perfect example of minimalism at work," he wrote. Just as important to his work were his sketches from nature. "I would go out and draw trees," he said in an interview. "I loved the way a tree grew out of its stand then developed into two branches and from there into more branches. The whole concept of growth was fascinating to me." Kagan also studied human and animal anatomy, noting how his earliest furniture mimicked the "flayed-out legs of a young filly" or the elegant attenuation of a well-turned wrist. "I wanted to create vessels to hold the human body and my early chair shapes had elements of that," he said.

Father and son worked together making radio and phonograph cabinets: one mahogany cabinet had leather handles and a screen made of interwoven strips of pigskin. Father Illi supervised the workmen, mother Hildegarde and sister Tanya managed the showroom,

and Vladimir dealt with design and commissions for interiors. The craftsmanship of a Kagan design was distinguished enough to garner appreciative articles in the *New York Times* in 1949.

Kagan's first notable chair, renamed the Barrel chair in 1947, was part of the Sculpture Form collection. Inspired by a zeppelin he had seen as a child in Germany, he designed the chair in much the same way: as a curvaceous armature sheathed in fabric. Or, as Kagan liked to put it, "frame follows function." A considerable success from the start, the chair has remained in continuous production.

Upholstery work, Kagan said in an interview at the time with *Interiors* magazine, gave him "the chance to be animated." With typical pragmatic aplomb, Kagan later described how it was actually the hydraulic stapler that allowed the process of making complex sculptural shapes feasible. At a time when the norm was inner springs and down-filled cushions, Kagan was revolutionary in introducing rubber strapping and foam rubber. And with that one stroke, comfort no longer depended on adding cushions.

From the start, he wanted to open a cosmopolitan shop that would sell not only furniture but also ceramics and art pieces. His model was Rena Rosenthal, a major client of Kagan Designs, whose shop on Fifty-seventh Street was a mecca for recently arrived and visiting European artists, ceramicists, and designers, among them Tommi Parzinger. Cross-fertilization remained a source of creative vitality throughout Kagan's career.

In 1948 Kagan opened a shop on East Sixty-fifth Street. Artists were invited to exhibit their wares. Several made tiles that were inlaid into the tops of Kagan-designed coffee tables with tapered, grooved legs. Among them were the artist Alexandra Kasuba (known for horsey shapes) and the Dutch artisan Warner Prins, who made reinterpretations of traditional Delft tiles (and the occasional porn-inspired image). The showroom also carried work by the noted textile designer Dorothy Liebes, who also worked with Samuel Marx. For a time, a weaver was installed in the storefront window, an advertisement for the bravado of Kagan's entrepreneurial sensibility.

Through the Italian artist Emanuel Romano, Hugo Dreyfuss entered the picture. Dreyfuss was a retired Swiss lace manufacturer who also had a reputation as a ceramic artist and textile designer. He offered to underwrite Kagan Designs with $20,000 and Kagan-Dreyfuss was formed in 1950, selling furnishings, art, and accessories, both retail and wholesale. The partnership, after relocating to 125 East Fifty-seventh Street, lasted ten years and is considered by many collectors to be the golden age of Kagan's productivity. Artists continued to bring in their work for display, among them Louise Nevelson, whose famous painted-wood sculptures were often made using scraps collected from the Kagan factory.

In addition to offering "personalized" interiors through which he could advance his philosophy that "art and beauty are part of everyday living," Kagan began playing with the animated organic shapes that would become his signature. In 1950 the Serpentine sofa muscled its way into postwar living rooms, where it sat sprawled across the space like an upholstered centerfold model. Arguing that the times demanded new forms for new tastes (he even thought

ABOVE RIGHT In the late fifties Kagan increasingly received private commissions, including complete interior decoration projects, such as the Robert Graham penthouse on Fifth Avenue, shown here. Kagan's shop on Fifty-seventh Street in Manhattan attracted a cultured clientele and several gallerists chose to furnish their city and weekend homes with his pieces.
LEFT At the Troy residence on Long Island Sound, the most impressive element was the ten-person tangerine unicorn sofa with a twenty-four-foot diameter. The sofa could rotate either to face floor-to-ceiling windows looking out at the water or a music room with two grand pianos.

OPPOSITE PAGE The Crescent desk was a popular choice for the many high-profile offices that Kagan designed in the seventies. Experimenting with the desk's components, Kagan included retractable arms, built-in compartments, and cantilevered construction. This example from 1979 is made of a curvaceous piece of zebrano wood supported by thick beveled acrylic legs. (Kagan had been using Lucite and Plexiglas in his creations since 1956.)

E. Romano

The Kagan-Dreyfuss store opened in 1950 and was located on East Fifty-seventh Street. The shop offered a refined mix of Kagan's designs complimented by ceramics, textiles, and fine art by up-and-coming artists, including the bronze head sculpture by Modigliani on the far left. The store was partitioned in order to create decorating vignettes, including a section with brick walls and a fireplace and another domestic corner with silk wall coverings.

ABOVE LEFT This coffee table from the fifties embellished with Venetian-glass tiles on the surface shows Kagan combining materials and shapes. The mosaics here are applied to a thick rosewood base. **CENTER** The Barrel chair (1947) was one of Kagan's earliest signature pieces. As part of the Sculpture Form collection, it eventually appeared in many different heights and with various legs. The form was also adapted for sofas and love seats and stayed in near continuous production. **RIGHT** The One Arm Contour chaise shows Kagan's designs becoming more attenuated and delicately sculptural towards the end of the fifties. The tri-symmetric base, which was once made in wood, started to appear in mirror-finished aluminum or black steel.

the square room had to go), Kagan wanted to make conversation pieces as much as furniture. His predilection for sofas that could seat as many people as possible was something of a lifestyle revolution, introducing a sophisticated informality that quickly caught on. Heedless of the grumblings from the old-guard craftsmen in the factory, Kagan also experimented with different mediums, including metal, aluminum, bronze, and ceramics. A collection of wrought-iron chairs inspired by the sculptures of Harry Bertoia included the Savanarola chair, which was selected to be in the Museum of Modern Art's *Good Design* exhibition of 1952. In 1958 he introduced a collection of metal garden furniture exclusively for W. & J. Sloane department store. The Capricorn Collection was extremely difficult to make, involving a fire-escape manufacturer (later known as the furniture company Brueton), and for that reason did not stay in production very long. As a result it has become one of Kagan's most sought-after vintage designs.

In the mid-fifties, Grosfield House, a New York manufacturer that specialized in trend-oriented contemporary furniture, commissioned Kagan to design a fifty-piece collection to furnish living rooms, dining rooms, and bedrooms. Sketches of the collection show a full selection of chests and tables with "sprawling filly" legs. Also at this time came a series of glass-and-marble-topped tables on "tri-symmetric" bases (Kagan invented the word and in the late fifties turned the bases upside down to become three-point supports). Inspired by root and tree-node formations and displaying an idiosyncratic organicism, these distinctively shaped tables were made of exquisitely carved and honed wood, often maple.

The Unicorn base was, if anything, even more pronounced, its acute angled thrust suggesting something between a bird's claw and the nose of a rocket ship in orbit. Kagan said the shape was inspired by Constantin Brancusi's *Bird in Flight*. After designing it in wood as part of the Unicorn table (1957), he later used the shape as a base in cast and polished aluminum for chairs as well as large sofas.

The Contour Sculpted rocking chair (1955) with its elegant protoergonomic styling was an instant success, as well as an extremely demanding piece to produce. In 1958 Kagan made a version in highly polished steel with a companion ottoman, both upholstered in elephant gray leather. Only a few were produced, with one selling at Sollo Rago Auctions in 2005 for $22,325.

As the fifties progressed, pieces like the Multi-position Reclining chair and the One Arm Contour chaise lounge appeared, looking ever lighter and more delicate as Kagan strove to make furniture pieces that were sculptural tours de force. The VK 100 of 1958 (Kagan started signing pieces with numbers and a date in the late fifties but sometimes postdated them to make a piece seem even more up-to-the-minute) took two years to make in collaboration with a clock designer and an engineer. Based on the Multi-position Reclining chair, it included a pullout footrest made of aluminum slats. *Interiors* magazine called it "mystifyingly flexible." But due to its structural complexities, only fifty were ever made.

From the start, Kagan attracted numerous discerning celebrity clients, including Gary Cooper, Lily Pons, Xavier Cougat, and Marilyn Monroe (who shopped but never bought). The penthouse home on Fifth Avenue for the gallery-owner Robert Graham was a showcase of Kagan's

most popular designs. There was a Contour rocker in glove leather, a Serpentine sofa nestled into a custom wall cabinet, and a boomerang coffee table inlaid with a splash of gold Venetian mosaics. The dining table was a free-form curve cantilevered off the wall, and the entrance hall was adorned with marbleized wallpaper by Erwine Laverne.

On the business side, the Kagans were forced to close the Fifty-seventh Street showroom and discontinue the partnership with Dreyfuss, relocating it to the factory on Eighty-first Street. Kagan's designs were increasingly attractive to a corporate clientele. But he never turned his back on private commissions: for one couple, Rosalie and Matthew Weinstein of Merion, Pennsylvania, he made more than a dozen signature pieces for their living and dining room in the early 1960s, including a one-of-a-kind rosewood dining table with a hand-chiseled ebonized mahogany base that sold at a 2007 Sotheby's auction for $36,000.

In 1963 a division of Monsanto Chemicals asked Kagan to contribute a "Room for Total Living" to an exhibition at the Park Avenue Armory. That led to a commission to design the Monsanto House of the Future for Disneyland in Anaheim—an experiment in plastics that Kagan ultimately found disappointing. He went on to design the product presentation for General Electric at the GE pavilion at the 1967 World's Fair. A devastating fire burned down the factory on East End Avenue and Eighty-first Street in 1972, propelling the family to move production facilities to Long Island City and open a new showroom on Fifty-ninth Street, where Kagan's office featured a zebrawood desk, above which hung one of his stalactite Plexiglas and chrome chandeliers.

In 1969 Kagan designed and furnished a ten-room apartment for Doris and Alan Freedman on Central Park West. He was an industrialist, she was director of cultural affairs for New York City, and they had an impressive collection of artworks by Frank Stella, Mark Rothko, and Susan City Rothenberg. Kagan built recessed niches and cove lighting (refusing to consider track lights), as well as floating partitions supported on acrylic pedestals for the art. The furniture was more architectural and rectilinear than anything he had done before.

ABOVE In the late forties and early fifties Kagan's upholstered pieces tended towards oversized organic shapes, here exemplified in the Serpentine sofa. Curvaceous and grand, Kagan's sofas toyed with the then-popular idea of the kidney shape on a massive scale. Many of Kagan's best clients were art collectors and the shape of the sofa enabled them to get closer to the works hung on the wall. In the 1970s, the furniture company Directional reproduced a similar but shorter version of the Serpentine sofa. This photo of a private home represented Kagan's design aesthetic so well, he chose to put it on the cover of the Kagan-Dreyfuss catalogue of 1950.

William Rubin, curator of painting at the Museum of Modern Art, and Barbara Jakobson, a trustee and art-world personality, both furnished their homes with signature Kagan pieces. Ironically, Kagan himself lived much more traditionally, at least at his Nantucket home, where his English-born wife, Erica Wilson—with her own major career focused on teaching and promoting the domestic art of embroidery and crewel work—had furnished the rooms with English antiques, Victoriana, and ship models.

The seventies signaled a new direction in Kagan's style. He told Cara Greenberg in *Op to Pop: Furniture of the 1960s* that he had "reached an apex in terms of organic shapes, and could only end up going baroque" if he continued, adding that sculptural shapes had become prohibitively expensive to make. He was now working more with the trade than on individual commissions. But the Omnibus was a modular concept that could be adapted to almost any use. Called "interior landscaping" by Kagan, it was born in the late sixties out of his interest in animating small spaces. With its interchangeable multilevel slabs that could be stacked and rearranged—and even included built-in lighting—the Omnibus quickly became a new hallmark, both of the period and of Kagan's career.

The Kagan business operated at full speed well into the eighties (Illi and Hildegarde had retired and moved to Switzerland in 1971), with eight national showrooms and some thirty employees in the factory. When it became too much to handle and Kagan's designs of the period proved too easy for competitors to duplicate, he decided to close the factory and get out of the business in 1987. Customer lists, and the jigs and patterns for much of the furniture, were all lost.

With the revival of interest in midcentury modern in the late nineties, Kagan's furniture returned to the limelight. William Sofield, the designer for Tom Ford, who was then heading up the creative effort at Gucci, sought out Kagan at home on the Upper East Side of Manhattan, where the apartment is chockablock with vintage Contour chairs, Omnibus elements, and sculpture that his father made in retirement. The dynamic energy of even the oldest pieces (not to mention the designer himself) must have been hard to resist, and Ford soon ordered 360 of the Omnibus elements to furnish every Gucci boutique worldwide. It was the beginning of a new phase for Kagan, in his seventies, who started selling "Vladimir Kagan Classics" on a small scale at various elite trade shows. In a 1996 *House & Garden* magazine profile, Kagan was dubbed "a living legend." And in 2002 the Brooklyn Museum of Art presented Kagan with a Modernism Lifetime Achievement Award.

Kagan has been careful to distinguish between what he calls "multiples," which are mass-produced, and "originals." The Kagan New York Collection, manufactured abroad by Club House Italia, offers updated versions of the classics but is made with plywood frames and foam rubber. Kagan's "originals" are limited-edition pieces available through Ralph Pucci International that replicate as closely as possible with hardwood frames and innersprings the way they were made in the fifties and sixties. And according to Kagan, now eighty-one, they are selling even more briskly than they did when first made, making his dream of being a Thomas Chippendale for the twentieth century well within reach. **J.I.**

ABOVE The Floating Seat and Back sofa debuted in 1952. It synthesizes two important Kagan characteristics: biomorphic shapes and sinuous carved-wood legs. Its spirit is echoed in the Tri-symmetric coffee table from 1955. The travertine boomerang-shaped top seems to hover above an undulating rosewood base.

OPPOSITE PAGE A rare glimpse of the designer's own home. Kagan furnished his Manhattan residence with some of his most popular designs: a Contour armchair, a mosaic-topped table, and a library ladder. A metal sculpture by Kagan's father, Illi, completes the room.

GEORGE NAKASHIMA

George Nakashima (1905–1990) was surely one of the most recognized of the so-called studio furniture makers emerging from the postwar period. His name was constantly linked with the likes of Charles Eames and Eero Saarinen. However, while those designers were dedicated to the cause of mass production, Nakashima remained adamantly a craftsman, ever suspicious of the dehumanizing effects of the machine-made. "My relationship to furniture and construction is basically my dialogue with a tree, with a complete and psychic empathy," he said in a 1977 lecture.

Nakashima did collaborate occasionally with such manufacturers as Knoll and Widdicomb-Mueller, but his approach was essentially very different from other preeminent midcentury furniture makers, harking back to the traditional methods of colonial American craftsmen and the Shakers, and stretching even further back to what he liked to call his ancestor's "samurai heritage" in Japan. And yet, whatever the source of his inspiration, his furniture reflects a distinctly American blend of innovative form and intense craftsmanship.

He called himself simply a woodworker. This distinction has allowed his daughter Mira to continue the Nakashima legacy of exquisitely conceived handmade wood furniture.

Nakashima's story is as far flung and compelling as any in midcentury modernism, taking him from Paris in the 1930s, to an American internment camp during World War II, and then finally allowing him to flourish in the unlikely artist's arcadia of Bucks County, Pennsylvania.

He was born in 1905 in Spokane, Washington, and spent his youth traipsing through the forests of the Northwest that in turn inspired him to study forestry at the University of Washington, although he switched to architecture after two years.

In 1930 Nakashima received his master's degree in architecture from the Massachusetts Institute of Technology, and for a time he worked as a mural painter and designer on Long Island (for the State Park Commission) and in Albany. With jobs scarce during the Depression, and Nakashima never having been much of a materialist, he sold his car and jumped a steamship with the idea of traveling around the world, winding up in Paris. Though he didn't stay, he remained long enough to be fascinated by the construction of Le Corbusier's Pavillon Suisse in Montparnasse out of reinforced concrete, learning lessons about the plasticity of a hard material that he would later apply in his own buildings and designs.

OPPOSITE PAGE This detail of the Arlyn table, which Nakashima designed for the Krosnicks in 1988, is a monumental piece reaching over seven feet wide. It was made from a redwood burl; in true Nakashima form the beauty of the tree speaks for itself in its form and color.

ABOVE LEFT Portrait of George Nakashima, c. 1942, in the internment camp in Minidoka, Idaho. After over a year of confinement in Idaho, Nakashima and his family were released when former professors at MIT (where Nakashima earned his master's degree in architecture) petitioned on his behalf. The family was allowed to relocate to New Hope, Pennsylvania, under the agreement that Nakashima would be working on a chicken farm. **CENTER** Nakashima with his new bride, Marion, in Tokyo c. 1940. **RIGHT** Nakashima, c. 1945, working at his New Hope home, shortly after his release from Camp Minidoka where he honed his skills as an architect and furniture designer.

OPPOSITE PAGE The careful selection of wood was paramount to Nakashima's practice. While living in Japan during the 1930s he learned how lumber was cut, evaluated, and chosen and he applied these lessons to his furniture with unique sensitivity and spirituality. He believed he was giving a second life to the trees he worked with. Once his studio was established he sought out the highest-quality materials such as American black walnut and Japanese textiles.

His travels brought him inevitably to Japan to visit his mother's ancestral home in Kamata. He took a job in Tokyo working for a Czech-born architect named Antonin Raymond, who had worked with Frank Lloyd Wright.

Nakashima was in Japan right as the Mingei movement, which called for a return to ancient craft traditions, was gaining momentum and spreading the belief that true beauty in objects was irregular and unique and could only be achieved by a craftsman whose long experience allowed him to trust his materials and tools so completely as to let them guide his hand.

His work for Raymond took him to Pondicherry, India, to oversee the construction of a dormitory at the Sri Aurobindo ashram, where every piece of furniture and even the hardware was custom-made. These simple teak dormitory pieces were the first pieces of furniture designed by Nakashima. Impressed with yoga's philosophy, Nakashima gave up his salary and joined the community for two years.

When Nakashima left in 1939, he traveled home by way of Japan, where he became engaged to Marion Okajima. Together they returned to the United States in 1941, settling in Seattle, where Nakashima worked as an architect and part-time furniture maker using the basement of a Maryknoll Boys' Club as his shop. According to his daughter Mira, it was there that he accepted his first private commission to make furniture for a cosmetics executive, Andre Ligne, including a splay-legged coffee table (an early version of the piece he made for Knoll), a grass-seated chair, and a cabinet with a version of his signature "free edge."

Mira Nakashima was born in February 1942, a tragic time for Japanese-Americans during World War II. Like thousands of other citizens, the Nakashima family was sent to an internment camp; theirs was in Minidoka, Idaho. Though day-to-day life there was extremely hard, Nakashima was lucky enough to meet a traditional Japanese carpenter with whom he worked to make their quarters more livable, and from whom he learned about traditional Japanese joinery. In memory of those hard days, Nakashima kept a branch of bitterbrush from Idaho mounted on his studio wall.

The family was released from the internment camp in 1943 through the sponsorship of Nakashima's former boss, Antonin Raymond, who was living on a farm in New Hope, Pennsylvania. He was hired to take care of the chickens, but Nakashima was soon making furniture again. His work habits quickly assumed the shape they would maintain for the rest of his life.

Trained in the camp to work with scraps, Nakashima was happy to receive wood not suitable for use as veneer from the Thompson Mahogany Company in Philadelphia. Later his sources expanded to include wood from tree surgeons, construction projects, and people calling to tell him about fallen trees.

Nakashima believed profoundly in allowing the wood to speak for itself, seeing himself as merely a guiding hand to make sure that technique never overwhelmed the true character of the wood. Rather than reject defective logs, Nakashima cherished the knots, cracks, cavities, and worm holes as part of each piece's life story. Wood was air-dried for years and then baked

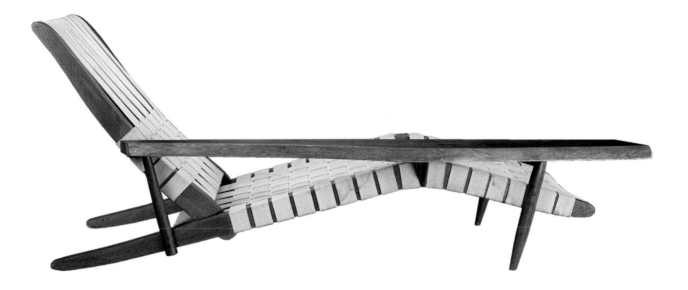

in a kiln; he often compared cutting planks to cutting diamonds. "Hours spent by the true craftsman in bringing out the grain, which has long been imprisoned in the trunk of the tree, is an act of creation in itself," he wrote in 1941 in *California Arts & Architecture* magazine.

In the beginning, Nakashima worked alone out of a garage attached to the house where the family lived on Aquetong Road. When he later built a workshop, three assistants came on, and at the time of his death in 1990 that number had reached fifteen. He always made freehand sketches (rather than drawings) that each assistant would have to interpret with Nakashima himself in constant attendance to make sure things were done correctly. Following the Mingei craft tradition, pieces were never signed, and those scraps of paper with his sketches (or a bill of sales) are sometimes the only proof that something was made by Nakashima. That is, until around 1980, when so many fakes were turning up on the market that Nakashima was forced to start signing the undersides of pieces in India ink and later with an indelible felt pen.

His early pieces made in New Hope, such as the Milk House table of 1944 (made from teak that a friend saved in Seattle while the family was at the internment camp) and the Trestle table (1944) with its signature butterfly joints, show a clear affinity to Shaker furniture, with which he was most likely familiar from books given to him by Raymond. Nakashima's unique ability was to explore the resonant simplicity of rural American forms through the perspective of an Asian minimalist sensibility.

At the sprawling family compound in New Hope that still looks much as it did in his day, Nakashima took the same approach with the home, showroom, and studio that he built by hand, where peeled posts stand alongside traditional Japanese sliding shoji screen doors.

In the mid-1940s Nakashima began to seek outlets for his furniture beyond his own show-room and arranged for pieces to be sold through Rabun Studios in New York. He was then approached by Hans Knoll, the furniture manufacturer, who was already working with the designers Alvar Aalto and Harry Bertoia. Nakashima was wary of mass production and considered it dehumanizing. His collaboration with Knoll lasted from 1945 until 1954. With such Knoll pieces as the Windsor-back armchair and splay-leg table (the earliest of which were made in New Hope), Nakashima's name quickly spread to a much wider audience. However, still determined to maintain as much control as possible over the entire process, Nakashima always maintained production rights, selling the same pieces out of his work-shop that Knoll was making with fewer refinements at its factory.

A second mass-produced line, Origins, was created for Widdicomb-Mueller, a Grand Rapids furniture maker. Produced between 1957 and 1961, the collection, writes Mira Nakashima in *Nature Form and Spirit: The Life and Legacy of George Nakashima*, represents her father's most extensive experimentation with long curves, exotic woods, veneers, and various finishes. (In his own studio, pieces were always oiled with many coats of Tung oil varnish.) The collection also included several of the Conoid chairs, frames, and room dividers that were inspired by his architectural work involving large parabolic and curved shapes made in his Conoid studio in New Hope.

ABOVE In the forties and fifties, modern interpretations of the traditional chaise lounge were popular. Nakashima's American black-walnut Long chair from 1951 is distinctive due to its dramatic single oar-shaped armrest. Compared to earlier examples, this version is slightly more elongated and the webbing is in canvas rather than cotton or twisted grass.

OPPOSITE PAGE The image below, taken around 2007, shows a living room on the Nakashima compound, which has changed little over the years. Nakashima considered himself a "Japanese Shaker." The chairs pictured in the Nakashima's kitchen, above, allude to the classic American Windsor chair. With its simplicity and form it also harkens back to traditional Americana. Knoll would manufacture a version of this chair, but Nakashima negotiated the right to continue making it by hand in his studio as well. Although Nakashima had doubts about working for a major manufacturer, the relationship was beneficial as it exposed his work to a wider audience.

Opposite page top: Ezra Stoller © Esto. Opposite page bottom: © 2008 Leslie Williamson.

ABOVE TOP This piece is a fine example of Nakashima's benches. Hickory spindles were inserted into an uninterrupted slice of walnut. At nearly ten feet long this bench is not only notable for its size, but also for its provenance. In the mid-seventies, Nakashima created over two hundred pieces for Governor Nelson Rockefeller's Japanese-style residence in Pocantico Hills, New York. Upon completion it was the largest-held collection of Nakashima's work in the world.

BOTTOM During his lifetime Nakashima completed only a few projects for corporate collections. The pieces commissioned for the International Paper Company's New York City headquarters are some of the largest pieces he made during his lifetime, as well as some of the most distinctive. The Odakyu cabinet is made from his signature American black walnut with the decorative lattice in cedar. The lattice was constructed without nails or glue and is held together by pressure and placement. Nakashima began using this lattice motif in the early seventies, and it remains a rare example of ornamentation in Nakashima's oeuvre.

The *New York Times* wrote in 1958 that the Origins collection offered a "New American look, a giant step in contemporary design." One of Nakashima's most recognizable and copied pieces, the Conoid chair was designed in 1960 with two legs using a cantilever also inspired from architecture.

Nakashima was already very well known in the fifties. The Museum of Modern Art had presented his work in 1951, and in 1952 he received a gold medal in craftsmanship from the American Institute of Architects, the group's highest award of recognition. Perhaps the most important private commission came in 1974, when he was asked to design the furnishings (that he labeled "Greenrock") for Nelson Rockefeller's home in Pocantico Hills, New York. He used many exotic woods, including French olive ash burl, East Indian laurel, and Persian walnut, and created several unique shapes, such as an inverted sled-based bench and a canopy bed never to be duplicated. Other major public commissions included furnishings for the president's house at Rockefeller University, Carnegie Mellon University (including an office suite in the Conoid style), Columbia University, Mount Holyoke College, and the International Paper Corporation. There were also invitations from abroad to make furniture in India and Japan, as well as a collection (the only one in the world authorized for production outside New Hope) for the Sakura company in Japan with several recognizable Nakashima shapes rendered with slight variations to accommodate Eastern expectations. (For instance, the Sakura version of the Conoid chair has a more V-like shape in the seat.)

Though Nakashima liked to call himself the world's "first hippie" or an American "druid," his approach was anything but far out. Making furniture was for him an all-consuming task requiring his complete attention whether he was in his workshop or not. Everything fueled his art.

Should a client ask for something different, he told them they had better go shop at Macy's instead. (Mira herself recalled being "fired" many times for not following his orders precisely enough.) This uncompromising approach gave birth to the mythology of the sole artist—which was not entirely true. The entire family was involved in supporting the workshop, whether it was his wife, Marion, keeping the books, or Mira and her brother helping in the studio; and, except for at the very beginning, there were always woodworkers under Nakashima's direction.

In the 1970s Mira's role expanded when she returned to help her father in New Hope after studying architecture and living in Japan and in Pittsburgh, where she started to raise a family of her own. She began to organize and prepare more detailed drawings for the furniture.

In his later years, Nakashima turned to ever-more exotic woods, saying "my wood is better now as my work is better now," and a more layered style, including multiple free edges and complex butterfly joinery. In the 1980s he was commissioned to design more than one hundred pieces for Dr. Arthur and Evelyn Krosnick of Princeton, New Jersey, a collection that was almost entirely destroyed in a 1989 fire. One of the surviving pieces, a large table made of California redwood, was featured in the fifty-year retrospective of Nakashima's work at New York's American Craft Museum in 1989. It was then sold at a Sotheby's auction in December 2006 for $822,400, a record for the artist.

George Nakashima died in 1990 at the age of eighty-five, and, according to lore, one of his favorite trees, a five-hundred-year-old Columbia oak, split on that day. If true, there could be no better tribute to a unique artistry representing the rare convergence of heart, hand, and intellect.

ABOVE AND OPPOSITE Nakashima has traditionally commanded the highest prices in the secondary market, including nearly twenty-five examples that have achieved more than $100,000 at auction. For younger collectors, manufactured pieces like this Gentleman's cabinet (Widdicomb-Mueller) from 1958 in walnut and Carpathian elm, are more accessible, but still quite expensive. In December 2007 Knoll reissued Nakashima's straight-backed chair.

PREVIOUS SPREAD This is the living room of the reception house, also known as Sanso Villa (Japanese for "mountain villa"), c. 1977 at the Nakashima studio workshop. It is one of fifteen buildings on the New Hope property that Nakashima built by hand with local woods and fieldstones. The reception house, which includes a traditional tearoom and an artist's studio, is open to the public for tours. Many of his signature pieces are visible, such as his Conoid chairs in the dining room (far right), a crosscut burl coffee table, Mingei (Japanese for folk art) textiles, and square ottomans.

Previous spread: © 2008 Leslie Williamson.

ABOVE The James A. Michener Art Museum in Doylestown, Pennsylvania, celebrates the contribution of many studio artists who worked in New Hope and across the state. A few years after Nakashima's death the institution created a reading room in his honor. Nakashima's daughter, Mira, who took over the studio and completed projects such as Melody Woods III, worked on the furnishings for the room. The large coffee table is made from an uninterrupted slice of claro walnut burl.

OPPOSITE PAGE Another impressive example from the International Paper Company's commission, this room divider stands over eight feet tall. Several of the pieces that Nakashima created for the executive offices were made from English-oak burl.

In the years following Nakashima's death, Mira and her brother, who managed the business side, imagined that they would merely complete existing commissions and then close the studio. Gradually, however, new work continued to flow in, and interest in Mira's creations grew. A turning point came when the James A. Michener Museum of Doylestown, Pennsylvania, commissioned a reading room for which Mira made both signature pieces and her own designs. The popularity of a 1998 show of Nakashima's works at the Moderne Gallery in Philadelphia helped Mira resolve to keep the Nakashima studio open for the production of both familiar pieces and new designs by Mira, whose aesthetic tends to be more geometric and controlled but shares the same reverence for the wood. Auction catalogs started to create separate sections for her work alongside that of her father. And when Mira unveiled her own first collection in 1998, she called it fittingly "Keisho," or continuation. **J.I.**

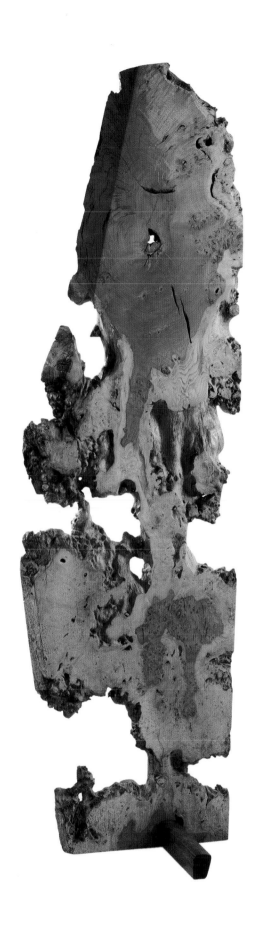

SILAS
SEANDEL

Born and raised in a place and time that bred artistic excellence and nihilism, Silas Seandel (b. 1937) forged his way through the trenches of New York City's pulsing art world in the 1950s and '60s. As a metal sculptor, Seandel pushed the limits not only of his skills but also of his forms in furniture and decorative art; his fluid structures in metal are a testament to his creativity and undying effort to perfect his craft. From wall sculpture and flowers to large outdoor installations and furniture, Silas Seandel's amazing talent and excellent craftsmanship shines.

Like many artists, Silas Seandel, born in 1937, considered sculpting a hobby, not a career. With no formal training beyond clay modeling at the University of Pennsylvania, Seandel took his sculpture career from mere interest to a fruitful design studio in New York's art gallery district of Chelsea. Inspired by Alexander Calder's mobiles, Seandel experimented with model making but considered it only a pastime—one he still enjoys.

While serving in the army between the Korean and Vietnam wars, Seandel spent time making emblems out of wood and metal or fixing the colonel's furniture. After the service, Seandel attended business and law school, but in 1961 he returned to service in Europe. During this tour he realized that working with his hands was his passion and never returned to law school. Instead he returned to New York and worked part time at B. Altman department store as a stock boy.

A 1963 exhibition at the Walter P. Chrysler Museum was a catalyst for Seandel. On his way to Cape Cod, Seandel had an hour's wait for his friend to pick him up in Provincetown, Mass., so he walked through the exhibition *Sculptors of the Fifties*. Seandel recalled being blown away by artists such as John Chamberlain, Richard Stankiewicz, and Jason Seley: "I just went out of my mind. And I told myself, 'I can do that. That's what I want to do!'" Obsessed and focused, he skipped Cape Cod, went home, and bought books on welding.

In his apartment on the top floor of a six-story Greenwich Village building, his kitchen-cum-welding studio lined with tin cans and bricks became his laboratory. Without a welding permit allowing for delivery, two or three times a week Seandel carried home everything from torches to oxygen tanks, some pieces weighing 130 pounds. He practiced nonstop, and with every mistake he made, his passion burned brighter to create unique forms and styles all his own.

His first break as an artist came in 1964, when B. Altman renovated the Old Oaks Country Club in Purchase, New York. His friend, the head decorator for the project, knew Seandel was

ABOVE LEFT Silas Seandel in 2007 in his Chelsea studio in front of his Ribbon wall sculpture. **RIGHT** The wall sculpture was designed for the Bell Telephone Company in the early 1970s, not long after Seandel began his sculpting career in the early sixties when he won his first commission to design a wall sculpture for an upstate New York country club.

OPPOSITE PAGE TOP The Picasso table is made in cast bronze with a natural finish. The inset plate-glass top cantilevers to give this piece a lightweight, sculptural feel. The table shows Seandel's skill in creating a sculptural and functional piece of furniture out of metal. **BOTTOM** The table sculptures that earned Seandel recognition and success were his delicate flower sculptures. Each one made by Seandel and his two-man crew is different from the other, making it all the more astonishing to realize that these unique pieces were sold through department stores nationwide.

an aspiring sculptor and asked him to make wall sculptures for the dining room. Seandel created four golfers in different phases of a golf swing in a three-dimensional design using twisted wire, rods, and planes. The pieces were seen by several interior decorators who contacted him for commissions.

Shortly after this move, Seandel's entrepreneurial spirit and his need for an income drove him to create his delicate flower sculptures—thin wires growing out of a simple metal circle, ending in small, round petals teetering above. He wanted to add to his table-sculpture oeuvre but needed to design something that connected to a wider audience, specifically those who shopped at Saks Fifth Avenue. He presented a sculpture to the merchandising managers at Saks, and they loved it so much they fronted Seandel the money to fill the orders. This business venture encouraged him to approach other department stores and ultimately secured him nationwide sales from such companies as Neiman-Marcus, C. D. Peacock in Chicago, and Gump's in San Francisco. The revenue from his flower sculptures allowed him to produce more pieces for his showroom and to finally hire help; Raymond Quinones and Rupert Williams have worked in the studio for thirty-eight and thirty-six years respectively. Upon his return from the nationwide department stores tour, another friend mentioned a new Design & Decoration (D & D) building going up on Fifty-eighth Street and Third Avenue. So, with his indomitable drive and earnings from his flower sculptures plus cash borrowed for six months' rent, Seandel became one of the original tenants in New York City's D & D building, remaining there for thirty-five years.

One day Seandel got a call from a friend asking if he was showing his art in Texas; he was not and quickly realized people were copying his designs from his catalogues. Therefore, Seandel's start in sculptural furniture—a craft he knew involved great skill, engineering, and patience—resulted from the need to ward off copycats. His first piece was an adaptation of his most successful wall sculpture. His forms are mostly abstract: some geometric, others more fluid; some three-dimensional, others two-dimensional but with planes and rods alluding to three-dimensionality. Even though each piece is unique to him, Seandel has still found designers copying his designs, such as his amorphic table, which copies have been found in a high-polished chrome version.

Seandel's process involves a simple chalk sketch drawn on a steel-slab worktable, a necessary tool of his trade. He notes that the machinery has changed little throughout the years, so many of the tools he bought in the sixties are still used in his studio today, although on occasion they make tools when existing ones don't meet their needs.

Many of the forms and techniques are based on the mistakes he made in his formative welding years, with Seandel and his two-man crew creating each piece by hand to the client's specifications. Once his sketch is drawn he makes a three-dimensional model in wood, clay, plaster, or wire. Then the team manipulates the raw materials: bronze, brass, steel, or copper are transformed from rolls, sheets, plates, rods, or coils by cutting, burning, welding, and brazing them into shape. Seandel's obsession with the perfect weld and durability makes some

Seandel was one of the first tenants in the Design & Decoration building in New York City on East Fifty-eighth Street, near Decorator's Row. This photograph was taken in 1967 and shows how Seandel displayed both sculpture and furniture in the same room. Seen here are early versions of pieces that remain popular for his clients today, among them the amorphic stainless-steel table (center), which is similar to the Monet piece on view at his Chelsea studio. The showroom also exhibits the breadth of finishes that Seandel employs—from a polychrome patina to a mirror finish.

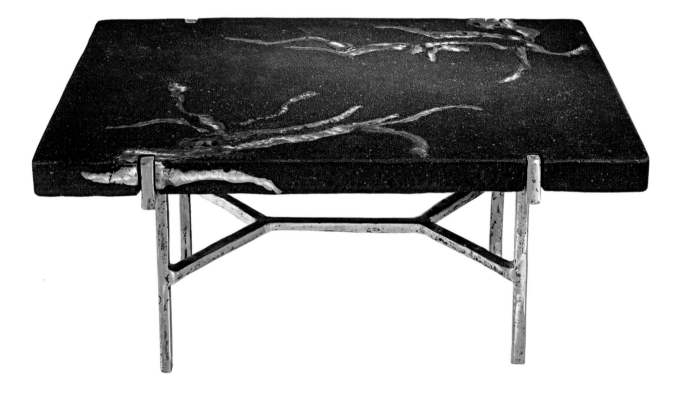

materials preferable to work with than others. His brazing technique, which he believes is a lost art, involves gas fusing two dissimilar metals, allowing for stronger joinery and a perfect union of the materials. His welding technique involves the electrical fusing of two similar metals, which allows for perfect joinery.

The finishing process is the lengthiest part. Once a basic shape is formed and the metals are fused, its surface needs to be chased and grinded, and its edges need to be cut and smoothed. This is where Seandel's perfectionism really comes out. The process is most similar to stone sculpting, "where the rough parts are removed and the image is released."

Seandel prefers working with brass, copper, steel, bronze, and cast stone—this final material took him four and a half years to refine. He favors the malleability of bronze and uses nitric acid to create beautiful colors and aged looks. Blends of pewter wash on bronze or "tortured bronze" techniques are exclusive to the Silas Seandel Studio. His Ortago cocktail table exemplifies his abstract forms and use of bronze. A thick glass top sits on rounded strips of bronze that crisscross at varying points, creating shapes that are abstract with animated properties—they appear to move through space, using bended strips to form tails, legs, and arms that support the clear top, resulting in a lightweight feel.

Stainless steel is Seandel's least favorite material, because the bending and hammering process not only makes the steel harder but it also puts gouges and indentations on the surface that need to be removed and smoothed. It also has limited coloring ability that does not last. In spite of this, Seandel creates fluid forms in stainless steel, with lustrous finishes. The Monet dining table shows his use of finishes in stainless steel and demonstrates his skill in transforming this stubborn material. By using two biomorphic shapes as pedestals supporting a glass top, Seandel gives the shapes a right angle, then faces them toward each other, allowing the negative space to allude to a more substantial, solid form.

His cast-stone material is a secret process that uses a cement-base binder. On a trip to Italy in the 1970s, Seandel noticed the beautiful terrazzo floors and decided to create a variation of this look by creating polychrome cast stone incised with metal. At first the pieces were incredibly heavy, but in the past twenty years he has been able to make them 35 percent lighter. Another major challenge has been getting a perfectly flat, maintenance-free surface in any shape, size, and color. Seandel can make the material look antiqued and rough with a deckled edge, as if it was from an archeological dig, as seen in his Cycladic table—one of his more representational pieces that harkens back to ancient Greece. Or he can make the material look colorful and shiny, like marbleized paper with bright strips of metal meandering throughout, as seen in his Terra table.

As the consummate artist, he continues to produce sculptured furniture but still receives commissions to work on outdoor installations as well. His latest commission was for the Greenwich Hospital; the hospital lost many of its employees on 9/11 and hired Seandel to create a memorial for its garden. Seandel used his scorched-bronze technique to create his Twin Towers sculpture. As for furniture, Seandel has a mantra: "I want you to use it. I want you to love it." His biggest concern is giving the best and making the best. Through what he calls luck, Seandel single-handedly built a career out of his passion. **E.J.**

ABOVE LEFT The *Colorado* wall sculpture is a variation of *Dimensions*, the wall sculpture that Seandel based his first piece of furniture on. **RIGHT** The coffee table is from Seandel's first furniture series; it's made from copper, brass, bronze, brass welded-steel nails, and glass. Seandel also used brass welded-steel nails plus copper and brass in the wall sculpture of a similar pattern. Creating a three-dimensional table that was not only beautiful but also well made was another way Seandel introduced art into everyday life.

OPPOSITE PAGE TOP The Ortago table made of cast bronze is one of Seandel's favorite pieces. He has made many variations of this form, from small end tables to consoles to dining tables, and all can be done in any finish. **BOTTOM** The Terra table is made from a cast-stone material; it took several years of refinement for Seandel to get his formula to behave according to his specifications. The material can be made in any color or any size, and can be buffed to a high shine or left natural. Stonelike veins of any metal can also be incised into the surface.

CHARLES HOLLIS JONES

Although various synthetic materials found their way into postwar furnishings, it was not until the 1960s that plastics truly came into their own. (It was 1967, for example, when Mr. McGuire advised a young Benjamin Braddock in *The Graduate*: "I just want to say one word to you—just one word… plastics. There is a great future in plastics. Think about it.") Charles Hollis Jones (b. 1945), whose career began in 1961 (when he was just sixteen years old), arrived on the scene at a pivotal moment—although by a somewhat indirect route. "I really fell in love with glass," recalled Jones, "but it couldn't do what I wanted it to do." Acrylic—the material that would become his signature medium—wasn't Jones's first choice. Nor was he the first to design acrylic furniture—Grosfeld House, for example, produced traditional furniture designs from acrylic in the 1940s. But Jones was among the first to treat acrylic as a unique material, to meet it on its own terms—and apply it to distinctly modern designs. Numerous designers experimented at one time or another with this highly seductive medium, but none pursued acrylic with Jones's dogged determination. Jones built his entire career around acrylic (although he also designed scores of all-metal accessories early on), creating everything from table lighters to four-poster beds and custom staircases from the material. This innovative approach—combined with a broad range of manufacturing processes—allowed Jones to transform acrylic's image from slick to chic. Of course, not everybody approached acrylic with Jones's sensitivity. And, "the uneducated use of acrylic," said Jones, "is a disaster."

In the early 1960s, acrylic's future was still rather uncertain, despite its early promise. An article by Robert Medill in the April 1940 issue of *Arts & Decoration* described acrylic as a nearly miraculous material, one that "looks like quartz crystal but can be carved, turned on a lathe, or worked like metal." Within just a few years of its introduction (DuPont's acrylic resin formula, Lucite, was introduced in 1936), acrylic was destined, it seemed, for a bright future. "Its great virtue in the decorative and architectural fields," wrote Medill, "is its versatility in the workshop, for, capable of being cast into sheets, rods, and tubes, it serves as basic materials for manufacturing into a thousand and one usable objects." In fact, little of acrylic's potential was realized prior to World War II, when it was molded into aircraft canopies, nose cones, and gunner turrets. More often, acrylic "reflected a stylish frivolity," wrote art historian Jeffrey L. Meikle in *American Plastic: A Cultural History*, "as it became available to manufacturers who made jewelry from it or embedded flowers and sea horses in it to create desktop novelties."

OPPOSITE PAGE The Swedlow showroom at the Pacific Design Center in Los Angeles around 1979 featured Charles Hollis Jones's Le Dome table and Arch armchairs. The Le Dome table required extensive experimentation before it met the designer's strict requirements. Its 1/16" diameter base was made as a single casting, including a custom steel anchor used for attaching the top. The concept for the anchor itself was inspired by Jones's memories of space-capsule splashdowns. Jones made the prototypes for the Arch armchairs himself, using his kitchen oven (with its rear panel removed) to heat the acrylic enough so that he could then bend it by hand.

ABOVE LEFT The László game table (c. 1970) was named for architect and designer Paul László, one of Jones's earliest and most-loyal clients. **CENTER** The bathroom and bar shelf (c. 1961) of brass, mirror, and wood were manufactured by Roide Enterprises, where Jones started working when he was sixteen; they were sold at the West Hollywood showroom, Hudson Rissman. **RIGHT** Jones made a tableau with a lead-crystal chandelier, dining table, and Arch armchairs, all of his own design, for an exhibition at Showcase House around 1973.

OPPOSITE PAGE At the Los Angeles home of Loretta Young. The award-winning film and television actress was one of Jones's best clients, and a frequent visitor to the Hudson Rissman showroom. The L'Ami cocktail table (1963), one of Jones's best-selling designs, and the Blade Line desk (c. 1969) are fine examples of Jones's cast-in-place manufacturing technique. Also shown are Jones's Cantilever chair (c. 1970), Let's Make a Deal table lamp (1970) and pedestal. The folding screen (c. 1968) seen in the background was designed to coordinate with his Wisteria chairs with their circular designs machined into the acrylic. Over the years, Jones's work was specified by three different interior designers for the Young estate; the second iteration, c. 2001, is shown here.

For Jones, though, acrylic has never been a "stylish frivolity." Although acrylic furniture was, according to an article in the October 1970 issue of *Progressive Architecture*, "surprisingly slow in gaining acceptance," Jones's work was attracting the attention of some of the twentieth century's most important architects, designers, and decorators from the very start. Interiors by Paul László, Arthur Elrod, Hal Broderick, Steve Chase, and John Woolf featured countless Jones designs. In addition to his impressive client list (Lucille Ball, Dean Martin, Frank Sinatra, and Sylvester Stallone, to name just a few), Jones has an equally impressive list of awards. His Edison lamp, a celebration of Edison's original carbon-filament lightbulb ("to get people to look at the lightbulb again and get what a great difference it made in the world," suggested Jones), was one of three Jones designs selected for the seminal *California Design 11* exhibition in 1970. In 2007 he was nominated for the Lifetime Achievement Award by the Cooper-Hewitt National Design Museum. It's quite a career for a kid from the heartland, who, as a boy, Jones confessed, "didn't even know what an architect was. My mother kept talking about Frank Lloyd Wright, but her idea was, she hoped I'd become a manager of Howard Johnson's."

Charles Hollis Jones was born in the rural community of Bloomington, Indiana, in 1945. According to his sister Jan, his creative spirit and desire to build were evident from an early age. He "rebuilt" a discarded tricycle, using a metal coffee can lid as a makeshift wheel, when he was just eight years old. At the same age, Jones was drawing cars (a passion that continues to this day). He designed and built his first piece of furniture—a cabinet for his father's office—when he was fourteen. At sixteen, he landed a job with Roide Enterprises in Los Angeles. Initially, his role was, said Jones, "cleaning up" designs that weren't selling well—removing the "froufrou." Success was immediate, and what was supposed to be a one-month visit lasted all summer. He worked for Roide again the following summer, and in 1963, Jones moved to Los Angeles, quickly becoming an integral part of its growing design community. For his next career move, at Joe Roide's suggestion, he went to work for Hudson-Rissman, the West Hollywood showroom featuring, according to its catalog, "the finest in quality decorative accessories for the home in the modern idiom." Though hired as a driver and delivery boy, he became head of the design department within six months, designing everything from desk accessories to elegant acrylic étagères.

Although Jones had turned down an art scholarship to Indiana University to move to the West Coast, he was an eager learner and on his own went through all three libraries at UCLA until, he says, "I was totally educated… I was after knowledge!" His formal education would come later, when, with the support of Hudson-Rissman and one of its generous clients, he attended the Art Center College of Design in Los Angeles. "They picked up the $144 a unit, and I went to school for three years, nights." Today, Jones calls those three years at Art Center "God's gift to me."

For seven years, Jones continued to work for Hudson-Rissman, helping to establish the company's growing reputation as the best accessory showroom in town. Interior designer Ron Fields, who grew up in the Los Angeles design scene, said Hudson-Rissman was the showroom for "modern, high-end, good looking" furnishings. "There were other accessory showrooms in Los Angeles at that time," said Fields, "but Hudson-Rissman was in a class by itself." Ultimately, however, Jones wanted to work less in accessories and more in furniture. "I liked art you bumped

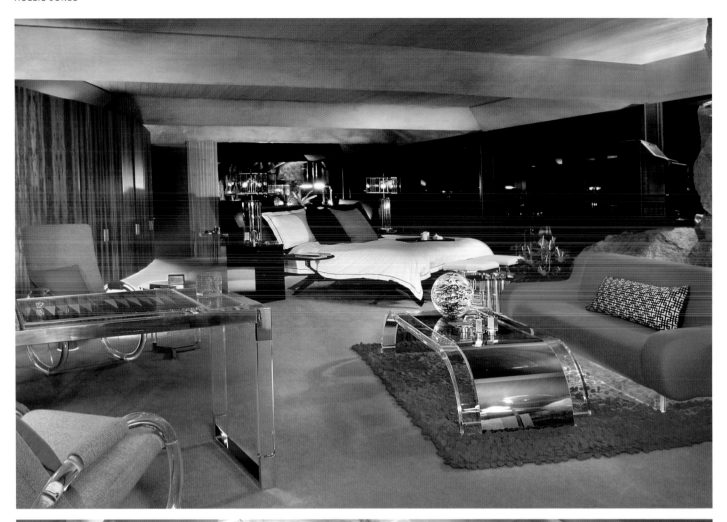

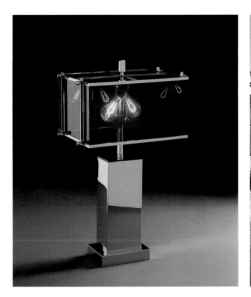

into," he recalled, "not that you looked at on a shelf. I wanted to make big furniture. I wanted to make beds—they wouldn't let me put a bed in their showroom." So, after seven years, Jones decided to open up his own showroom.

As an independent designer, Jones was able to work in any scale he wished. Just as important, however, was the opportunity to spread out creatively. Concepts that had, until that point, been explored only tentatively could be expressed more fully. Although the origins of Jones's work are often traced to the geometric tendencies of the Bauhaus or the repetitive rectilinear elements of art deco, his greatest inspirations are to be found not in Europe but in the American Midwest. His first exposure to acrylic was his mother's "Jelly Belly" pins (costume jewelry designed in the shapes of various animals, each having acrylic centers). And the quilts his mother and other family members made—with their various colors and geometric structure—were among his earliest visual influences. "My mother was not afraid of color," said Jones. "If colors went together in the garden, she could put them in the quilt." And the "pattern houses" (complete kit houses sold as economical postwar housing solutions) produced by his father's lumber company helped foster his growing interest in design and building. During the 1970s—freed from the demands of a "boss"—Jones was able to explore these early influences, to work in a more experimental mode (and, often, with increasingly generous elements of acrylic).

As much as Jones enjoyed the freedom of his own showroom, his creativity was sometimes limited by the manufacturing capabilities he had at his disposal. Swedlow Plastics had no such limitations, having grown to meet the demands of the booming Southern California aircraft industry. Of particular interest to Jones was Swedlow's ability to make large acrylic castings and scratch-resistant acrylic sheets. So in 1977 he teamed up with Swedlow to produce the Charles Hollis Jones Signature Collection of furniture, lighting, and accessories (including some of Jones's most monumental pieces, such as the Le Dome table). Unfortunately, what Jones had gained in manufacturing capability, he had lost in creative freedom. After almost two years, when the costs began to outweigh the benefits, the deal fell apart. Eager to move on, Jones wasted no time getting settled into his second showroom and reopening his showroom at the Pacific Design Center.

Since the early 1980s Jones has continued to work as an independent designer. He has had his own showrooms and even his own factory at one point. He sells through a handful of select showrooms in Los Angeles, but most of his contemporary designs are commissioned by interior designers or directly by clients.

Joining two pieces of acrylic is not complicated. "A good joint between two pieces of Lucite," read a DuPont catalog from the 1960s, "is strong, transparent, and practically invisible." However, this is rarely the case in practice. More often, glue joints are done sloppily—and rather than a welded bond, the result is a fragile mass of tiny air bubbles. For this reason, Jones uses glue only when the design demands it—and then only a special nonacidic version, applied with a craftsman's skill. "I insisted on my joints being better than anybody else's," he said. "I wasn't going to do this unless it was going to be better than what I'd seen." His joints are nearly invisible— no bubbles or discoloration, only the smooth edges of two transparent planes of acrylic.

ABOVE LEFT Edison lamp (c. 1970). One of Jones's best-known designs, the Edison lamp was his homage to the original carbon-filament Edison lightbulb. It was selected for the *California Design 11* exhibition in 1970 at the Pasadena Museum of Art, and won a Brilliance of Design Award from the German government in 1971. **RIGHT** At the Charles Hollis Jones showroom in Los Angeles, c. 1971.

OPPOSITE PAGE At the Elrod house in Palm Springs. Nearly one hundred pieces of Jones's work were showcased for the 2006 *Dwell on Design* reception sponsored by *Dwell* magazine. For Jones, the project was a homecoming of sorts. Arthur Elrod, for whom the architect John Lautner originally designed this iconic home, was perhaps Jones's best client. In fact, several of Jones's pieces can be seen in photos of Elrod's original interior, designed in 1969. Since the Elrod house had always been meant for entertaining, said Jones, the *Dwell* event was an opportunity to celebrate both the home's design and the vision of its namesake.

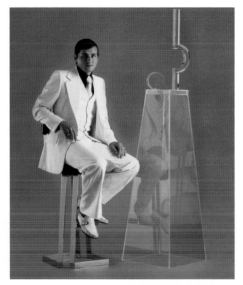

ABOVE Charles Hollis Jones and his *Ball and Pole* sculpture (1975). Jones's sculptures are used for the *Hollywood Life* magazine's Breakthrough Award, as well as a number of awards commissioned by community organizations.

Jones's preference is to avoid the glue altogether, which can be accomplished by casting molten material into a gap between two pieces of acrylic. It's a demanding and time-consuming (and therefore expensive) process, but the results are unlike anything that can be accomplished with glue. Jones has applied this cast-in-place technique with great success in his Blade Line series of furniture and accessories. The Wisteria chair, one of Jones's most recognizable designs, is actually a precursor to the Blade Line (and employs its cast-in-place joining technique). Inspired by Tennessee Williams's *The Glass Menagerie*, Jones designed the 1968 Wisteria chair, which gives the illusion (especially in the version with the acrylic edges dyed green) of plates of glass floating in space. The detail cut into the chair's back inspired Williams to name the chair (he said the circles reminded him of "modern" wisteria) and gave Jones another technical challenge, because it "makes them twice as hard to make—not putting the circles all the way through."

Although Jones is known as the pioneer in acrylic furniture, many of his designs actually combine acrylic with metal, creating a delicate tension. But because acrylic cannot hide the screws and other fasteners commonly used to assemble a piece of furniture, Jones either finds a clever way to hide them or eliminates them entirely. For his Metric Line, the acrylic members are joined with metal by way of a proprietary process in which the acrylic is cooled—forcing it to contract—before assembly. As the assemblage returns to room temperature, the acrylic expands snugly into the metal sleeve. The result is a clean, solid joint—free from the usual clutter of nuts and bolts.

In addition to his innovative designs and manufacturing techniques, Jones—perhaps more than any other designer—has tapped into the inherent properties of acrylic. One of the greatest differences between acrylic and glass has to do with a physical property called transmissivity. While light tends to reflect off glass, it tends to go through acrylic. This is particularly evident in Jones's work, as he rarely uses acrylic less than an inch thick. With a thicker material (Jones has made the tops of consoles and dining tables as thick as three inches), the acrylic absorbs more light, giving it a dramatic presence. In this way, even Jones's largest pieces have a mysterious lightness to them. Some of his best-known—and best-selling—designs take on a truly sculptural look and feel, as can be seen in the L'Ami table. By "carrying the light," as Jones likes to say, the acrylic highlights the table's understated form. And the sheer volume of acrylic gives it the appearance of being lit from within.

Thin sheets of acrylic can be sculptural, too, as Jones has demonstrated with his 1969 Sling chair, one of his most recognizable designs. Indeed, its dramatic presence is created precisely because of its thinness. Here, Jones has stretched the acrylic under carefully controlled heat—a technique adapted from the World War II–era aviation industry. The result is a sheet of acrylic just over a quarter of an inch thick, but with incredible tensile strength. Made from a thicker sheet, the Sling chair would lose its sublime beauty. It would simply become too visible.

Today Jones is as busy as ever. His 2007 Nouveau Vu line is a radical departure from his largely geometric oeuvre and was inspired more by nature than technology. "I studied art nouveau for years," said Jones, "and I always wanted to make furniture as good as art nouveau." Jones's take on art nouveau—rendered in ghostly acrylic, naturally—was inspired by a friend's Palm Springs garden. Jones was admiring the trees loaded with ripe fruit. "I thought," said Jones, "I have to start drawing more things from where I come from." There was a substantial gap to be bridged between inspiration and implementation, however. "It's taken me over two years to develop the machinery to do it," Jones said. "I didn't even know how to make it when I first designed it." It's a situation Jones has become comfortable with. As the pioneer in acrylic furniture design, he has done some of his best work when the way forward was *not* clear.

Jones's work began to show up in the secondary market in 2001, when he offered eighty pieces of his vintage work as part of the Christie's Los Angeles "Innovators of Twentieth-Century Style" auction. Wright featured eighteen lots of Jones's designs in October 2007. A pair of Elrod Spider occasional tables (a design that was a personal favorite of legendary designer Arthur Elrod) brought $3,000. A pair of Metric Line lounge chairs and ottomans sold for $5,500, and a pair of Edison lamps brought $6,500. **P. W.**

ABOVE LEFT Wisteria chair (1968). Edge-dyed acrylic with upholstered cushion. The Wisteria chair was originally designed as a commission from playwright Tennessee Williams. "He wanted to sit in it every morning, to start his day in it," said Jones. Each joint is cast in place and no glue is used. Jones would return to this technique and the general concept behind the design for his Blade Line series that debuted the following year. **TOP RIGHT** The Blade Line dining table was originally designed for decorator Welter "Bud" Holden (c. 1969). Rather than using glue, Jones decided to use his cast-in-place technique for manufacturing his entire Blade Line series. The time-consuming process involves carefully pouring molten acrylic into the small gap between two pieces of acrylic. Once the joint is cooled, cleaned up, polished, and cured, the result is seamless. **BOTTOM LEFT** The Flying Ziggurat cocktail table (c. 1975) was designed for the Hotel Le Mondrian in Los Angeles.

PHILIP & KELVIN LAVERNE

The LaVernes were a family of artisans stretching back three generations. Paterfamilias Max was a muralist who painted in churches, synagogues, hotels, and office lobbies. Of his nine children, Philip and Erwine became famous designers, the former known for bronze art furniture that he made by hand with his son, the latter establishing with his wife a highly profitable company that manufactured wallpapers and furnishings. Another brother was a well-respected interior decorator. Less typical was the reputation that eldest son Philip (1907–1987) established in collaboration with his son Kelvin (b. 1937) in the rarefied field of custom–furniture making, or as Philip described it, "functional art." Father and son made patinated and sculpted bronze tables and cabinets combining innovative techniques with traditional styles.

Max LaVerne, originally Levine, emigrated to America from Eastern Europe in the later half of the nineteenth century. As an itinerant muralist, he would sometimes travel for months at a time, leaving his son, Philip, in charge at home in Brooklyn.

Max expected Philip—and his other sons—to follow in his footsteps, sending Philip to the library to paint birds and trees from books. (Years later, Philip and his own son Kelvin kept mum about their patented, secret technique for the distinctive finish on their ornately produced and sculpted bronze furniture, which turned out to have been extricated largely from books at the New York Public Library.)

By age sixteen, Philip had dropped out of school. He was working for his father to help set aside money for brother Erwine to go to the École des Beaux-Arts in Paris. This pattern would repeat itself with Kelvin, who studied in Paris and Florence for a year before becoming his father's creative partner.

Meanwhile, Erwine followed his own route to fame and fortune. Through LaVerne Originals, Erwine and his wife, Estelle, became known for their wallpapers with contemporary motifs and their plastic furniture collection.

Philip and Kelvin, who sometimes signed their name La Verne, were determined to operate as artist–furniture makers, creating one-of-a-kind and limited-edition pieces that would be both functional and aesthetic. Their unique production methods and goals were far more aligned with today's avant-garde furniture designers than they were with either the high-end upholsterers or the mass-production modernists who dominated the scene in their own day. For advertisements that appeared in the 1960s, Philip penned the tagline: "It's not just functional and not just art, it's an investment."

OPPOSITE PAGE The Bathers, shown here in a detail, was made by Philip and Kelvin LaVerne in 1968. The nude figures, according to Kelvin, were inspired by swimmers he used to observe on Shelter Island. Only one or two pieces are believed to exist using the Bathers as decoration.

ABOVE LEFT In 1968 the *New York Times* featured the father-son team in an article boasting the pair's secret formula for their patinated bronze technique. The formula was said to consist of a mysterious soil that originated in the Far East, a fitting detail since many of their bas-relief designs featured historical Asian motifs. **RIGHT** In 1963 an article in the *Nashville Banner* covered a solo exhibition at the Tennessee Fine Arts Center displaying the LaVerne's metal furniture and metal paintings. The article quoted Philip explaining his works as "the poetry of the soul" that were products "of a lifetime." With each piece Philip and Kelvin attempted to resurrect historical motifs enhanced with an array of colors and aged with expeditious care.

OPPOSITE PAGE These are typical examples of the work that came out of the LaVerne studio as Kelvin became more interested in sculptural forms. A round table is decorated with nude figures in high relief, hand cast with a lost-wax process, while the figures in the four cast cubes have a smoother burnished bronze surface. Such molds were cast in their New York studio until the early 1970s when the city banned casting within city limits. Subsequently, Kelvin became interested in using a torch technique, or brazing, which he had seen in the work of sculptor Seymour Lipton.

Although Philip trained at the Art Students League in New York, he was also quite entrepreneurial, and at some point, though records have been lost, he seemed to have opened a business that created smoked mirrored furniture in the Venetian style. Later he began casting porcelain, before moving onto brass and bronze, making his own molds. (Kelvin recalls that his father always favored working in an undershirt topped with a blacksmith's apron.)

By 1950 Kelvin joined his father, and the pair started making their signature pewter-etched bronze tables and cabinets. Philip called it "functional art," a concept he did not invent but that the LaVernes brought to a wider audience through their gallery/showroom at 46 East Fifty-seventh Street and an aggressive advertising campaign.

The process for creating the patinated bronze series that started to appear around 1954 took six years for the LaVernes to refine. With its flat bronze and pewter surfaces articulated with classically inspired images, the series lived up to the name of functional art (also called "sculptural functionalism"). Slabs were set atop different supports—sometimes legs, sometimes a pedestal—that were not always fully integrated into the piece. In earlier pieces the surface alone had received attention, as though it were a canvas. Later pieces were more sculptural and three-dimensional. The Four Cubes from the early 1970s were especially dynamic, with mythological and Michelangelo-esque figures made to look so muscular they literally burst out of the cubes' surfaces.

The technique used by Philip and Kelvin was based on centuries-old bronze-casting methods, tweaked to give each piece its own distinctive patina. A hand-carved bas-relief was cut into a layer of bronze that was then set on a layer of pewter (enamel detailing was sometimes added); another layer of bronze completed the sandwich. The entire section was buried for six weeks in a container full of special soil (Philip indicated vaguely to reporters that the sod came from the Far East, and it may have been imported through Hong Kong) that was mixed with the family's secret chemical brew (another brother, Albert, was a chemist). Once buried, the bronze would oxidize naturally, causing the metal to turn different colors at specific stages, a process known as the "rainbow cycle." Philip and Kelvin would carefully monitor the progress to achieve the exact color and patina they wanted. By sealing sections with wax they could set a color, or they could add more chemicals to alter it. Smelted enamel created its own color variations. In order to lock a slab "into lasting brightness," as Philip said, it would be frozen in subzero temperatures. To get a darker, mottled look in spots, they zapped the surface with a torch.

Though their process was radical, the LaVernes's designs were conservative: a combination that was intentional, they often said, so that their functional art would adapt to traditional or modern furnishing styles. Motifs were drawn from history (inspired by more trips to the library). Chinese scenes adorned some of their most popular cabinets and tables, particularly from the Chan series. Chan table 142 depicted peasants bearing gifts to a young prince on a forty-eight-inch round top on an octagonal bronze base, while Chan 132 was a four-foot-long rectangular table with a variation on the same scene in a more architectural setting. The key differences were the variations in color. There were several decorative themes in the popular Chinese series, including Tao, Chi Liang, Chin Ying, K'ang-Hsi, Lo Ta, Ming, T'ang Sui, Shang Ti,

and Su Tao. They all blended well with the oriental style so popular in decorating at the time. Most pieces in the Chan series were sold in limited editions of twelve, but, due to demand, the LaVernes made many more, said Kelvin in an interview. Still, a catalogue from the mid-seventies described a Chan Li cabinet, with four sculpted panel doors and bronze-edged interior shelves sitting on a modified key-scroll base, as available upon request only in a limited edition. When it surfaced at Sollo Rago's modern auction in October 2007, it sold for $22,800.

A nearly six-foot-long Chin Ying coffee table of 1972 was especially notable for its rich range of colors resulting from smelted cloisonné set into pewter and bronze. Such cabinets now sell at auction for $45,000 to $100,000, usually depending on the subtleties of coloration and design. The LaVernes were also inspired by Etruscan, Renaissance, eighteenth-century French, and abstract modern styles. An ornate design with a theme from *The Odyssey* was commissioned by Aristotle Onassis, the Greek shipping magnate, and was elaborated with astrological signs from his own horoscope. To this scene of heroic striving, Kelvin remembers adding his own figure disguised in a beard. Another singular design was the Bathers cabinet, made by father and son in 1968. The nude figures, according to Kelvin, were inspired by swimmers he used to observe on Shelter Island in the summer and show off his ability to render dynamic, semiabstract figures. Only one or two versions of the Bathers are believed to exist; a Bathers cabinet sold at a Sotheby's auction in November 2007 for $91,000.

Whether limited or not, all pieces were signed by both father and son. Signatures were sometimes cut out and laid in pewter or engraved directly into the bronze. Kelvin said in an interview that the more painterly wall plaques were made by his father, and usually only Philip signed those. If they were particularly happy about a piece, he added, they signed it two or three times. Philip was so delighted with one table that he scrawled his name right across the top, and the client complained. "Not negotiable unless signed by Philip and Kelvin LaVerne" was one of Philip's favorite catchphrases, used on all marketing materials.

Before the LaVernes had their own showroom, they sold their tables and cabinets through the Baker Company. It was the closest they would come to commercial distribution; custom designs and limited editions ultimately suited their production style best. Famously, their showroom looked more like an art gallery than a commercial space. Walls were stripped of all but the pieces on display; extraneous decorations were eliminated. The serious intentions of these furniture artists were clear.

The company flourished in the 1960s and '70s, fulfilling orders and selling through dealers in Boston, Chicago, San Francisco, and Dallas. Pieces were also sold at the high-end furniture store Sloane's. In 1963 the Tennessee Fine Arts Center in Nashville hosted an exhibition of the LaVernes's work, about which a local reporter wrote, "These works add a modern chapter to the long history of man's infatuation with enduring metals." While Philip and Kelvin presided over production, Philip's wife and their second son, Seymour, handled business affairs (until he died in the early '70s).

ABOVE LEFT The bronze plaque is one of the many acid-etched paintings that Philip LaVerne created, although this one is signed by Kelvin. The scenes were often abstract, deriving their shape from the properties of the metals used. **RIGHT** The wall hangings were produced in bronze, pewter, brass, or a mixture of metals; the colors ranged from yellow gold and turquoise green to dull silver. To enhance the surface, they also applied deep reds and glowing blues, which can been seen especially well on this Chin Ying tabletop.

OPPOSITE PAGE The LaVernes tried to make the base of each piece as expressive as their acid-etched surfaces. Here, thin sheets of bronze appear to melt down the column of an Etruscan-inspired dining table. On its top, the design shows an abstract array of ancient-looking letters as both border and pattern.

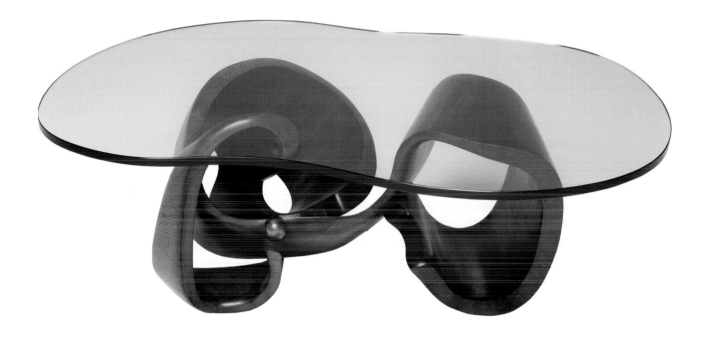

ABOVE TOP A rare oak table from the early 1960s shows Philip LaVerne branching out to explore different media; Kelvin LaVerne stated that only a handful of these tables were made. Signatures were an important part of the creative process and marketing of the LaVernes' output and this piece was incised Philip LaVerne Galleries. Sometimes the duo would be unaware that their partner had already signed a work and therefore many extant pieces can be found with two signatures. **BOTTOM LEFT** The Bathers, which sold at Sotheby's in 2007 for $91,000, is a rare piece illustrating how the LaVernes' furniture complemented both traditional and modern interiors. And, in this instance, the artists were so delighted with their creation, they signed it twice. **BOTTOM RIGHT** Another nod to early twentieth-century artists is the Kiss table, inspired by Constantin Brancusi's sculpture of the same name.

Kelvin called the scene on East Fifty-seventh Street a hive of activity spread over three floors, with cutting machines running, assistants welding, and even a mold-maker hired from Naples, Italy. Kelvin lived in the neighborhood and usually came to work at 6 a.m., completing projects and monitoring workmen; Philip took over in the afternoon, whipping out his latest thumbnail sketches and dictating ideas for his son to execute. "We had an understanding of how we wanted things to be," said Kelvin, noting that as the years went on Philip gave Kelvin increasing latitude in developing his own designs. Whether sculpted or cast bronze, each piece took up to twelve weeks to make. Prices were reasonable considering the materials, with small tables selling in 1960 for about $166 and larger coffee tables for $500.

In the late seventies, the laws for casting and smelting within city limits became too restrictive, and the LaVernes closed the showroom on East Fifty-seventh Street. Work continued in a work-shop on Wooster Street that Kelvin still occupies. When Philip died in 1988, Kelvin was tired of making art furniture to order and eager to take up sculpting again. After completing three years' worth of back orders, that is exactly what he did, leaving behind a legacy of inimitable creativity.

ABOVE LEFT Designed in the late 1950s by Erwine and Estelle Laverne the Invisible Chair series was an early example of acrylic furniture. The pieces were appropriately named for the flowers that inspired their shapes: jonquil (shown), lily, buttercup, and daffodil. Erwine Laverne once said it was the people not the furniture that made a room complete, thus the invisible furnishings. **RIGHT** However, as seen in the tall Tulip chair, sculptural qualities were very important to these artists whose work covered a variety of media from acrylic and metal furniture to hand-painted textiles and hand-painted aluminum planters.

OPPOSITE PAGE This interior is from an interior-decorator show house in 1973. The A.I.D. (American Institute of Designers) designer chose many Philip and Kelvin LaVerne pieces, such as the dining table. Its base is made from plates of bronze that have figures in high relief designed on each panel. The "painted" metal panel on the wall is a Philip LaVerne piece that features a female nude, which is atypical of his wall plaques as they were usually abstract designs.

PREVIOUS PAGE The Tao cabinet is a finely sculpted bronze and pewter cabinet featuring such fine details as pierced drawers with delicately molded flower knobs. Its surface tells the story of life in ancient China depicting a scene of small village life. The cabinet's base is a hand-chased bronze form with a Greek key motif. The mirror shows ancient Chinese architecture, nature, and people. Both pieces were highlighted with brilliant, colorful enamels.

LAVERNE ORIGINALS

Erwine and Estelle Laverne met at New York's Art Students League in 1934, just a few years after Erwine won a gold medal for faux-marble painting at the 1929 International Exposition in Brussels. After marrying, Erwine and Estelle went into business on their own, combining fine arts and applied design in furnishings that mixed Old World craft with the latest production technologies and materials. In the early 1940s they founded Laverne Originals (later Laverne International), creating wallpapers, textiles, and furniture, and quickly establishing themselves as designers with a finger on the pulse of modern design trends. Erwine's wallpapers, especially the dark blue and black Marbalia series, reflected his talent for faux finishes and abstract organic styles, while Estelle's designs were often witty and representational. In 1958 Laverne Originals released their most memorable collection, the Invisible Group. Made of a type of plastic (newspaper reports refer to a German manufacturer called Enreviglas) and inspired, the Lavernes said, by Eero Saarinen's Tulip chair of 1956, the chairs were named after the flowers they somewhat resembled: buttercup, lily, and lotus. Lightweight and durable (they were tested by freezing and scorching with cigarette ash), and with prices ranging from $140 to $250, the collection was revolutionary for its time. Recalling the impression the Invisible Collection first made, Rita Reif of the *New York Times* told a reporter in 2004, forty-five years after the fact, "I knew immediately what it was, how innovative: it was the first time we saw full-fledged modern design in acrylic…. [It was] really the most important thing they ever did." The collection also included an unusual settee with shag seats made of Lucite on metal legs. When a settee with original shag seat cushions came up for sale at a Sollo Rago auction in 2006, it sold quickly for $7,200.

Working from a carriage house on the Tiffany summer estate on Long Island, where they moved in 1948, the Lavernes became known for entertaining and making studio and exhibition space available to artists. Attracting new talent was integral to the success of Laverne Originals, resulting in such successful collaborations as the T-chair (1952) by industrial designers William Katalavos, Ross Littell, and Douglas Kelley. In the Contempora Series of the late 1940s, Alexander Calder, Alvin Lustig, Oscar Niemeyer, and others contributed designs for textiles and wallpapers. In 1949, 1952, and 1953, the Lavernes received prestigious Good Design Awards from the Museum of Modern Art. Their wallpapers were often exhibited in context with work by Charles and Ray Eames, George Nelson, and Isamu Noguchi.

Erwine and Estelle Laverne fully participated in the design movement of the 1950s and '60s, embracing modernism and modernist motifs while maintaining an interest in high-quality craftsmanship and hand-painting techniques more often associated with a traditional approach to interiors. **J.I.**

JAMES MONT

Roué, rogue, and man-about-town, James Mont (1904–1978) was a charismatic charmer with high-profile clients and an anger-management problem. Along the way—and his way was wayward—he is said to have designed interiors for such show-business marquee names as Bob Hope (the best man at Mont's wedding), Irving Berlin, and Lana Turner. More firmly documented is the work he did for East Coast mafiosi, including Frank Costello and Lucky Luciano. Hot headed and mercurial, Mont had a bad temper and willfulness that repeatedly got him into trouble and debt during a roller-coaster career lasting four decades. His creativity, perfectionism, and delight in innovation produced both elegant, high-style interiors and over-the-top kitsch. At its best, Mont's work was synonymous with Hollywood glamour, captured in sumptuous materials and luxurious, patently expensive finishes. To this idiomatic American style he often blended Oriental flourishes: film noir in vivid color; Rita Hayworth meets Charlie Chan.

Demetrios Pecintoglu—a.k.a. James Mont and James Pess—was born to a Greek-Turkish family living in Istanbul, the son of an antiques-loving inventor and a mother from a distinguished family of judges. According to Mont's nephew, architect John Karfo, when the family emigrated to the United States in 1922, eighteen-year-old Mont was detained in France, where he was treated for syphilis—a possible explanation for a lifetime of uncontrolled rage and occasional violence.

Settling in Brooklyn, Mont opened a little electrical supply shop, and after selling some lamps to a Brooklyn mobster and his girlfriend, his career took off. He soon had a waterfront lamp shop in Atlantic City, New Jersey, and increasingly useful friendships with the big boys. According to Karfo, "the gang would pull up in their cabin cruisers with their girlfriends and Jimmy would cook up a feast because he was quite a gourmet."

By 1932 Mont had a flourishing design business and a well-located shop on Fifth Avenue in midtown Manhattan reputedly bankrolled by his gangster pals. Having spotted a need—call it a social need—soon after his arrival during Prohibition, he had begun designing custom bars, not only for mobsters, but for homes and businesses. From this early success, Mont built a business designing a broad line of home furnishings, although his association with bars, some of them remarkably clever, lasted through most of his career. Mont held patents on two designs: a decorative service bar (1937) and a collapsible, fold-up home bar (as late as 1953).

OPPOSITE A cinnabar lacquered and gilded chinoiserie console server that was originally purchased from Mont's showroom in Manhattan for a Sutton Place, Manhattan apartment. Designed and built in the late 1950s, this piece reflects an interesting convergence of art-deco, modern, and Asian design that typifies Mont's work. The centerpiece of the cabinet is an antique Chinese carved and gilded screen, salvaged from a defunct Brooklyn theater, then backed by a smoked mirror. The console comprises four pieces: the base is one unit with a large drawer flanked by two cabinets, the top center is a shallow decorative chinoiserie grill flanked by two cabinets with gilded faux lanterns mounted on each. Mont's pieces are distinguished by luscious finishes created by lacquering over a dozen polished layers and then gently sanding them to reveal a nuanced luminosity; the antiqued cinnabar surface here is an exceptional example.

ABOVE LEFT Mont was often the life of the party and both behaved and positioned himself as a celebrity. Here he is on his wedding day in 1937 flanked by his new bride and best man, Bob Hope. RIGHT Mont's image and identity varied (above right, in glasses), but he was always a ladies' man. Here he is with Sophie Tucker, a popular vaudeville singer and actress, and friends, c. 1950.

OPPOSITE PAGE TOP This carved- and limed-oak breakfront from 1946–47 illustrated an article and was selected for an being paradigmatic of his originality and unique style. In an interview around the time the breakfront was made, Mont described his aesthetic as "modern with a high-collared look, formal but comfortable." BOTTOM The gold- and silver-leaf camouflage technique, applied to this console and to several of the pieces from the King Cole penthouse, is Mont's most glamorous and innovative finish. Both ingenious and outrageous, this unprecedented technique is an allusion to antiquity, evoking a past era of finishes that are part visible and part concealed. Pieces with this camou-flage-patterned surface in gold- and silver-leaf finishes are rare as the process was labor intensive and time consuming. In the late 1990s a rediscovery of Mont's work was sparked when Christie's auctioned a handful of his major custom pieces from a New York collection. Beth Vilinsky, Christie's decorative-arts specialist, wrote one of the first articles about Mont to appear in decades.

The Fifth Avenue shop was followed by 37 West Fifty-seventh Street, where he did business as Maison Decors, Inc. (1937); 548 Madison Avenue at the corner of Fifty-fifth Street (1938); and, after the war, 310 East Fifty-ninth Street. Over the years, he had numerous other shops (in Atlantic City, Amityville, Miami Beach, and even Greece). His leases changed hands with the speed of a three-card monte dealer, as he nimbly dodged bill and tax collectors, often successfully, but going bankrupt three times (in 1934, 1946 as James Pess, and 1952). According to a 1950s radio interview on the famous "Tex and Jinx" show, Mont at his peak was running three New York shops: in the San Moritz Hotel and on both Park and Madison avenues. According to Karfo, "He was on top of the world. He drove around town in a custom-built Packard car. He used to drive up to the stage door of a new musical comedy. He'd load his Packard with beautiful girls. Then he would drive them to an expensive dress shop, a shop for which he had designed the interior. And he would take his payment for the [interior decorating] job… in clothes for the girls."

Mustached and balding, more suave than handsome, Mont loved the notoriety of celebrities and gangsters, and the kicks of fashionable nightclubs, booze, and bimbos. His salacious personal life was anchored, oh-so-briefly, by his 1937 marriage to a twenty-five-year-old Korean-American stage actress named Helen Kim, who committed suicide in their Park Avenue apartment twenty-nine days after their wedding, landing Mont on the front pages of New York's newspapers. It was not the last time: he sat out World War II in a Sing Sing cell, sentenced to five to ten years for assaulting a female business associate who thereafter killed herself. In many quarters, both of these deaths were suspect.

But loosey-goosey as he was in his personal life, Mont was serious when it came to his work. As a custom designer, his taste always ran to opulence and drama, and a typical Mont interior was filled with large and usually comfortable pieces. He designed for people who had or wanted to look as if they had plenty of money. Some of his pre–World War II work leaned toward too-muchness, but over the years he somewhat refined his sensibilities. His later work is characterized by a strong Oriental flavor, then in vogue but perhaps also the influence of his natal land, and he is closely identified with "Chinese modern," a term he claimed to have coined. Never accused of subtlety, he nonetheless was able to produce dramatic interiors of elegance and high style, frequently managing to stay just this side of excess.

In a 1996 article in the New York Times, Mitchell Owens described Mont's work as "a stylish uptown fusion of Eastern silhouettes and Western modernism." Owens later described his style as "a look that could be called Runyon Moderne, beefy, broad-shouldered objects imbued with a Pacific Rim flavor that appealed to gun molls and their brass-knuckled protectors." When Mont was on his game, he produced custom pieces on a grand scale that flashed a distinctive Hollywood glamour and the exoticism of the East: mirrors, faux animal skins, vivid colors, and plenty of silver and gilt. Pieces were large, sleek, exquisitely crafted, and often fabulous. He was equally capable of unrestrained and flamboyant designs that were more grandiose than grand.

Many Mont pieces are distinguished by wonderfully sumptuous surface textures—luscious finishes that included distressed, wormy, and limed woods, layers of silver and gold leaf, and lustrous, deeply lacquered pieces—and fourteen or fifteen hand-polished layers were typical. A *New York Times* article in 1945 described one of Mont's techniques for adding texture to wood: "the wood is grooved by sandblasting, then treated with stale beer and rottenstone" and, finally, given a pickled finish. Pieces often had four different undercoats in different colors, then three or four layers of gold or silver leaf, then graining with steel wool to create an antiqued look, and a tinted finishing lacquer. Mont said that he learned many of his techniques through extended experimentation during his years in prison.

Given the labor-intensive and time-consuming processes involved in making his one-off pieces, it is not surprising that his work was expensive for its time. According to Karfo, "The lamps he called octopus lamps he sold for $1,000 each"—an enormous sum in the early 1950s. But his craftsmanship and attention to detail were unsurpassed. Mont had the zeal of a perfectionist. He was genuinely finicky about his work but also theatrical to the core, known to occasionally destroy a piece with (or without) a slight imperfection, to demonstrate his extraordinarily high standards to a stunned client who might immediately sign on the dotted line. According to the son of Mont's longtime lawyer, David Friedland, if Mont didn't like a customer, he threw him out. And he was tyrannical—people took what he wanted them to take.

Much of Mont's best work was created in the five years following the war and his release from prison. Partnering with Karl Gephardt, a skilled craftsman in woodworking and cabinetry (who brought a level head and, probably, the financing), Moderne Modes was launched, operating from a five-story building at 214–216 East Fifty-second Street, employing some fifty workers. According to Karfo, who as a youth worked for Mont, the basement housed a drafting room and storage for the exotic woods Mont favored. The first floor was the showroom, the second was upholstering and the metalworking shop, the third and fourth were woodworking, and the fifth was finishing—sandblasting and pickling with a color ground and then graining color. Friedland said that Mont claimed to be the first designer to set up his showroom as individual room tableaux, to indicate the kind of work the client could expect when hiring Mont for his custom design work.

In 1952 Mont was in deep financial trouble again. His inventory and his personal collection of Oriental arts were sold at a forced two-part public liquidation sale at Savoy Galleries. He rebounded, of course, but by the 1960s the parade was passing him by. Nonetheless he snagged a large commission in Miami Beach: a three-thousand-plus-square-foot penthouse on Bay Drive in a fancy building called the King Cole. Although most of Mont's other custom interiors were not photographed, this showcase apartment was the exception. The home is archetypical Mont. The classical Greek mise-en-scène is established on the outside of the front door, with a massive medallion-studded cream and gold pediment and fluted columns flanking marble niches and a black paneled and lacquered door. A Greek key theme undulates through

ABOVE Mont built his career on clever constructions and claimed to have invented the sofa bed. In the 1930s he established his reputation by designing clandestine, often collapsible bars during Prohibition. Many of his later pieces similarly include secret compartments.

OPPOSITE PAGE TOP Indulgent in terms of its lush materials, finishes, and details, this elegant dining set is classic Mont with pierced-back chairs upholstered in a shining silver-beige wool, the original fabric. The graceful form of the chair back is echoed in the shape of the beveled marble tabletop. Expertly carved caryatids in silver gilt wood create an elegant base. **BOTTOM** The Opium Den sofa (1948/1963) epitomizes "Chinese modern," a term Mont coined. The upholstered one-arm sofa rests on a long platform in oak. Its luminous gilded bronze sheen is the result of silver leaf over orange and black primers and an antique lacquer finish.

RIGHT Interior shot of the 1963 King Cole penthouse in Miami Beach taken in the 1970s. The Orlowitz family had previously worked with Mont on two other residential projects prior to the design of their Florida residence. It was the end of his career, and only a loyal patron who understood Mont's vision could offer him such an ambitious and grandiose commission. Mont had carte blanche to realize this Greco-Roman Chinese fantasy. He was involved with all aspects of the project, including designing door handles, moldings, a custom piano, and matching furnishings. During this period Mont lived on an Asian-themed houseboat of his own design. Inspiration for the penthouse may have come from the equally opulent film *Cleopatra* starring Elizabeth Taylor, which opened in 1963.

the entire apartment, decorating every conceivable surface, from the lacquered black baby-grand piano to table aprons, chair arms, and closet drawers. Greek columns are incorporated in the living room design. The "entertainment room" escaped—it is Asian themed, paneled and lacquered in orange and black, in contrast to the rich Roman style in most of the other rooms—with recessed orange niches holding Oriental objets d'art. (During this period Mont was also said to have built an Orientalized houseboat on Indian Creek, where he lived with one of his girlfriends.)

Mont didn't limit himself to big jobs. A small-scale project was featured in a *New York Times* article called "Space-saving Devices to Expand a Tiny Apartment," which described Mont utilizing built-in cabinets, shelves to replace tables, and sofas that serve as beds. (Friedland reported that the article featured Mont's actual apartment.) And, deploying profound self-confidence and a quirky imagination, he could respond to challenges by producing innovative and problem-solving pieces. For example, he designed a table that converted to a ten-foot-long library ladder, and a coffee table with optional secret compartments. He claimed credit for having invented the sofa bed, and did, in fact, patent a sofa design in 1947.

Ever the showman, Mont was a facile and playful marketer. One example is the goofy self-promotional book he wrote, *The Young Physician's Road Map*, illustrated with clever cartoons showing Mont as he was—gambler, boozer, ladies' man—all to promote an inventory sale prior to doubling his space at the 214 East Fifty-second Street premises. Another Mont-penned pamphlet, "All Gall Is Divided into Three Parts," was described as an "amusing and instructive booklet on interior decoration."

Actually, it was Mont who had many parts, including gall. Extravagant, hot-tempered, impulsive, theatrical, generous, egotistical, unstable, even dangerous—he was not your typical genteel designer. He was an original. **R.M.**

ABOVE James Mont's lamps are arguably the most precious pieces from his oeuvre and demonstrate a fusion between chinoiserie and Hollywood Regency. Each lamp was truly a work of art and was realized using an array of elaborate treatments and finishes. Lamps, despite their functional nature, engendered Mont's fascination with Eastern cultures and flaunted his innovative lacquering or gilding techniques. Exotic found objects would often be incorporated. Although many of his lamps, which were always ornate, were made in the forties and fifties, they defy the prevailing interest in modernism, embracing ornament and glamour instead. **FAR LEFT** Here, a silver-plated metal falcon sits on aperch, while the structure alludes to both a Japanese torii, or sacred gateway, and the Greek letter pi. The shade was constructed with interwoven patinated parchment strips and a white gold–leaf finish. **CENTER LEFT** The shade, on the sculpted and sanded oak lamp, intensifies the sculptural presence of the grid by using interwoven cardboard strips covered in layers of brushed bronze finishing. The lamp's weathered base is sculpted and sanded and finished with a glue patina and silver base. Mont devised many original treatments for softening and distorting wood. **CENTER RIGHT** The ceramic Thai deity is another reclaimed exotic object used for ornamentation. The figure was antiqued and gilded on a similarly treated gilded wood base. Mont used sculpted and applied plaster to create the band that surrounds the shimmering gold-leaf paper shade. Once applied, the plaster was hand carved and polished. **FAR RIGHT** Mont's artistic expression manifested itself in many moods, from the exotic and ornate to the sculptural and sometimes naturalistic. The Octopus lamp from c. 1950 cost $1,000, a tremendous sum for the period. The legs were cast bronze and were affixed to a curvaceous black lacquered wood core.

OPPOSITE PAGE Many of Mont's preferred touches and signature motifs are united in these elongated white gold-leaf shelves, including stylized bamboo, expert gilding, and reinterpreted Asian forms. The pagoda shelf would reappear in several different guises throughout Mont's career.

A magnificent mirrored-panel screen done in 1950 in Mont's Chinese-modern style blended details from his Turkish roots. Each panel is hand finished with an Ottoman inspired verre églomisé design in gold metal leaf then backed with a white-metal leaf. The mirrors are framed in Mont's smoked-silver metal-leaf technique and formed with pierced bases and pagoda-style tops.

TOMMI
PARZINGER

Tommi Parzinger (1903–1981), for all his continental training and appreciation for traditional craftsmanship, was an American iconoclast who, in riding against the prevalent tide of modernism, utility, and antiornamentalism sweeping the country, still managed to secure his own place in the canon of midcentury modern furnishings.

His distinctive pieces, with their exquisite finishes, hardware flourishes, and elegantly attenuated proportions hinting at roots buried in some mythic kingdom, could not have been made anywhere but in America, where the designer found the freedom to invent, combine, and alter according to his own inspiration, using whatever materials, finishes, and silhouettes he cared to imagine. Freed from the constraints of any specific historical lineage, he rigorously adhered to a personal code of perfectionism and an interest in exploring new effects in his designs that were in their own way very much in keeping with modern sensibilities. An extremely consistent level of high craftsmanship guaranteed an appreciative audience for Parzinger's work both then and now.

Anton Parzinger (the insouciant "Tommi," so perfect for his American years, came later) was born in Munich in 1903. Little is known about his family apart from his father being a sculptor, although his aquiline features, polished bearing, and penchant for bespoke clothing, indicate that he came from a privileged background.

In 1920 he attended the Munich Kunstgewerbeschule (School of Applied Arts), a magnet at the time for talent in the emerging fields of applied arts and industrial design, where a philosophy of turning art to the creation of everyday objects was championed. There he immersed himself in the complete range of designing and producing decorative arts—glass, metalwork, ceramics, furniture, as well as drafting, modeling, joinery, and gilding. He likely studied as well with the noted graphic and poster designer Julius Diez.

Parzinger was also attracted to the holistic teachings and philosophy of Rudolf Steiner, the philosopher, educator, and social thinker who was so popular at the time with the creative intelligentsia, and Parzinger remained a committed anthroposophist throughout his life.

After graduating from the Kunstgewerbeschule, where he had been known to sell some of his student ceramics on the side, he worked in Vienna and Berlin, designing porcelains for the prestigious KPM or Royal Porcelain Manufacturer from 1923 to 1928. His social savoir faire

OPPOSITE PAGE A version of this console debuted at a furniture fair in New York City in the early 1950s. Although it was subsequently custom-made in a selection of colors, the console was first realized in marigold yellow, and was always complemented by brass hardware. Parzinger's studio never used a simple primary color but instead experimented with the lacquer to produce an original shade. The console also appeared in dark mahogany and variations of orange and red. In the forties and fifties they avoided black and most shades of blue lacquer. It was a practical consideration rather than an aesthetic choice as dark lacquers were not adequately developed and were prone to fading. Parzinger is known for the subtle but glamorous hardware that embellishes his creations. Several of the brass forms he used were inspired by medieval furniture and ornamentation. Shortly after the fair the console was photographed for *House Beautiful* and over the years the console and the color have become signatures of Parzinger's work.

ABOVE LEFT A 1943 portrait of Parzinger, age forty. Throughout his lifetime he would invariably be described as elegant and refined. CENTER Parzinger's prize-winning poster design for the steamship company North German Lloyd provided him with tickets for his first trip to New York City. RIGHT Parzinger's first design projects included packaging and perfume bottles for Hattie Carnegie and John Frederics' Golden Arrow.

OPPOSITE PAGE Parzinger's experience working for the avant-garde shopkeeper Rena Rosenthal was crucial to his artistic and professional development and his success in America. Her shop was one of the chicest and most exclusive in the country. Most of the items she offered were sourced in Europe and were available only in her shop at Madison Avenue and Fifty-second Street in New York City. Parzinger's experience working for Rosenthal enabled him to develop a unique style and visual language. Perhaps more importantly he became acquainted with decorators, designers, and tradespeople familiarizing himself with the tastes and demands of the city's affluent. TOP A vanity designed by Parzinger that was offered at Rena Rosenthal's. BELOW Rosenthal's storefront featured some of Parzinger's early designs.

helped him to develop important contacts in the design and fashion worlds, among them the French fashion designer Jean Louis Berthault. These connections would be important when he came to New York.

Although Parzinger was already making a reputation for himself with his ceramics and decorative art pieces that appeared in numerous arts journals, his big break came when he won a poster competition in 1932 sponsored by the steamship liner North German Lloyd. First prize was a trip to New York City aboard the *Bremen*, one of the more famous ocean liners carrying emigrants from all points around Europe to the land of opportunity. About a year later, when he returned to Munich, Hitler's home base, he did not recognize the place. He entered another poster competition, again winning first prize. The story goes that when he went to the mayor's office to collect his prize, he was told he would first have to join the Nazi party, whereupon he promptly went to Hamburg and sailed for America, leaving everything behind. He never returned, apart from an occasional visit in the fifties to see his sister, one of the few in his family to survive the war.

When he arrived in New York at age thirty-two, Parzinger took advantage of his old contacts and started working for Rena Rosenthal, whose fashionable shop on Madison Avenue specialized in gift items and decorative arts, many made in Austria or commissioned especially for the shop. Parzinger's ceramics and metal pieces could soon be seen featured in Rosenthal's window displays. Rosenthal was able to expand the designer's circle to include the fashion and jewelry designer Hattie Carnegie, also from Austria, and the flamboyant costume and fashion original Norman Norell, both of whom would not only hire Parzinger, but also introduced him to key clients in the future. For Carnegie, Parzinger created everything from perfume bottles to display cases.

In New York, Parzinger was a workaholic who spent his leisure time attending Friday night anthroposophy meetings and going to art galleries and museums on Saturdays, after lunch at a fashionable restaurant. With a reputation in Europe already established, his work quickly attracted attention in the United States.

In 1938 he was approached to design a small collection by the Charak Company of Boston, a fine furniture manufacturer known best for traditional styles, that was then pursuing a more modern look that would not alienate established clientele. Parzinger's furniture—so beautifully made, so clearly rooted in recognizable past shapes and yet stripped of outmoded clunkiness—fit the bill. Parzinger's collections for Charak, often displayed in the Charak showroom at 444 Madison Avenue, exhibited all the designer's talents for creating fully integrated spaces, sometimes as many as five rooms completely accessorized down to the placement of lighting fixtures. (Parzinger attracted immediate attention by deleting the expected chandelier over the dining table and replacing it with wrought-iron standing lamps.)

His hard work and prolific output were noticed, and, in 1940, Walter Rendell wrote in the *New York Times* how designers like Parzinger, who had been trained in Europe, were transforming the American design scene by combining "American simplicity with smart cosmopolitan styling."

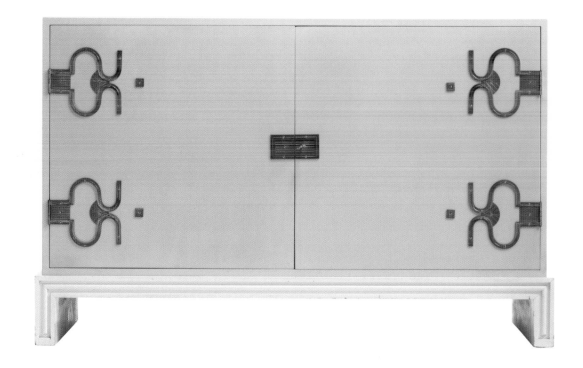

At a time when fine materials were becoming scarce and the machine-made was no longer so novel, Parzinger's designs with their intense workmanship—the hand-tooled leather, ornate marquetry, customized hardware—were deeply appealing to an audience in search of greater resonance. The richly jewel-toned, leather-covered pieces tooled in gold that he created for Charak Modern were nothing short of eye-popping. While other designers were exploring large-scale methods of production, Parzinger, along with T. H. Robsjohn-Gibbings and a small elite, took another route, focusing on limited production and rarified, labor-intensive finishes. At least one reviewer suggested that it was actually these designers who were the most able to respond quickly to new ideas, whereas large manufacturers were forced to focus on the less progressive tastes that go with mass production.

Parzinger was no fan of commercialization and disliked the pressures that came with even small-scale market production—the dog and pony shows for salesmen, the need to be seasonal as opposed to classical. He would just as soon exhibit his latest work at handcraft shows sponsored by the Society of Designer-Craftsmen, and often did.

But Parzinger was already enough of a success to open his own shop, Parzinger, Inc., at 45 East Fifty-seventh Street in 1939. It was a good year all around: people could see his furniture at the 1939 World's Fair, buy it at his own showroom, see his interior decorations at Hattie Carnegie's, or take home his packaging commissioned by Mark Cross.

His approach to design was very consistent over the years. He created a look that offered the most refined shapes along with the barest hint of exoticism through the use of strong lacquer colors, gold or precious-metal nail heads, velvet-lined drawers, and the slight flip of a slender leg encased in a brass or silver shoe. Nothing was overblown or crudely themed. Parzinger was too modern for that, even if he did dismiss modernism itself as "cold and scientific." His goal was to make pieces with "soul and charm," harboring a sense of the past but never creating literal reproductions. Emily Genauer in the *New York Times* wrote that Parzinger belonged to "an entirely different breed from what we have known as modern," adding that his pieces appealed more to emotional than functional needs.

A six-piece bedroom set from the 1940s displayed at the New York Coliseum National Home Furnishing Show included a bold and nearly incongruent four-poster bed made of polished mahogany with elongated posts thinning out into small bursts of a finial. Alongside the bed was a dresser finished in white lacquer with bronze starburst hardware supported on a dark mahogany base.

Dark lacquers were a favorite finish in the 1940s, as precious dark woods became scarce and prohibitively expensive during the war years, according to Donald Cameron, who met Parzinger in 1944 (becoming the designer's most trusted business and creative partner in 1949). Parzinger's favorite colors were cream, blue, raspberry, and gold—never black (the way he liked pieces to be lacquered called for a scratching technique that would turn black to gray)—and may have been inspired in part by the blue and white Munich flag. Parzinger was proud of his Bavarian roots.

In 1941 Parzinger, Inc., closed shop, and Parzinger himself, who was not a citizen at the time, moved to Bermuda to wait out the war, doing illustrations for Condé Nast and drawing up fabric designs. His later enthusiasm for incorporating shell and other sea motifs in his textiles and wallpapers was probably inspired by this period.

After the war, Parzinger seemed less inclined to work for the Charak Company. According to Cameron, Parzinger loathed the monthly sales meetings for which he produced exacting models that the salesmen then critiqued, wanting cheaper hinges and manufacturing shortcuts. The relationship ended, with Parzinger designing one last fifty-piece collection for Charak in 1949, which was reviewed admiringly alongside pieces by Charles Eames and Alvar Aalto.

Parzinger was more determined than ever to follow his personal vision. Exotic woods were once again available, and Macassar, madrone, Koko, fir chestnut, and mahogany became staples. He constantly experimented with new finishes as well, whether pickling the mahogany to achieve a blush of pink or inventing a large-scale crackled lacquer. His update on the traditional metal shoe slipped over a leg involved painstakingly inlaying the metal to make sure it was perfectly flush and the leg completely streamlined.

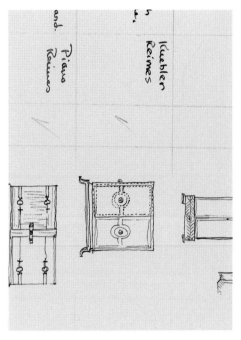

ABOVE Parzinger was a talented draftsman and illustrator who kept meticulous records. Many of his drawings and showroom photographs are archived at the Cooper-Hewitt, National Design Museum in New York City. His unique talents and organizational skills have prevented misattributions on the secondary market, even though his designs and overall aesthetic have been widely copied.

OPPOSITE PAGE Parzinger used brass studs on his pieces to accent his simplified forms, as in the white lacquered nightstand shown here. His wonderful use of color is seen in this lacquered marigold cabinet. With his trademark hardware and subtle details these pieces, both for Parzinger Originals, are wonderful examples of this classic designer's style.

Above: Tommi Parzinger Collection, Cooper-Hewitt, National Design Museum, Smithsonian Institution, Gift of Donald Cameron, 1998. Photograph by Matt Flynn.

ABOVE FAR LEFT This was one of the first lamps Parzinger designed in wrought iron. During the late forties it was considered daring because of its unusual height and scale; even more unusual was Parzinger's use of torchères in dining rooms instead of overhead lighting. Parzinger continued to make floor lamps that often measured over five feet tall. CENTER LEFT Throughout his career Parzinger worked closely with metalworkers to produce his designs both under his name and also for other companies. This silvered metal backlit torchère is over five feet tall and has a ribbed shaft and a saber-legged base. It was designed for Lightolier in the early forties. CENTER RIGHT This lamp from the early 1970s is one of the few examples with a painted base that was part of a collection of lamps that Donald Cameron hand painted. Many of the shapes along the shaft are derived from designs Parzinger had done in metal. FAR RIGHT Parzinger's lighting often reinterpreted candelabra forms, his nod to the history of decorative arts. In many of his creations, Parzinger worked in historical iconography, which he admired in European pieces. The forms and details that make up this seven-foot-tall enameled iron floor lamp also resemble the hardware that appears on his furniture. The inverse double "J" hook recalls the brass detail featured on the marigold console from the fifties.

OPPOSITE PAGE Parzinger provided detailed drawings for all of his clients. Here he wanted to show how natural light would fall on the furnishings. Finished interiors, whether residential or commercial, would closely resemble his renderings, with only minor color changes. Renderings, like these done on 24" × 30" boards, would often show the final design before implementation.

Above center right: Tommi Parzinger Collection, Cooper-Hewitt, National Design Museum, Smithsonian Institution, Gift of Donald Cameron, 1998. Opposite page top and bottom: Tommi Parzinger Collection, Cooper-Hewitt, National Design Museum, Smithsonian Institution, Gift of Donald Cameron, 1998. Photograph by Matt Flynn.

Not everything he tried was practicable, and he revealed an almost perverse glee in designing such blatantly noncommercial designs as dining tables with unmoveable iron bases or tops at a nonstandard height, making it impossible to use any chairs but his own matching ones. "He went a little crazy," recalled Cameron in an interview, "but then he learned to compromise."

By 1951 Parzinger had or was soon to establish relationships with an assortment of manufacturers, including Hofstatter (furniture); Dorlyn (brass); Willow & Reed (rattan); Lightolier (lighting); Schumacher and Katzenbach & Warren (wallpaper); and Salterini (wrought iron). In 1952 he reconceived his own label as Parzinger Originals, probably in part to distinguish his work from copycats and even from designs made through licensing agreements with companies unauthorized to use his name.

In addition to his manufactured pieces and custom designs for individual clients, he also designed the furniture for a 1952 housing development, called Morton Village in Plainview, Long Island. The development built by Emil Morton was conceived, as many were at the time, as an upscale Levittown to respond to the housing needs resulting from the postwar baby boom. The houses ranged in price from $9,999 to $11,999. When Parzinger added twenty-five fabrics to his offerings at 32 East Fifty-seventh Street, he was by now providing decorators with a full range of furnishings.

Business was brisk, and the showroom was a popular destination for a discerning crowd, from Olga Gueft, inimitable editor of *Interiors*, to Mrs. Arthur Miller, a.k.a. Marilyn Monroe, who used to drop buy for a chat and borrow select furnishings for her parties. Parzinger's press breakfasts and cocktail and holiday parties were anticipated events. The showroom itself was meticulously designed in a way that set it apart from other venues, and the walls were hung with paintings by Miró, Braque, and Pissaro, some on loan from client-turned-champion Vincent Cymes (who could be counted on to send down fifteen pounds of steak tartare on short notice). Even the ashtrays were special, with Parzinger swapping out the caterers' standard issue with his own exquisite dishes.

Parzinger's private clients were typically drawn from mainline society in Philadelphia, Pittsburgh, and Florida, including assorted Whitneys, Fords, and Mellons, for whom Parzinger did the complete interiors at their Snapper Creek home in Florida. (New York society was not a major source of work for the designer, according to Cameron, although Hilla Rebay, Solomon Guggenheim's art consultant, muse, and first director, owned several pieces.) Parzinger also won the commissions (possibly over Billy Baldwin and Robsjohn-Gibbings) to design executive office interiors for advertising kingpin J. Walter Thompson, and also for the publishing offices of McGraw-Hill.

Parzinger's furniture was not inexpensive, even in the mid-fifties, and prices were in line with a couture level of production where a dining table cost $900 to $1,500, an armoire $2,300, and a dining chair $198. Typically Parzinger prepared full-scale drawings for every piece, and for many details as well, a level of attention atypical at the time. (According to Cameron, the drawings were made because the business couldn't afford to make mistakes.) Much of the

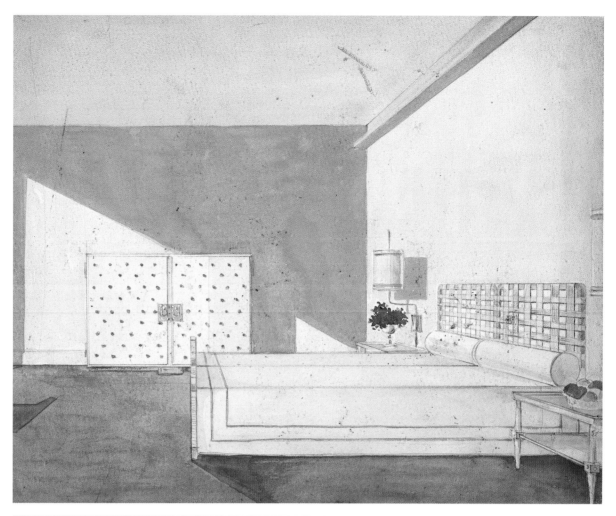

custom furniture was made at a small factory under the Queensboro Bridge where some sixty craftspeople worked on the relatively small batches commissioned by a range of designers, including Parzinger as well as various architects working on the United Nations.

Cameron, who met Parzinger when he was barely twenty years old and had a background in art, became increasingly involved over the years. While Parzinger painted at a home studio every morning until noon, Cameron oversaw production and was the liaison with clients; he contributed to designs as well. He remembered well Parzinger's fluency with a pencil, noting that he could design ten chairs in an hour while still adhering to his meticulous eye for detail.

Parzinger belonged to an era in American design and entrepreneurship, in general, when optimism and opportunities for defining new ways to be creative flourished. With his concept for furniture that was luxuriously elegant, studiously hand produced, and imbued with the resonance of the past, Parzinger created pieces that might be described as nongeneric modern. Eighteen years after the designer's death in 1981, gallerist Pat Palumbo, in collaboration with Cameron, reproduced some twenty-five Parzinger pieces from the designer's later years, including a mahogany dining table with strips of holly inlay and silver-plate firedogs. Parzinger strove to create pieces with a singular beauty that managed to straddle past and present, connect America and Europe, and inspire sleek modern furniture with the warmth of emotion, and he achieved nothing less. **J.I.**

ABOVE LEFT Here, an announcement for the opening of Parzinger's new showroom on Fifty-seventh Street published in a trade magazine. Located on the sixth floor, the showroom was open only to the trade. **RIGHT** This is a rare image of a private home designed by Parzinger. Interior photography was expensive, time-consuming, and many clients did not want their homes photographed.

OPPOSITE PAGE Parzinger redecorated the Fifty-seventh Street showroom every other year. He worked with the best photographers of the era like Hans van Ness. Parzinger first sketched how he envisioned the final image before a photographer would shoot each vignette. He completed numerous 8" × 12" drawings with special attention towards light sources. Parzinger was very involved with how his work was represented but such exhaustive preparatory efforts reduced both improvisation and expenses.

Above left: Tommi Parzinger Collection, Cooper-Hewitt, National Design Museum, Smithsonian Institution, Gift of Donald Cameron, 1998. Photograph by Matt Flynn. Right: Tommi Parzinger Collection, Cooper-Hewitt, National Design Museum, Smithsonian Institution, Gift of Donald Cameron, 1998.

RIGHT Vignettes in the showroom. Parzinger knew that furniture and accessories enhanced an interior, an understanding that was probably developed during his experiences working with Rena Rosenthal. These photos show two handsome and exemplary cabinets surrounded by elegant decorative objects and works of art.

OPPOSITE PAGE The German baroque mirror in pine that appears in this showroom vignette was found, according to Donald Cameron, while Parzinger was antiquing and it was ultimately sold to Billy Baldwin. This neo-Biedermeier console, possibly in Macassar, is a rare example of Parzinger working in an exotic wood.

HARVEY PROBBER

If the public has only recently become aware of Harvey Probber's vast body of work, it is not because he wasn't prolific. For more than forty years Probber (1922–2003) designed and marketed his furniture designs, winning over interior designers and discriminating consumers with his clean lines, expert craftsmanship, and a range of luxurious materials and exquisite finishes rarely seen in modern furniture design. In fact, Probber's success was anticipated almost from the very beginning. Before he was twenty years old, one of his sketches—of a residential interior appointed with modern, low-slung furniture—was published as part of an "Interiors to Come" magazine competition. When he took his first full-time job in the furniture business in the mid-forties, with Trade Upholstery in New York, a mailer announced to clients that Probber was a "brilliant newcomer, whose freshly original approach… marks him for prominence." His early Sling chair and Nuclear seating group were chosen for MoMA's *Good Design* exhibition in 1951. Yet despite his impressive list of accomplishments and enviable career, Probber's work was not included in the first wave of the midcentury modern revival that began in the 1990s. But by that time, Probber had grown accustomed to (if not entirely comfortable with) what had become a recurring theme: he was simply ahead of his time.

Probber was born in Brooklyn in 1922. As a young man, he worked in his father's showroom on Saturdays, selling furniture. He sold his first furniture design, a sofa, for $10 when he was just sixteen. After being honorably discharged from the Coast Guard (he had enlisted when he was seventeen), Probber set his sights on a career in the furniture business but was temporarily derailed by wartime shortages. For about a year, he worked as both furniture designer and pop singer/songwriter, before settling on what he presumed would be the more stable of the two careers in 1945. He opened his first New York showroom on Fifth Avenue the following year. There, Probber created complete residential and office settings in which his furniture could be seen in context, an approach adopted by only a handful of progressive designers (e.g., Jack Lenor Larsen), manufacturers (e.g., Herman Miller), and importers (e.g., George Tanier). He also resisted the common practice of releasing two new lines of furniture each year, which, to Probber, only encouraged bad design. Indeed, "the classic Probber look," as described in a 1967 *Interiors* article, was characterized not by trendy style changes, but by "a deceptive simplicity of line and proportion, one which, with constant refining, remains the epitome of timeless good taste." In an age of planned obsolescence, Probber was swimming against the tide. "Don't be intimidated into thinking last year's purchases are obsolete simply because a new style appears on the market," he warned in a 1957 interview with the

OPPOSITE PAGE Probber periodically used enameled copper panels on his occasional tables and case goods, as in this mahogany cabinet (c. 1960) with brass sabots. The vibrant colors and playful patterns of the enameled copper stand out beautifully against his dark-stained woods and sober forms, creating an exciting contrast. The relative rarity of these examples makes them a favorite of collectors.

ABOVE LEFT Harvey Probber, c. 1950, is seen here probably in his office working on the next innovative form or application of a new material. RIGHT Probber's occasional tables, such as these elegantly spare ones with fashionable mint-green terrazzo tops, brass inlay, and green lacquered mahogany legs, combine a sophisticated understanding of casual postwar lifestyles with a sure sense of sophistication and attention to detail.

OPPOSITE PAGE TOP The Sling chair (1949), made with a birch frame and an upholstered foam sling seat, was critical to Probber's early career and illustrates his willingness to experiment. "There are many chairs that assure the sitter comfortable support in any one position—as long as the sitter can be comfortable in any one position," sniffed *Interiors* magazine in 1949, but Probber's Sling chair, the article added, "assures absolute support no matter how the sitter shifts."
BOTTOM The Mayan sofa (1983), made of upholstered foam over a hardwood frame, was Probber's contribution to the art-deco revival of the 1980s. With its elegantly simple forms, it borrows from the past without imitating it. The result is an unmistakably contemporary design statement.

Philadelphia Inquirer, "good furniture doesn't have to change with the seasons, leaping in and out of fashion like a woman's hat." Probber's unconventional but highly successful practices were made possible, in part, because he was in total control. He had learned the business through experience rather than training (his only formal education was by way of evening classes at Pratt Institute). From the outset, he tackled not only the design work, but also the business and marketing chores of Harvey Probber, Inc. In 1979 *Interior Design* called Probber, "one of the few furniture designers who doesn't have to defer to the boss."

As his own boss, Probber had the freedom to pursue innovative designs that weren't easily justified by the bottom line—an enviable situation that led to a number of unexpectedly bold designs. His Python table of 1950, for example, combines a square glass top with a frame made of a sinuous solid oak. The result is a remarkably spare, organic form that looks like it might have been designed yesterday. In 1951 *Interiors* called his debut line of case goods "a sophisticated embodiment of the ideals of modern furniture—unfussy, unforced, unpretentious, and quite lovely." But those same pieces, admired by *Interiors* for their "strict geometric shapes— rectangles and squares… insisted upon throughout, and ornament… practically non-existent," were occasionally decked out in flower-pattern door fronts of enameled copper.

Probber's later work, too, includes some unconventional pieces. During the 1970s, for example, he wrapped chair and sofa frames in woven *latania*, a palm species from Haiti, enthusiastically mixing the "high" and "low." Probber's Mayan sofa of 1983 may be one of his most recognized designs. Its simple geometric slabs, a nod to the period's art deco revival, create a dramatic presence through their utter simplicity and precise scaling.

As the one person overseeing all aspects of his business, Probber was able to appreciate the value of developing and perfecting new manufacturing processes. An article in the September 1949 issue of *Interiors* described the "knotty technical problems" he faced while developing the Sling chair, a design that helped launch his career. "More than just a new model," the chair was "a design based on new principles of construction and new uses of materials. In order to produce it, designer-manufacturer Harvey Probber had not only to sit over a drawing board but to experiment at length with foam rubber, bonding materials, fabrics, and laminated plywood. He has obtained a patent." Twenty-three years later, in 1972, when he introduced his Cubo line of modular furniture, Probber took on the challenge of molding the self-skinning urethane foam in-house. It was perhaps the first such production facility in the country—a milestone in American furniture manufacturing—and a move Probber later called "foolish audacity."

Probber's greatest contribution is generally considered to be the modular furniture concept, something he began experimenting with as early as the 1930s. "The key to salvation was in bits and pieces of plane geometry," he later reflected in an unpublished article. Probber's early experimentation would first take shape in the form of his Sert Group (named for architect José Luis Sert, later the dean of Harvard's Graduate School of Architecture), the first of his modular furniture designs. According to professor and author Judith Gura, the Sert Group "consisted of 19 different elements—in simple upholstered forms like half-circles, quadrants, wedges, and corner sections that could be assembled into any desired seating configuration." Gura, curator

of the 2003 Baruch College exhibition *Harvey Probber: Modernist Furniture, Design, and Graphics*, noted that Probber's modular concept made for endless possibilities. "The upholstered elements could be ordered as a single seamless piece, or separate, individual ones," and clients could "adapt the same basic form to any styling—loose cushions or tight, skirted or plain."

Although Probber's innovative concept of modular seating offered nearly infinite flexibility, the benefits were not always immediately obvious (or, just as likely, clients might have been overwhelmed by the range of options). So Probber—who had as much marketing savvy as design talent—created scale models for his showrooms, allowing clients to experiment with their own furniture arrangements. Later, Probber extended his modular concept to "nuclear furniture," which included occasional tables available with a variety of tops and bases. And in the 1960s, he applied the concept to case goods, creating a vast array of offerings by way of different finishes, bases, heights, and hardware (an economical approach that helped make possible the very high level of quality and materials). During the early 1960s, Americans cooled to the idea of modular seating (even while it enjoyed great popularity in Europe), but by the end of the decade, they had reversed their course. With its updated forms and exciting new materials—and a flexibility that fit well with the unconventional spirit of the period—modular furniture experienced a renewed popularity.

During the 1970s Probber shifted his attention away from residential furniture design to the more lucrative contract furniture field. In 1986 he sold his company, and it was closed soon afterward. He continued his involvement in both the design and business aspects of the furniture industry, serving as a consultant and lecturer. Probber passed away in 2003, following a series of strokes.

Throughout his career Probber resisted the temptation of chasing furniture fashions. In a January 1990 *Interior Design* article, he argued that fashion, as applied to the furniture industry, is "just another crafty way to titillate and then entice youngsters with unformed taste (oldsters should know better) to invest when setting up house on limited budgets… [in] major expenditures they are bound to regret." And yet, when it came to sweeping trends, Probber was often well ahead of the curve—especially when it came to adapting interiors to the increasing presence of technology. As television began to transform the way Americans lived in the 1950s, for example, Probber's modular concept proved an ideal complement. "When living in a theatre," he said in a 1979 interview with *Interior Design*, "conventional seating becomes inadequate." Probber's designs recognized the increasingly informal American lifestyle, while at the same time bringing an undeniable sophistication to "living in a theatre." He adopted a similar approach with his Advent III series of executive office furniture, introduced in 1977, by employing built-in ambient lighting and tackling the growing issue of "wire management."

Just as Americans began yielding more and more living space—both residential and office—to encroaching technology, Probber was providing a luxurious counterbalance. "Though he considered himself a modern designer," wrote Gura, "his approach to modernity favored exotic woods, highly polished lacquer, hand-rubbed finishes and opulent upholstery fabrics—material

ABOVE Probber's Nuclear line of furniture, an early application of his modular furniture concept, was included in the Museum of Modern Art's 1951 *Good Design* exhibition. Its flexibility reflected the increasingly informal lifestyle of the period. According to a Probber ad from 1950, his Nuclear tables made of stained mahogany could "be arranged in endless ways," for "buffet entertaining, as serpentine cocktail tables, as end tables, even one above the other to make a smart service device."

OPPOSITE PAGE TOP The versatility of Probber's design instincts can be seen in the range of forms and materials seen in this showroom photograph from around 1960. The sofa and cabinet are typical of his early modular furniture, with their strong geometric lines. The Oval side chair, on the other hand, with its generous curves and woven-cane back presents a somewhat softer look. The occasional tables round out the grouping, offering an interesting counterpoint by way of contrasting color. **BOTTOM** To create this residential line of furniture, the Artisan collection (c. 1970), Probber worked closely with craftsmen in Haiti who used woven latania, a species of palm, to expertly wrap his furniture frames, which were then paired with upholstered cushions. The resulting furniture, whether a bedroom set or a seating arrangement, displayed an interesting juxtaposition of textures. Joan Probber, Harvey Probber's wife, holds the trademarks for the Artisan and Nuclear collection shown here, as well as the Inner Office, Advent, Advent III, Houston, and Cubo lines.

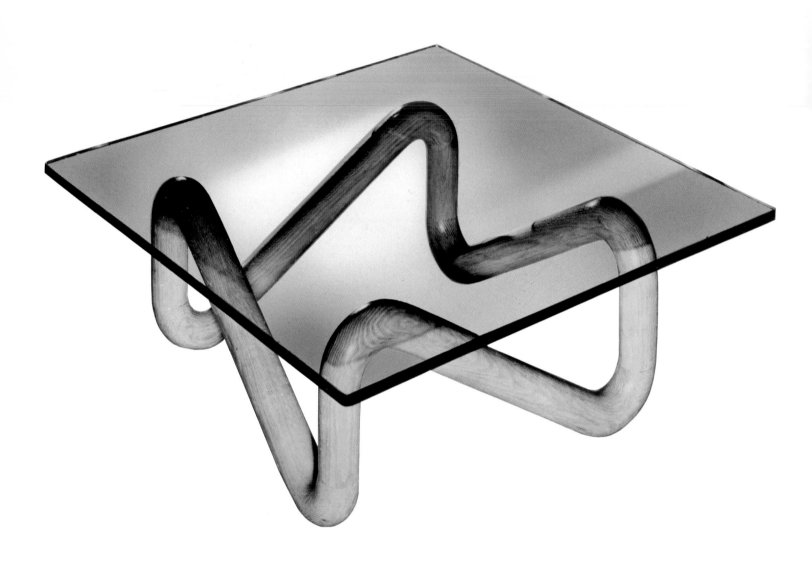

largely abandoned by more radical, Bauhaus-influenced designers." So the fact that Probber's designs are now perhaps more popular than ever should come as little surprise. Surrounded by all manner of high-tech devices (themselves often fashionably impermanent), we look to the furniture of Harvey Probber for some much-needed grounding.

Probber's extensive use of the modular concept led to a tremendous range of different designs, making it a challenge for collectors to focus on a handful of iconic pieces. As they are discovering his work, therefore, collectors are typically drawn to early designs, unusual variations, or pieces with compelling histories. A Nuclear coffee table in bleached mahogany, for example, brought $14,000 at a Sotheby's New York auction in 2005. A desk of bleached African rosewood commissioned for President Lyndon B. Johnson sold for $9,000 at Sollo Rago in 2006. That same year, Wright sold a Sling chair for $3,500 and a set of three occasional tables with terrazzo tops, in an unusual celadon lacquer, for $8,400. **P. W.**

ABOVE TOP Probber's modular furniture offered clients near limitless options. Combinations such as this modular seating arrangement plus storage and tables (c. 1952) look as though they were custom designed. In fact, Probber's strategic design decisions (and his role as both designer and manufacturer) allowed him to create such solutions with relative economy. The white laminate surfaces reflect Probber's practical side as well as his understanding of his clients' workaday needs. **BOTTOM LEFT** This bleached African-rosewood desk with mahogany legs was designed in 1968 for President Lyndon B. Johnson. It illustrates Probber's fondness for showcasing exotic woods—especially those with pronounced grains. **RIGHT** This zebrawood cabinet (c. 1955) with brass hardware stands on slim legs, a style that Probber frequently employed in his case goods, creating an overall effect of sophisticated lightness, and perhaps led *Interiors* magazine to refer to his 1952 line as "buoyant."

OPPOSITE PAGE The Python table (1950) has an oak frame supporting a plate-glass top. Although Probber's early work was often characterized by strong rectilinear forms and careful detailing, this table demonstrates a decided turn to a more organic, sculptural—and minimalist—aesthetic.

T. H. ROBSJOHN-GIBBINGS

Sometimes known as "Gibby," T. H. (Terence Harold) Robsjohn-Gibbings (1905–1976) was a prodigious furniture designer, interior decorator, and writer. Both his custom-built and mass-produced furniture pieces introduced a new aesthetic into the American home, redefining contemporary style. Gibbings was interested in functional design, purposely avoiding the constraints of being labeled modern or fashionable at a time when that was the aspiration of many designers and manufacturers. For Gibbings, the early modern period did not reflect the individuality, comfort, and warmth he sought to create.

With his lifetime partner, Carlton W. Pullin, an interior designer who specialized in fabrics and textiles, Gibbings pursued a distinctly American form of contemporary furniture, the architectural equivalent of Frank Lloyd Wright, whose work Gibbings admired for heralding a new form of contemporary American architecture. Born in England, where he spent his formative years before emigrating to the United States in 1930, Gibbings studied at the University of Liverpool and London University, earning his bachelor's degree in architecture. He received additional training in the decorative arts in Paris and at the Slade School of Fine Art in London. As a teenager, prior to his formal education, Gibbings had worked as a draftsman for the London-based design firm of Heaton, Tabb and Co., designing interiors for passenger ships. In 1929 Gibbings was introduced to Lord Duveen's brother Charles, who imported Elizabethan furniture and antiques to the United States under the name Charles of London. Gibbings left his native London that year to work for Charles in New York City. Their association lasted six years and undoubtedly provided additional incentive for Gibbings to formulate his own discriminating ideas about design.

In 1936 Gibbings opened his own design studio on Madison Avenue in New York City—the showroom for his first line of furniture. The small collection that he called Sans Époque (without time) expressed his earliest and lifelong thoughts about creating interiors independent of time and free of specific styles, past or present. As Gibbings explained, "we have exhausted the ponderous Gothic, the stuffy Victorian, and the Jacobean, and relegated the 'modern' to commercial limbo. Gradually we are achieving a new form of clear-cut beauty based on ancient traditions of purity of line. These forms are without period because pure beauty is everlasting—only materials change." This philosophy evolved over time and became an underlying theme in Gibbings's career and personal life.

OPPOSITE PAGE The Klismos chair was introduced in 1961 as part of the Furniture of Classical Greece collection. Manufactured by Saridis of Athens, it was made of Greek walnut with woven strap leather seating. Robsjohn-Gibbings based the design on a fifth century marble gravestone from Hegeso. Commenting in the *New York Times* about the design, Robsjohn-Gibbings said, "It's the most beautiful chair in the world. It is to furniture what the Parthenon is to architecture." The designer's fascination with Greek culture and furniture first appeared in 1936 when he featured a pair of Klismos chairs with Greek accessories in his Madison Avenue showroom.

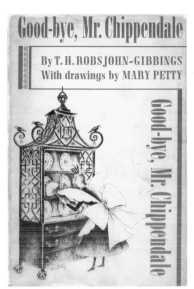

ABOVE LEFT Robsjohn-Gibbings in 1961 lounging among classical ruins in his daybed he designed for Saridis of Athens. **CENTER** This portrait of Robsjohn-Gibbings in his signature grey suit shows the designer looking very much the thoughtful lifestyle arbiter that he was. **RIGHT** The first of several books written by Robsjohn-Gibbings, *Good-bye, Mr. Chippendale* (1944), a bestseller with playful drawings by Mary Petty, was an instructional satire about reproductions of antique furniture and styles.

OPPOSITE PAGE This bleached lime wood, carved Griffin console table (1937) was executed for Gibbings by the Peterson Studios in Santa Barbara, California, as part of his Sans Epoque furniture line for his Casa Encantada in Bel Air, California.

Gibbings's most significant commission representing the Sans Époque aesthetic was Casa Encantada (House of Enchantment) in Bel Air, California. The house was completed in 1938 for Hilda Boldt Weber. Gibbings designed the interiors and furniture for the Georgian house, producing more than two hundred custom-made pieces for use throughout the sixty-four-room estate, which included sixteen bedrooms, twenty-six bathrooms, and twelve fireplaces, each with a different color of marble. Gibbings worked closely with craftsmen at the Peterson Studios in Santa Barbara, California, to execute many of the designs for this multiyear project. A precise and sophisticated combination of Egyptian, Greek, Roman, and Asian influences was interpreted with finesse. Gibbings ensured it was "neither antique nor modern. Neither tricky nor an 'exact copy.' It projects a timeless quality, a pure good taste that seems to have evolved from many centuries. Yet it is completely without epoch." His fondness for taking inspiration from ancient Greek vases can be traced to this commission, along with the form of animal legs for tables and chairs that eventually appeared in his formal line of furniture based on ancient Greece. For Casa Encantada, Gibbings produced his earliest Klismos chairs, consoles with seated sphinxes for bases made of bleached sycamore, as well as Griffin tables carved from bleached lime wood, all striking focal points for the most visible areas of the house. Pieces from the commission were included in the 1986 exhibition *High Styles: Twentieth-Century American Design* at the Whitney Museum of American Art in New York. Casa Encantada eventually became the home of Conrad Hilton, who bought the house fully furnished in 1950, but today the original pieces no longer remain with the house.

With an imperious streak and holding many strong opinions, Gibbings became one of the most widely published designers at the time, fiercely advocating independent thinking, individuality, and personal taste in numerous magazine articles for *Harper's Bazaar, Town & Country, House Beautiful*, and others. At a time when Americans were experiencing new affluence and a desire to improve their lifestyles, coupled with nagging insecurities about aesthetic matters, Gibbings's books were natural best sellers. *Good-Bye, Mr. Chippendale* (1944), with drawings by Mary Petty, addressed his disdain for European and Colonial American furniture reproductions. *Homes of the Brave* (1954), with drawings by Mary Petty, was called "a real service to art and architecture" by Frank Lloyd Wright, and *Mona Lisa's Mustache: A Dissection of Modern Art* (1944) offered Gibbings's views about the "quasi-religious-mystic" influence of theosophist Madame Blavatsky on modern art. As these playful titles suggest, the books were leisurely, though informative, discourses on design. Gibbings's last book, *Furniture of Classical Greece* (1963) was the culmination of his studies of ancient Greek furniture and the accompanying line of furniture he designed.

The largest and most influential line of furniture Gibbings designed was for the Widdicomb Furniture Co., which introduced his first collection in 1947. Gibbings commented, "in 1946, ignoring the fashionable plastic, plywood, and metal approach to furniture, I attempted to bring timeless design to Grand Rapids," referring to the Michigan furniture industry. Gibbings wanted to avoid what he called the "skin-and-bones machine for living" of postwar modern

design prevalent at the time, stating "I don't believe that you have to design *down* for mass-produced furniture, nor do I think that you have to visualize the future American home in terms of a sort of slick bargain-priced machine for living."

Gibbings applied this philosophy to creating clean, simple, well-proportioned sofas, chairs, tables, cabinets, chests, benches, and other pieces that were thoughtfully coordinated from year to year. The Widdicomb furniture also provided the opportunity for Gibbings to put into large-scale production a signature feature from his custom-made pieces: the louvered front drawer. In 1941 he began placing a slightly staggered or angled space between drawers to eliminate the need for handles or drawer pulls on case goods. Although this appealing and functional element was first seen in Gibbings's studio pieces of the 1940s, a range of manufacturers including Knoll Associates and Heywood-Wakefield eventually made variations of the louvered drawer. Gibbings considered the drawer one of his contributions to the field of furniture design and wanted to be remembered for it, along with his "use of rawhide on furniture; the large, low sofa table; the use of bleached birch in cabinetmaking; and the one-inch plate glass for large tabletops." In 1950 Gibbings received the Waters Award for Outstanding Achievement in Design, an honor from the Grand Rapids furniture industry, to acknowledge his innovations and impact, including the use of molded foam on upholstered pieces for more precise shaping instead of the common practice of cutting seat cushions and backs from large, flat foam sections.

One of the most widely recognized pieces from Gibbings's association with Widdicomb is the Mesa table of 1951. The monumental-size coffee table, measuring nearly nine feet long and about six feet wide, was most often finished in a brown walnut color called Cordovan. The design, influenced by the aerial views Gibbings saw from his window on flights to and from the West Coast, was an interpretation of the mountains in the southwest. The three cloudlike, cascading levels of the coffee table were flat on top with undulating vertical sides. The effect was a stylized outline, combining a plateau rock formation. A smaller, six-foot-long-by-four-foot-wide version of the Mesa table was one of the thirty-five pieces Gibbings designed for his 1952 collection. He also added a new walnut finish called sienna to the standard finishes of sorrel, bisque, saffron, and cordovan.

The ongoing design challenges for Gibbings—to keep adding new pieces to the Widdicomb line while ensuring compatibility with past work—was unpleasant and constraining for him. He ended his association with Widdicomb and the Grand Rapids industry in 1957, remarking that "leaving greedy assembly lines and hungry home-furnishing floors to their own devices, I returned to my private clientele and custom-made furniture."

Gibbings's passion for ancient Greek furniture was a constant influence throughout his career. His strong affinity for this furniture developed over a nearly thirty-year period before he designed his own line of ancient Greek furniture in 1961. After completing his university studies, Gibbings read about ancient Greek civilization and participated in archaeological research while still living in Europe. Over the years, he supplemented his enthusiasm and fascination for the subject by traveling and visiting museums to study Greek antiquities—particularly vases,

ABOVE LEFT Gibbings designed over 200 pieces for Casa Encantada in Bel Air including this dining set from 1938. Many of the pieces were in his Sans Epoque aesthetic, which he considered timeless, describing it as "…neither antique nor modern. Neither tricky nor an exact copy." **RIGHT** The sitting room at Casa Encantada, Bel Air, California, c. 1938. Gibbings designed the furniture and interiors for each of the estate's sixty-four rooms. It is considered his most significant commission.

OPPOSITE PAGE One of two made of combed oak with rosewood inlay, this cabinet (1938) has two doors concealing six drawers, brass handles, and animal claw feet. Gibbings designed it for Casa Encantada, the house that Conrad Hilton purchased in 1950 with all the furnishings, including the silverware.

ABOVE LEFT The Mesa walnut coffee table for Widdicomb Furniture Company was introduced in 1951 and measured nine feet long and about six feet wide. A smaller six-foot long version was offered in 1952. The Mesa table is one of Gibbings' most recognized designs. **RIGHT** The walnut sofa was designed for the Widdicomb Furniture Company in 1950. Made of naugahyde with cotton webbing, the sofa came as part of a set that included benches and chairs available in a variety of fabrics.

OPPOSITE PAGE A patio setting for the Widdicomb Furniture Company showroom in Grand Rapids, Michigan, features Robsjohn-Gibbings' Mesa coffee table and other designs, c. 1950. A Pre-Columbian stone carving hangs over the walnut sofa. The designer used it to highlight the gold and brown tones of the furniture. The setting was photographed for the cover of *House Beautiful*, c. 1950.

paintings, and any renderings that illustrated furniture. Gibbings would have produced custom-made Greek furniture pieces for commissions, but it was not until he met Eleftherios and Susan Saridis, of Saridis of Athens, that his Greek furniture designs reached a larger, international clientele. The Saridis company, a group of master cabinetmakers, is the largest furniture manufacturer in Greece and continues to make Gibbings furniture to this day. When the line was first introduced, Gibbings created nineteen pieces, all based on designs from the sixth to fourth centuries B.C. that were exhibited at the Saridis showroom in Athens. After the 1961 exhibit, three additional pieces were added. Before Tommi Parzinger of New York became the exclusive agent for the line in the United States, miniatures of the furniture were put on view in the windows of Tiffany and Co. in New York City to announce the forthcoming collection. The Saridis group included chairs, tables, and stools made primarily with walnut or beechwood, and brass and leather. Two of the most admired and representative pieces are the Klismos chair and couch, both made with walnut and leather supports. Gibbings described the wide back of the Klismos chair as "curved with the delicate grace of a new moon" with "concave, angular—sloped legs," largely based on an etching he had seen on a fifth-century marble gravestone of Hegeso. The Klismos couch, with its backrest shaped similarly to the Klismos chair, was inspired by an image on a fifth-century red-figured urn.

After completing the line of classical Greek furniture for Saridis, Robsjohn-Gibbings designed a collection of thirty-two pieces for Baker Furniture in 1961. He described the furniture as "neither modern or contemporary," yet it retained the clean lines and quality widely associated with his past designs. Using one of his favored woods, American walnut, he bleached pieces to highlight the grain. The finish, called tourmaline, had a hazel tone and offered buyers a warm color alternative. In keeping with his minimal use of metal, Gibbings selected brass accents: either routed or leaf-shaped handles for cabinets, dressers, and other case goods. The centerpiece of the collection was a pedestal dining table. The dining chairs were slightly larger than standard to make them more inviting and comfortable. He also created a new furniture silhouette, increasing the back height of the sofas and chairs. The upholstered pieces were offered in unmistakable colors, such as powder blue, pale pink, peach, apricot, and pale yellow. The collection is notable because it was the only one Gibbings designed for Baker and represents his last involvement with a Grand Rapids furniture manufacturer.

By 1963 Gibbings and his partner, Pullin, had become full-time residents of Athens. Their apartment, with close views of the Acropolis and the Theatre of Dionysus, was furnished with many pieces from the Saridis line, along with a Gibbings custom-made chest with cypress trees and flowers carved on the front. One of his early local commissions was the interior design of windows and display cases for a jewelry store in Athens. He also managed to design a line of furniture for the Urban Furniture Co. of Hicksville, Long Island, New York, in 1965. The collection of upholstered and case goods featured, in Gibbings's words, "classical designs with little-known traditional Greek island motifs." The furniture did not receive wide attention or sales. Consequently, pieces from the line were either made in limited quantities or not put into production, although a large sectional unit and several chairs sold well. The president and lead designer of Urban, Benjamin J. De Setto, wrote to Gibbings that the "taste of the

In 1963 Robsjohn-Gibbings and Carlton W. Pullin published *Furniture of Classical Greece* and included photographs of ancient Greek ruins, in an ancient theater on the island of Delos, as a backdrop to the classically inspired furnishings, including a Folding Stool made of Greek walnut with bronze accents and deer legs with hoofs based on an earthen plaque from the mid-sixth century B.C.; a three-legged Greek walnut table based on a design from a sixth century limestone statuette on the island of Cypress; and a Greek walnut stool with leather designed from a miniature fifth century terracotta stool. The collection was manufactured by Saridis of Athens.

buying public is toward gaudy Spanish and Italian furniture. We are beginning to wonder what is happening to good taste in America!" De Setto also alluded to Gibbings's book *Good-Bye, Mr. Chippendale* by writing, "the last two to three years has shown a return to almost borax furniture," referring to the type of poorly built, discounted, showy furniture (and bought with soup coupons, hence the name) that Gibbings had always stood so vigorously against.

While Gibbings was living in Athens and choosing fewer projects in his retirement, he designed the interiors for the Hotel Atlantis on the Greek island of Santorini in 1972. It was his last interior design commission and included custom-made furniture for the hotel's twenty-five rooms and public areas. Saridis created the handcrafted birch and upholstered furniture based on Gibbings's stylized sketches. The result was a contemporary update on the traditional motifs of the Greek islands. Gibbings used locally grown bamboo, complete with green leaves, to create a panel for the lobby and applied different shades of the wood to the bar. He also printed Greek wildflowers on fabric for furnishings used throughout the hotel.

Gibbings's interest in Greek art and culture continued until his death in 1976. He always thought he would be remembered above all else for his Klismos chair, which he first designed in 1936 and which remained popular throughout his career. And while Gibbings, as one of the key figures on the American design scene, was able to introduce a sense of quality and classical appropriateness, both in his works and his words, to a wider and newly empowered public, which is his true legacy as a designer, he would be pleased that there is also a Klismos chair in the permanent collection of the Metropolitan Museum of Art in New York. **J.H.**

ABOVE LEFT A circular table from Gibbings' Furniture of Classical Greece is made of walnut with three bronze lion legs and claws cast from an original bronze leg made in the late fourth century. A variation of this table included a circular bronze stretcher below the walnut top; both were manufactured by Saridis of Athens. CENTER The bleached lime oak table with cloven hoof legs is more naturalistic even in white than some of Gibbings' other animal-inspired supports. RIGHT The design of a Folding Stool made of Greek walnut with bronze accents, a single piece of leather, deer legs and hoofs, was based on an image from an earthen plaque from the mid-sixth century and manufactured by Saridis of Athens.

OPPOSITE PAGE The Goulandris apartment in Athens, Greece, was decorated by Robsjohn-Gibbings in 1962. For the commission the designer placed his Classical Greek furniture throughout the apartment including the fountain room with its white marble flooring and grill sunshade. His three-legged circular walnut table with bronze lion legs and claws stands in the foreground.

KARL SPRINGER

From window dresser and bookbinder to major designer and couture furniture manufacturer, Karl Springer (1931–1989) captured the spirit of his age, the raging 1970s and '80s. He was inspired by the deco classics from another indulgent period, the 1920s, but by taking advantage of a convergence possible only in New York—of free-flowing cash and the inexpensive labor of recent emigrants possessing old-world craft skills—Springer was able to transform existing styles into his own distinctive expressions.

Though born in prewar Germany and working off European classical forms, Springer developed an irreverent and nondoctrinaire idiom of bold proportions, highly exotic finishes, and a sometimes flashy palette that identified him strongly with his American clientele. His work spoke with the confidence and energy of the highest-end productions associated with the disco decade. With his death from complications of AIDS in 1989, Springer joined the tragically swelling ranks of designers felled by that scourge in those years. Above all, furnishings by Springer, whether python-covered desk accessories or a shagreen dining table, possessed the verve and contemporary glamour of enduringly popular classics.

Karl Springer was born in Berlin in 1931. His family background has never been part of his story, apart from references to his study of bookbinding and working as a window dresser at a prominent Berlin clothier. He arrived in New York in the late fifties, following a brief stint in California; his exit from Germany—the details of which remained vague—was probably arranged with the help of a gay American military officer. Aged twenty-six and with no formal training, Springer found work styling windows at Lord & Taylor. Eager to move on, he started applying his bookbinding skills to making animal skin–covered jewel boxes, desk accessories, and telephone tables. His work attracted the attention of a buyer for Bergdorf Goodman and, in a story he told often, a snakeskin phone table caught the eye of the Duchess of Windsor, whose patronage quickly moved Springer and his expanding line of furnishings onto a society fast track, where he reveled in keeping pace.

Springer opened a small shop on First Avenue, wrapping leather, applying faux finishes, and working for decorators interested in intriguing accent pieces. He then moved to East Fifty-third Street, known as Boutique Row, where the back rooms were crowded with refugees from Europe and Asia adept in refined craft skills—such as lacquering, batiking, and leatherwork—which were not particularly common to American furniture making, rooted as it was in more basic Colonial-style paint finishes and carving.

OPPOSITE PAGE This dining table from 1979 is an excellent example of Karl Springer's skill in designing furniture for a clientele that shared his opulent taste. It features a six-foot-diameter top detailed with feathers in a circular pattern underneath a glass top all resting on a brushed-steel base. Using only the finest craftsmen, Springer created pieces with stark silhouettes, which were embellished with minute details such as delicate, colorful feathers to enhance their beauty.

ABOVE Once a bookbinder Springer understood well how material worked when applied to a surface. He often employed the ancient art of wrapping shagreen to finish anything from a simple jewelry box to an armchair. This material is fitting for Springer's era since the French aristocracy used it throughout the eighteenth century; the material was revived again in the twenties by such French masters as Clement Rousseau and Jean Michel Frank, both admired by Springer. His use of other materials like chrome and Lucite further purported Springer's glamorous design sensibility, as seen in his version of a Chinese-inspired X-frame chair, center, where he uses chrome with Lucite and bronze details to give the ancient form an updated kick.

As his career flourished, Springer's own homes were a most convincing showcase of his evolving sensibility. From a sky-lit artist's studio at the top of a Greenwich Village town house, where a bedroom was squeezed into a hallway and a cabinet was retooled from an antique confessional that appeared in the *New York Times* in 1967, to the plush apartment on the forty-fifth floor of an Upper East Side tower published in *Architectural Digest* in 1989, these homes displayed his flair for glamour without ostentation. If the earlier place showed off Springer's early ingenuity, the latter one featured the extraordinary range of his aesthetic interests. There was a Chinese antique drum as a side table, alongside an Ashanti stool, a sixteenth-century Italian wrought-iron chest, and an eighteenth-century gold-leafed Japanese screen. The well-endowed proportions of his own upholstered pieces, metal tube lamps, and lacquered tables added muscle to this precious, eclectic collection. And a final layer of gloss came with walls and ceilings lined in antiqued copper-leaf and mirrored window niches. Even the closets were lined with lacquered bird's-eye maple, and his Lucite headboard was illuminated. The writer for *Architectural Digest* attributed a "well-burnished masculinity" to the place that was yacht-like, while the silver-maned Springer himself came across as an adventuresome sea captain.

Certainly, Springer was an omnivore of world styles and rare techniques well before globe-trotting became the favorite pastime of decorators in search of inspiration. He focused especially on materials with texture, from Japanese prints to African mud cloths, and his showrooms were stacked with such exotic finds as ostrich eggs and Venetian hand-blown glass. But his real signature was furniture covered in lacquered skins: goat, lizard, alligator, fossilized coral, shark, cobra, and even frog. He is often credited with having revived the fad for shagreen, long associated with such French deco masters as Jean-Michel Frank, Jean Dunand, and Emile-Jacques Ruhlmann. The Springer look, however, didn't derive from deco alone; it borrowed as well from ancient Greek and chinoiserie motifs, pumping up and simplifying familiar shapes, then reinvigorating them with exotic finishes in unusual colors (purple python was a favorite). "I may be inspired by other designers," he told *Architectural Digest* in the late eighties, "but the interpretations are strictly my own." It was a significant break from the more staid interior fashions of the day that tended toward ball-and-claw Americana, French Louis-by-the-numbers, and pervasive beige.

Mark Eckman, an industrial designer who worked for Springer in the sixties, specializing in making Lucite furniture, described Springer's style in an interview as "crude chic," noting that the designer "liked the material to be really out there, screaming." Gutsy simplicity remained Springer's hallmark. His most iconic pieces resonated with a sense of history while striking a clear contemporary note. One of his earliest classics, the JMF chair, which he named after his idol, Jean-Michel Frank, possesses the clarity of classical form injected with Springer's signature boldness. While the JMF chair was always very expensive, ranging from $1,400 to $2,200 according to Eckman, depending on the finish, it remained one of Springer's most popular and in-demand pieces throughout the seventies. He made numerous variations using different materials: shiny black lacquer, veneered oak, a leather that could be either smooth or scored, and in later years shagreen with bone inlays. Belying its simple form, the JMF

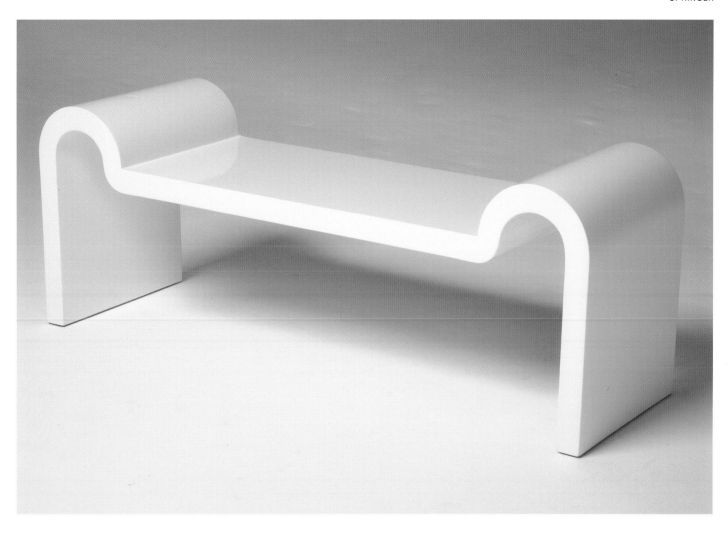

chair was extremely difficult to make. It was pieced together without distracting decorative flourishes, resulting in an elegance that depended on seamless lines and flawless craftsmanship. Each piece took about a week to complete, and lacquer finishes could require as many as twenty coats. The Regina chair, with an upholstered seat and back within a wood frame, was another iconic piece, one reflecting the slightly less rigorous side to Springer's later work and exhibiting his interest in ever-more-exotic finishes. But the most copied of all his pieces was most likely the telephone table on castors, with its slender proportions and two tiers with gallery edges. The originals, noted Eckman, were very low at twelve to fourteen inches, to stand alongside the low-slung slipper chairs made so popular by the decorator William Haines.

Springer was well attuned to society tastes, whether he was working for King Hussein or Tina Turner, Jackie Onassis or the soap-opera actress Loretta Young. When Diana Vreeland declared seashells were divine, no one was faster at coming up with a snazzy showstopper, such as a lamp with a sea-urchin base, or an irresistible ostrich-feather pillow. While individual clients encouraged Springer to produce over-the-top, tour-de-force creations (for instance, interior decorator Jane Baum commissioned a coffee table with massive eight-inch-diameter legs carved entirely from Lucite), he was equally happy producing what he called "stock," favorite pieces to have always on hand. That adaptable sensibility naturally endeared him to decorators at the highest end of the design spectrum, including Billy Baldwin, Valerian Rybar, Robert Metzger, and Jay Spectre.

Springer never advertised, and for a long time, his personal charisma—dashingly handsome even when his beard turned snowy white—was all that was needed to attract enough new business to keep a one-hundred-person-strong operation buoyant. At a charity auction in the eighties, Laurence Rockefeller declared furnishings by Springer to be the "antiques of tomorrow," a declaration reflecting how costly they were even in their own day. In 1980, according to an article in the *New York Times*, a glass-topped table by Springer with a Lucite base cost $12,630, while a parchment-covered side chair covered in twenty-four coats of clear lacquer sold for $1,450.

ABOVE This classic ivory lacquered bench epitomizes the chic and sleek look of the 1970s. The subtlety in form is enhanced by a hand-rubbed high-polish finish. Springer was known for his finishes and his commitment to meticulous craftsmanship; applying hand-rubbed lacquer is a laborious process that can easily show flaws, though Springer was a perfectionist, personally inspecting every piece before delivery.

Perhaps because he was self-taught, Springer tended to develop and convey his ideas for new furniture with models made of cardboard rather than drawings or blueprints. In this way, too, he could make on-the-spot alterations and variations as well as ornamental flourishes without concern for having to transpose his notions into a technical language that could be reproduced. Thus he was cleverly able to convert a shortcoming—his lack of training—into an asset, even a desirable commodity: "Because I insist on the same standards, there could never be any mass production in my workshops. We make one piece at a time," he once told a design journalist.

While the main Karl Springer showroom was opened on East Sixty-first Street in 1969, the workshops, where pieces were assembled in several stages by different craft specialists, were scattered all around the city, and eventually around the world. He turned to a Japanese woman living in SoHo for linen lacquer and batik. On the Upper East Side, Chinese men (by the 1980s they were mostly Vietnamese) did lacquering and parchment. His lamp fitters were on Fifty-ninth Street, near York Avenue; in Queens, there was a woodworking shop; and among artists manqué in Manhattan, he found virtuoso faux painters. Nowhere other than New York would it have been possible to find so many different people trained in different skills from different traditions.

Springer's product depended on all of their varying degrees of expertise, casting the designer himself into the role of constant quality-control master. This subcontracting allowed for a unique freedom of expression, with styles liberated from traditional strictures, but it also led to unforeseen dependencies as the most talented craftspeople eventually wanted to spin off on their own, while the occasionally unscrupulous ones sold unauthorized copies or watered-down knockoffs on the side. Springer's main workshop was managed in the seventies by Ron Seff, one of his closest friends who shared the designer's zeal about quality control. In the early eighties, however, the two had a falling out, and Seff opened his own showroom where he produced variations on key Springer designs with slight alterations but equally high standards. The Ron Seff showroom is now located in the Design & Decoration Building in Manhattan and is considered by some to carry on the legacy of Springer's designs in terms of quality if not always conception. For collectors, the situation is exacerbated by the fact that in the early years, Springer rarely signed pieces, only occasionally adding a leather flap stamped with his name. It was only in the late eighties that he introduced an official stamp for hides and sometimes engraved his name into Lucite; but signing for Springer was an inconsistent art.

ABOVE This magnificent rosewood dining table and chromium-plated steel and brass armchairs are fantastic examples of the cabinetmaker's skill. The rosewood tabletop is inlaid with a chromium-plated steel reed and is decoratively mitered at the corners; its square rosewood pedestal base ends with a chromium-plated steel band. The table has a polished lacquer finish and the incredibly heavy, solid chromium-plated steel chairs with leather seats and brass backrest accents bestow a formal feeling to the set overall.

OPPOSITE PAGE In 1990 John Esten with Rose Bennett Gilbert and photographer George Chinsee included Karl Springer's apartment in their 1990 book *Manhattan Style*. This photo from the book shows Springer's own executive desk made of ebony inspired by an art-deco original done in glass. Springer said his apartment felt "like being inside a little jewel box . . . the mood changes constantly." Even though the mood here appears dark and sultry, one can see that with the right light the high-polish finishes and glass and chrome furnishings sparkle in their every detail.

PREVIOUS SPREAD In the late 1980s Springer's apartment on the Upper East Side of Manhattan caught the attention of *Architectural Digest* for his superb design of combining pieces from Africa and Asia with art-deco-inspired furnishings and details. This spurred other trade magazines to photograph the interior, showing off not only its amazing view but also the decadent combination of textures. Seen in the center of Springer's living room is a low palisander sofa with Bauhaus-inspired upholstery complemented with a petite nineteenth-century African tribal stool fitted with a one-inch slab of glass. Situated to the right is the console that Springer designed as a tribute to Emile-Jacques Ruhlmann. A classic bronze patinated cylinder lamp with a mushroom shade sits in the foreground. The copper-leafed ceiling and walls lend the room a soft glow.

Previous spread: © Peter Aaron/Esto.

SPRINGER

Ultimately, and perhaps as a way to avoid such pitfalls as well as to get a handle on rising costs, Springer moved as much production as possible abroad. By 1983, at the height of his business, Springer furnishings were available not only in Manhattan but also in showrooms in Los Angeles, Munich, and Tokyo. Lacquered goatskin pieces were made in Mexico; shagreen and coral in the Philippines and Indonesia. Springer, whose lamps carved in Lucite and glass were especially popular, established a relationship with a Murano glass manufacturer, Seguso, and worked with glassblowers in applying an ancient antiquing technique, called scavo, to create a series of distinctive chandeliers, candlesticks, and sconces with a modern sensibility.

As the Karl Springer business expanded and became more complicated, Springer's brother Joachim joined in and took over the idiosyncratic bookkeeping. It was a heady time, and Springer himself was flush with disco fever, clubbing at Studio 54 and diving into the notorious Fire Island parties of 1982 and 1983. By the mid-1980s the Karl Springer dynasty was ending. Shortly before his death in 1989, Karl's health began to rapidly decline, and he was no longer able to pay the close attention to detailing and quality control that had always characterized his process. He sold the company, and subsequently, Karl Springer Ltd. filed for Chapter 11 in 1993.

In the late eighties, tastes were also changing. Ronald Reagan conservatism and Ralph Lauren traditionalism were in vogue, and American reproductions were outselling creative spirits like Springer, Tommi Parzinger, and Paul Evans. These designers, who all stumbled into highly successful businesses, at least for a time, may have sought glory and fame but never brand domination: keeping the artistry alive was their higher goal. And as the disco decades became an aesthetic punch line, with John Travolta's black-and-white rayon suit as a benchmark, a sense of the achievements of these exclusive artist-designers was lost. Further complicating matters in Springer's case, questions have lingered over how the sale of his company and existing inventory were handled in the nineties. For collectors, it is not easy to discern true Springer originals from the authorized and gypsy reproductions, the fakes and the copies that abound. Until recently, resale of Springer pieces did not even keep up with the original high prices. That is changing, and in 2006, at the Sotheby's sale of furniture from the Tony Ingrao collection, a rare Springer table from 1979 with a steel base and a top with feathers under glass sold for $66,000.

Collectors are again taking stock of Springer's work, recognizing that the early pieces have the allure of the twentieth-century masters Emile-Jacques Ruhlmann and Jean-Michel Frank. Exquisitely made for a short period of time by traditionally trained artisans, Springer's furnishings captured the look and vitality of a unique moment in modernity that flourished, then blazed out like a supernova. **J.I.**

ABOVE This portrait of Karl Springer in his Upper East Side apartment was taken around 1989. The designer applied his signature to various materials in different ways but it is not unusual to come across unsigned pieces as Springer did not start signing his work until the late eighties.

OPPOSITE PAGE These cantilevered tables in brass and glass seem to defy gravity. They teeter on the verge of falling over. With forms that suggest movement, the shine of the brass and glass only enhances the illusion. As an admirer of the machine-age aesthetic, Springer was often drawn to streamlined shapes and shiny materials; these epitomize the best of his new-deco aesthetic.

Above left: © Peter Aaron/Esto.

EDWARD
WORMLEY

Edward J. Wormley (1907–1995) produced furniture that was uniquely understated, finely crafted, and definitively American modern. Wormley disseminated the modernist aesthetic to a wider American public with styles that were instrumental in popularizing a fresh, forward-looking design for American homes. His inspirations ranged from art deco, Arts & Crafts, Scandinavian, and International Style, but his designs were timeless and compatible with the traditional, adaptable styles preferred by the mainstream and upper-middle classes alike. Through his long-term association with Dunbar Furniture Corporation, a leading producer of furniture in America from the 1930s through the '60s, Wormley demonstrated a sophisticated understanding of handicraft that inspired other American manufacturers to aim for a higher level of production.

Edward J Wormley (he left his middle initial undotted) struck a knowing balance between stark standardization and historicized forms by creating furniture with a modern feeling that made a graceful bow to the past. And though he was awarded several Good Design awards for modern furniture from the Museum of Modern Art, he made his philosophy clear: "I have a real admiration for the design of the past and I am quite frank to say that too little design today can compete in interest, ingenuity, and beauty with the best traditional designs." Wormley's concern for bringing quality and craftsmanship into the American home, rather than a standardized style, earned him an important place in the history of American mid-century design today.

Born in 1907 in a small town outside of Chicago, Wormley aspired to be a decorator. In high school he took a correspondence course from the New York School of Interior Design and after graduation attended the esteemed Art Institute of Chicago for three terms before training as an interior designer at Marshall Field & Company. Three years later Wormley was designing eighteenth-century English reproductions that Berkey & Gay in Grand Rapids, Michigan, produced for Marshall Field. Berkey & Gay provided him with a valuable apprenticeship studying antiques at various museums.

The Depression curtailed Wormley's job at Marshall Field in 1931. But he took advantage of the hiatus from workaday employment to travel to Europe with Edward Crouse, a childhood friend who became his lifetime companion. According to Judith Gura, curator of *Edward Wormley: The Other Face of Modernism*, a 1997 exhibition about his role in the popularization of modernism in America, he arranged to meet both the architect Le Corbusier, an arch-modernist, and Emile-Jacques Ruhlmann, craftmaster of art deco, a sure sign of his broadening tastes in design.

OPPOSITE PAGE These occasional tables in sap walnut from 1956 each have three inlaid iridescent Tiffany-glass tiles. Wormley was an avid collector of both pottery and Tiffany glass well before it became popular again. In the mid-fifties small individual Tiffany tiles and complete mosaics began to appear in his tabletops and, today, these are some of the most sought-after Wormley pieces.

ABOVE LEFT Portrait of Wormley, c. 1948. **RIGHT** This vignette entitled "*Business is Pleasure*" appeared in a 1956 Dunbar catalogue. It captures Wormley's philosophy as both designer and decorator. He did not believe in rooms that appeared to have been done by a single designer, and he specifically rejected matching suites of furniture. His interior projects always gave the impression that they were the result of time and taste, and had been furnished with pieces accumulated from different sources, styles, and experiences.

OPPOSITE PAGE TOP This grand desk from 1967 was another one of Wormley's designs that Dunbar produced in a variety of woods to considerable success over the years. **BOTTOM LEFT** This well-known Dunbar sideboard was described in the catalogue as a "complete living-storage-serving center." It was often topped with Portuguese marble, which complemented the tambour doors and facade of Tawi and mahogany. **BOTTOM RIGHT** The 1954 coffee table with an accordion-like walnut base is topped with aqua- and lapis-colored Murano-glass tiles.

Upon his return Wormley was hired to be the marquee designer at Dunbar Furniture Company, then a medium-sized manufacturer in Berne, Indiana, where he remained until his retirement in 1968. After designing a traditional line for Dunbar, he began making adaptations of Beidermeier, a "transitional" style, as he put it. With a strong sense of prevailing trends, Wormley was soon looking at Swedish modern. In a 1987 interview with *Interior Design* magazine, he said, "By 1935 I was designing two complete lines—a modern line and a traditional line." He often gave a nod to past designers by using derivative forms, such as his Three-Position chair (1947), which evokes Alvar Aalto's bentwood Paimio chair of 1931. His adaptation of Richard Riemerschmid's graceful 1899 musician's chair was based on a photo he saw in a magazine. He then contacted the German designer, who agreed to send Wormley his original sketches. The aptly titled Riemerschmid chair from Dunbar was designed in 1947 and is in the permanent collections at both the Metropolitan Museum of Art and the Museum of Modern Art.

During World War II, while domestic production ceased, Wormley took a job with the government as head of the Furniture Unit in the Office of Price Administration. He returned to Dunbar in 1944 as an independent consultant. While his collaboration with Dunbar was long and prolific, Wormley also succeeded as an interior designer, opening his own design studio in New York City in 1945. Independently, he also produced lighting for Lightolier, cabinets for RCA, globe stands for Rand McNally, and carpet, for Alex Smith & Sons. In 1948 Schiffer Prints selected him to create textiles as one of the six renowned designers in the Stimulus collection that also included Salvador Dali, Ray Eames, and George Nelson. A 1947 collaboration with Drexel Furniture on the Precedent line did not turn out so well. When Dunbar found out about it, they asked Wormley to end the relationship with the competing furniture company out of conflict of interest.

From the 1940s on, Wormley was described in the popular and professional press as "a modernist," "a brilliant designer," "an insatiable eclectic," "a gradualist," "a time-tested professional," and "ostensibly easy to understand." In 1945 *House Beautiful* summed him up by stating, "Wormley's outstanding characteristic is his ability to design modern furniture that fits into period homes, and period furniture with a modern cast to it." These traits were undoubtedly reflected in his interior designs and furniture.

A 1945 *House & Garden* article described Wormley's "all-season room": "deftly adaptable furniture, to be moved and grouped seasonally, and the considerate color scheme are the abracadabra that gives it year-round interest and charm." Wormley designed a lightweight L-shaped table that hugged a settee in the living room, using such fresh colors as "Soft Aegean Mist," "Athenian Smoke," and "Gringo Pink." The entire suite, produced by Dunbar, was meant to face the fireplace in the winter, then be moved to face the floor-to-ceiling windows in the summer. With leather dining chairs featuring handle-holds, and built-in cabinets positioned above a recessed sideboard, Wormley created a mobile, versatile space.

As an interior designer Wormley did not fill interiors with his own pieces as a matter of principle, stating that he "wanted to make furniture that would agree with other people's furniture, or with antiques." He used contemporary furniture by his peers, antiques, Siamese silks,

Moroccan rugs, basketry, and plants. And yet his interiors were never cluttered. The pieces
he chose were trim with minimal ornament, always functional, comfortable, and well proportioned. In a 1956 article for *Interiors*, Olga Gueft stated, "the key to Wormley's quality as a
furniture designer lies, of course, in his interiors. Wormley does not design furniture per se,
as a sculpture might be designed, but as a tool which must serve some given visual and
functional purpose in an interior."

The 1950s saw a revival of the International Style and a rejection of historical precedents.
Wormley, however, was part of another school of thought, as Katherine B. Heisinger and
George H. Marcus stated in *Landmarks of Twentieth Century Design:* "other designers
regarded the past as the source of a suitable repertoire of forms and details, expressed
interest in traditional handcraft, and devised pragmatic and unconventional solutions to
engineering problems, making it plain that no one modern 'good' design idiom had hegemony
in the 1950s." Wormley, with his innate skill at using the "heritage of design fundamentals,"
coupled with Dunbar's fine craftsmanship, helped the company become the preeminent
producers of good American design.

Originally a manufacturer of horse-drawn buggies, the Dunbar Furniture Corporation opened
in rural Indiana in 1912. The company moved in 1919 to Berne, a small town full of Swiss
immigrants with old-world craft skills. With such talented employees, Dunbar soon became
known for fine hand-rubbed finishes and quality materials. Dunbar never mass-produced its
collections; in fact, "the factory's operations were not automated," stated Gura. Without
up-to-date mechanization, Dunbar was able to customize each piece of furniture per the
client's request. Furthermore, Dunbar and Wormley wanted their collections to offer details
that would give owners more flexibility in their rooms. Wormley was not interested in factory-
made furniture: "it was all too pat, all matched suites, and matched detailing—legs of chairs
and tables all being the same," he stated in a 1987 interview with *Interior Design* magazine.
The Dunbar and Wormley idea, he continued, "was to make collections of furniture that were
based on antique originals or adaptations of old pieces of furniture but look as if the collection
had been assembled by someone of taste rather than bought in a block. I aimed for traditional
period pieces and for simplified contemporary pieces that were related, but not matching."

Specially proportioned furniture could be ordered with optional doors, drawers, and shelves;
many pieces came in a variety of sizes and heights; and some even had detachable metal legs.
Even Dunbar's 1959 collection of office furniture offered "some forty variations in desks alone,"
from general secretarial use to high-level executive pieces made to suit a variety of needs and
personal styles.

All Dunbar pieces could be made in the client's preferred materials. One could order legs,
hardware, or accents in brass with a glossy or satin finish. Exotic woods were available, like
zebra and olive or local mahogany and walnut, and could be bleached, stained, and finished
in many variations, like oil, open-pore lacquer, or glossy lacquer. Many tables offered wood
or marble tops, and case pieces with sliding doors could be made with cane, leather, or straw
inserts, or a webbing of laminated veneers. The highly skilled craftsmen could execute such

precise detailing as Murano glass inlays, veneers, delicately carved legs or aprons, and light or dark hand-rubbed finishes that clients requested from Wormley's vast array of design options.

Wormley's furniture had a simple elegance that was suitable for any room, but with adjustments to color and finish, a dark and dramatic setting could be transformed into a light one. A 1960 *House Beautiful* article showed a dining room furnished with a dining table, chairs, and a sideboard that were finished in a bleached mahogany with blue upholstery, creating a fresh and airy look. The same furniture finished in a dark high gloss with red upholstery offered a more sensual feel for its inhabitants. And by incorporating red Natzler glass tiles instead of blue, and matching the armchair's upholstery, Wormley and Dunbar could offer their clients more than just furniture—they could create a mood for them as well.

Even with the multitude of options, Dunbar still managed to release two lines a year with an average of one hundred pieces per annum for thirty-seven years. By the 1950s, furniture from Dunbar was considered "to be the most luxurious, expensive, livable, amusing, and exquisite of all the modern furniture on the market," according to *Interiors* magazine, and Wormley was described as an "eclectic...master at improving the ideas of other people, other times, other places."

Wormley's pieces were featured in the *Good Design* exhibitions from 1950 to 1952. From 1950 to 1955 the Museum of Modern Art and Chicago's Merchandise Mart set out to promote good modern design. Edgar Kaufmann, Jr., MoMA's head of industrial design department and Wormley's friend, based his choices on "eye appeal, function, construction, and price, with emphasis on the first." He defined good design as "a thorough merging of form and function...revealing a practical, uncomplicated, sensible beauty." And while most designers tended to box themselves in with labels of modern or traditional, Kaufmann stated, "Wormley rises to the challenge of the past, showing that grace is never dead except for those who ape it."

One of the best examples of Wormley's ability to design modern pieces with reverence for the past was his appropriately named Janus collection, introduced in 1957 for Dunbar. Named after the ancient Roman god of gates who simultaneously looked to the past and the future, the Janus collection incorporated original Tiffany glass tiles (Wormley's friend Kaufmann collected works by Louis Comfort Tiffany) into the rich woods of various tabletops

ABOVE The La Gondola sofa and the Pentagonal table with Natzler-tile inlay (lower left) were both part of the Janus collection (1957). Wormley's designs for the collection demonstrated a willingness to experiment with forms and proportions. Although Dunbar's pieces were always restrained and elegant, these pieces are some of the most original and daring examples. The coffee table, c. 1960, in rosewood and brass (lower right) was influenced by contemporary Italian design.

ABOVE LEFT These elegant occasional tables from 1957 are made in mahogany and topped with Wormley's signature aqua and lapis Murano-glass tile mosaics. **CENTER** These lacquered tables from 1959 carry walnut marquetry in one of the only such motifs he designed. The diamond pattern also appeared on sideboards and other examples of furniture even though ornamentation rarely made appearances in Wormley's work. **RIGHT** Wormley's admiration for modern Scandinavian design is clearly manifested in the Wing chair from Dunbar's Janus collection (1957).

OPPOSITE PAGE In a 1960 article featured in *House Beautiful* Wormley designed the same room with Dunbar's Today & Tomorrow collection, which featured a sofa with moveable arms to be set at the user's desired angle, an armchair that could be fully upholstered or not, and a cabinet that could, of course, be made in any variation of finishes—here it is done in a dark stained mahogany. Below left is a view of one of the Janus rooms shown in a cozy setting in the Chicago Merchendise Mart. Below right is Wormley's living room on East Fifty-second Street in New York City. This setting shows Wormley's appreciation for all decorative art, such as the handwoven rugs and the abstract painting.

and cabinets, and used carved Japanese woodblocks as ornamental door inlays. Inspired by Greene & Greene designs that Wormley had seen on a 1939 trip to Pasadena, he conceived seventy nostalgic yet modern pieces whose forms were influenced by the American Arts & Crafts movement and made from such natural materials as ebony, ash, and sap-streaked walnut.

Dunbar touted its updated Wing chair as "One of the most elegant pieces in the Dunbar line." Instead of the traditional rounded wings upholstered separately from the back, this piece had angular, almost square "wings" that were upholstered as a unit with the back. In 2007 a pair of walnut leather chairs from the Janus collection sold at auction for $2,880.

A line introduced in 1963 had the typical Wormley-Dunbar characteristics of subtle refinements and classical craftsmanship. Influenced by a recent trip to England, Wormley incorporated exotic woods of zebra, olive, and rosewood in natural, bleached, or dark finishes. The forms were Regency revival with a twist, such as a four-leaf clover game table "where players sit in the inner sections and the 'leaves' curve around either side," according to catalog descriptions. A conversation sofa was angled, but not on a curve, so that the sofa could be placed in a corner or parallel to a wall and a guest could easily converse with the person on the opposite end.

To say Wormley strictly revered the past does him a disservice. He understood the times in which he lived and for which he designed, stating in the Walker Art Center's *Everyday Art Quarterly* (1953) that admiration for the past "does not mean that I believe for one moment in reproducing old designs for present-day use." Interpretation was more his style. In fact, he believed it was necessary to "continue to work with contemporary materials, techniques, and especially within the framework of our own highly developed and ever-changing patterns."

In 1955 Wormley and Crouse, a journalism professor and theater director, together designed the interior of the Luxtrol bus for the Superior Electric Company. This "mansion on wheels" had dimmable lighting, something that was only used in commercial interiors at the time. Using all Dunbar furniture, Wormley proved his ability to make a cramped interior look airy and elegant and Dunbar's ability to produce pieces in any specification requested.

The late 1950s were a prosperous period for Dunbar. The company's ad campaign conceived by the firm Hockaday Associates was highly visible, and the advertisements always featured Wormley's name and displayed furniture in an imaginative and unpredictable way. Sometimes furniture appeared up in the treetops or stranded on hillsides; other images showed babies in drawers and squirrels on sofas. The copy suggested that the owners of Dunbar furniture "inevitably grow into collectors." The Dunbar name became synonymous with high status; ads could be found in design magazines and the *New Yorker*. The firm had showrooms across the country

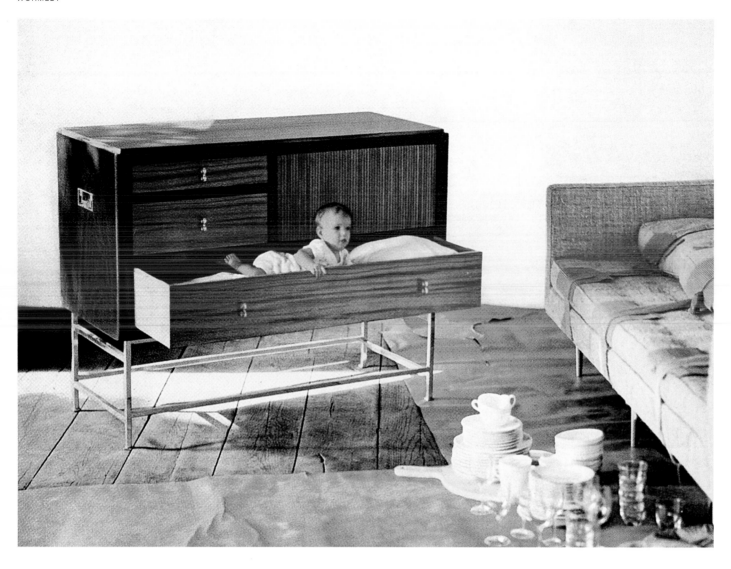

ABOVE AND OPPOSITE PAGE Dunbar developed a national reputation not only for craftsmanship and fine materials but also for innovative marketing. Many of their publicity images, such as the ones pictured here, were shot outdoors and prominently featured the Dunbar name in an early example of aggressive branding. As a result Dunbar became known as one of the first furniture "brands." The accompanying text always credited Wormley making his a household name. Hackaday Associates of New York was responsible for many of these innovative and expensive-to-produce campaigns in the fifties and sixties.

from New York to Chicago and Los Angeles to Hawaii. In 1956 the *Dunbar Book of Contemporary Furniture* was published to advertise current offerings, and in 1959 the company introduced a line of office furniture.

Wormley flourished in the 1960s. He had been teaching at Parsons School of Design since 1955, lecturing at the Architectural League, and traveling around the world. In 1962 he was awarded the distinguished Elsie de Wolf Award, named after the "mother of interior decorating."

Furniture that Wormley designed in the 1930s and '40s sold well into the '60s, reaffirming that the pieces reflected the continuing American lifestyle of cozy chic that he had been so key in popularizing during his early years. Some of his most popular pieces, like the Listen to Me chaise, Sheaf-of-Wheat table, and Tête-à-tête sofa, now attract strong prices at auction. In June 2007 Sotheby's sold a 1948 Listen to Me chaise for $66,000.

Throughout Wormley's expansive career, he consistently maintained a high level in his designs. His silhouettes were clean and sharp, whether in a bulky tufted sofa or his airy La Gondola sofa. Unimpressed with originality for its own sake, Wormley strove for function and adaptability in each line he designed. While American interiors became less formal, the desire to be in vogue was still important, and through Wormley's clean lines and lightweight forms, Americans were able to achieve the duality of comfortable elegance. **E.J.**

JOHN DICKINSON

It is difficult to imagine a designer or decorator limiting his color palette to just shades of beige, camel, gray, and white, yet San Francisco designer John Dickinson (1920–1982) did exactly that. And in the process he created a new aesthetic that was precise and imaginative. Although he designed furniture and interiors, Dickinson thought of himself as a draftsman, attentive to "line, proportion, and shape." He felt colors were a distraction, stating in *Interior Design* magazine that "vigorous forms and strong shapes take the place of color."

While the lack of color in Dickinson's work may initially have appeared bland or stark, his furniture was anything but that, with its classical forms and different styles combined in a modern, utilitarian way. This was especially true of the furniture he designed during the 1970s. His witty reinterpretations of eighteenth-century Georgian paw- or claw-foot tables and chairs are now considered to be among his signature motifs. The effect is surprising and, of course, reinforced with an understated use of color. Dickinson commented, "I think color is a big cop-out; in so many cases, it is used to cover up mistakes." Aside from the desire for perfection, Dickinson used a neutral color wheel to focus on texture and explore different materials and techniques. That chalky palette soon made his work instantly recognizable (but also easy for others to copy).

A native of Berkeley, California, Dickinson developed his style while studying at the Parsons School of Design in New York City. He was a student when the influential designer Van Day Truex was director and the decorator Albert Hadley was a faculty member. Dickinson's direct exposure to the modern decorative arts in New York—and especially the work of T. H. Robsjohn-Gibbings—was instrumental to his evolution as a designer. In particular, Gibbings's Klismos line of ancient Greek furniture featuring animal legs and hoofs must have impressed him. Years later, Dickinson's own animal leg furniture and his Greek X-leg table seemed to be an obvious tribute to Gibbings. Parisian modernist Jean-Michel Frank's elegant and minimalist designs were also an influence and reflected Dickinson's belief as quoted in Erica Brown's book *Interior Views: Design at Its Best:* "design is like vocabulary. There are so many ways to say the same familiar things, so originality is paramount. But one should never design with the idea of being extraordinary—after all, somehow, somewhere it's all been done before, and furniture must conform to the shape of the body."

In the mid-1950s Dickinson returned to California. His experience was unique for a West Coast designer, and he easily started to make a name for himself. Before establishing his

OPPOSITE PAGE A group of John Dickinson's most popular table designs made between 1976 and 1980: the "Y" table; the Square table; and the African table with feet. These monochromatic pieces were constructed from a plasterlike high-strength cement then painted. The handmade texture was the result of Dickinson's experience with clay molding. He later modified the tables to create versions that incorporated a lamp on top.

own design firm in San Francisco in 1956, however, he worked for Lord & Taylor's department store, the W. & J. Sloane furniture company, and individual designers on various traditional decorating projects.

In 1965 he established his residence and design studio in a former firehouse in the Pacific Heights neighborhood of San Francisco, restoring the Victorian building (and keeping the fireman's pole intact). Now on his own, Dickinson started to mix classical forms and African and Etruscan sources with a contemporary quality. He was unafraid of bold experiments, stripping and bleaching a Viennese art nouveau table to emphasize silhouette over decoration.

The table was a focal point in the development of the monochromatic furniture and interiors Dickinson started offering his own clients. He was also acknowledging the lasting influence of British interior decorator Syrie Maugham, former wife of author W. Somerset Maugham, famous for introducing all-white and one-color room designs during the 1920s and '30s. Decorator Francis Elkins in Monterey, California, who used white-on-white tones and white with gray, influenced by Maugham and Frank, also had a lasting effect on Dickinson.

Dickinson created a very small group of elaborate and colorful pieces for the Drexel Furniture Company's 1965 Et Cetera line. The collection included a trompe l'oeil piece that served as a storage unit with a brick-patterned Victorian town house facade. In its next catalog Drexel offered Dickinson's oak and ironlike bibliothèque side table, which was described as "three large simulated books covered in leather with gold-leaf edging, with the middle book as a drawer and a bookmark for a drawer pull." The Brighton Pavilion table was based on the exotic nineteenth-century pavilion in London for Queen Victoria and Prince Albert. The table was finished in a yellow lacquer and vermilion trim with brass tassels on each side. Dickinson's furniture was meant to complement the Et Cetera line of accent pieces, including the ornate, gold-leaf picture-frame mirrors with pediments and the nineteenth-century neoclassical cabinets with Doric column corners. The printed and hand-painted trompe l'oeil detailing made the furniture difficult to mass-produce, so only prototypes and one-offs were constructed. The collection marked the beginning of Dickinson's move toward more literal, graphical, and representational forms.

Interior designer Sam Crocker, a longtime friend and occasional collaborator of Dickinson's, described the designer in a February 2008 interview as "a one-man show who did his own drawings and clay maquettes. Although he did not do his own wood carving, he was very talented and creative with his hands." Dickinson typically turned his maquettes over to artisans with whom he worked very closely on prototypes. Dickinson's white plaster pieces were an extension of his ongoing practice of clay molding. Using a plasterlike high-strength cement, specifically created for handcrafted designs, Dickinson reintroduced *faux bois*, a technique first popularized in the late nineteenth century for making objects out of plaster that are usually created from wood. Among his earliest plaster pieces were framed mirrors, hangers, and other practical objects for the couture section of the I. Magnin department store in San Francisco. The recurring motif in these pieces was a twiglike stub from a tree that may have been inspired by an art nouveau bronze tree-trunk lamp base that Dickinson had at home.

ABOVE LEFT Dickinson often adapted African and Etruscan motifs into contemporary styles as with this three-legged African table, made between 1976 and 1980. The African tables came in slightly different sizes, typically ranging from 17" × 20" to 22" × 26." The development process for the stools started with a hand-carved model, then a mold was made and cast in plaster. Like most of his pieces, the three-legged tables had a tag or molded label marked "John Dickinson San Francisco." As one of his best-known plaster pieces, it is often copied. **RIGHT** Dickinson's interpretation of the Greek X-leg table made between 1976 and 1980 is made of painted plaster with animal legs and hooves, a design element that recurs often in Dickinson's plaster pieces.

OPPOSITE PAGE An Etruscan chair (1975–79) is covered in white leather with lacquered-wood animal legs, a reinterpretation of the Georgian claw-foot chair from the eighteenth century. One of Dickinson's Etruscan chairs is in the permanent collection of the San Francisco Museum of Modern Art.

His relationship with the Magnin family generated numerous commissions, including the interiors for the I. Magnin store on Chicago's Michigan Avenue in 1971. For this store Dickinson designed carved wood panels for the dressing rooms and castle-like displays to emphasize the landmark Water Tower building that was visible from several of the store's windows.

By the mid-1970s Dickinson was producing his three-legged, African-inspired stools and lamps in white plaster, now among his most popular pieces with collectors. During this era he was also working more with metals, particularly galvanized tin, folding it to look like draped fabric for his table designs. He varied the faux drapery by applying brass trim along the base to enhance the simulated fabric appearance, commenting to the *Chicago Tribune* in 1975 that "if it were a table skirted in fabric, you'd never look at it twice…in steel it presents a surprise." While these pieces were astounding for their inventiveness and perfect execution, it is possible they were Dickinson's nod to the tapered, skirted chairs of Syrie Maugham.

Dickinson achieved greater public exposure and success for his furniture in 1978, when Macy's department store in San Francisco commissioned him to design a suite of pieces for customers to purchase or custom order (Luten Clarey Stern, Inc., in New York City made the furniture available to East Coast buyers). The arrangement came about largely through the involvement of Macy's with the San Francisco Museum of Modern Art and Dickinson's Bay Area clientele, many of whom were involved with the museum. Approximately twenty-five pieces appeared in drawing-room, studio-apartment, and bedroom settings. Collectively they were seen more as an exhibition than a showroom. The San Francisco design firm Randolph & Hein produced the pieces for Dickinson—an arrangement that signified the creative apex of his career.

At this time, Dickinson also introduced a faux rock or "quarry-stone" interlocking slab table carved in wood with a high-gloss white lacquer that could also be ordered in a cement finish. A modular, staggered chest of drawers, horizontally expandable to eighteen feet, was also available in a stone finish. The most expensive piece was a set of stacked chests in ascending smaller sizes that could be built up to twelve feet, with a parchment finish of weathered fabric. But the most striking in the Macy's group were Dickinson's lacquered wood bone designs for chairs, tables, and lamps. In describing the furniture, Dickinson said "I was after something mock primitive and surprising.… Designers usually have gone the other way, taking primitive design and refining it way beyond recognition. That way you usually end up with something banal. If you go the other way, as I did, you usually end up with something very peculiar looking but quite successful." The bone furniture was among Dickinson's most expressive work for its scale, proportion, and unusual, lighthearted form. In their stark elegance and surreal sophistication, the bone designs may have also reflected an acknowledgement of mortality by Dickinson, who died just two years later.

Dickinson's last major commission was for Carlene Safdie, owner of the Sonoma Mission Inn & Spa in California. A friend and patron of Dickinson's, Safdie considered him "a designer's designer" and hired him to redesign the interiors of the one-hundred-room resort hotel. Dickinson created each room's furniture and accessories in a single color—camel, taupe, or terra-cotta—to contrast with the white walls. The interiors, completed in 1980, have since been altered by a new owner. The only remaining Dickinson interior known to be extant is the Northern California home of longtime client Leo Keoshian, a renowned hand surgeon.

One of Dickinson's wealthiest clients was Phyllis Wattis, a generous patron of the arts in San Francisco. She donated her collection of Dickinson's work, created specifically for her home, to the San Francisco Museum of Modern Art. One of the last pieces he made for her was an Etruscan side chair in 1979. With back legs bent as if ready to leap, the chair's animal form supports the feeling of both action and stability. It is now part of the museum's permanent collection of 250 examples of Dickinson's designs. In 2003 the museum featured Dickinson's drawings for various projects alongside work from his own home in the exhibition *Fantasy and Function: The Furniture of John Dickinson*. The Metropolitan Museum of Art in New York recently added a Dickinson galvanized tin-skirted table to its modern design and architecture collection. And international interest in his work, particularly in France, continues to grow as collectors recognize Dickinson's uniqueness and affinity with Jean-Michel Frank.

The San Francisco design firm Randolph & Hein, the makers of the pieces for Dickinson's Macy's commission, currently holds the exclusive rights to produce several of his upholstered seating pieces, including the Celebration chair in white oak. A stackable modular cabinet, hand-lacquered in pewter or marble and finished on all sides, is also available, in addition to several Dickinson design lamps.

Dickinson's restrained yet imaginative aesthetic avoided design clichés with a flair that was independent of a particular period or style. The result is a lasting, expressive contemporary look free of anonymous, passing trends. **J.H.**

ABOVE LEFT Dickinson's Twig collection included furniture, mirrors, hangers, hooks, and this painted plaster table. It was initially designed in 1971 for the I. Magnin Department stores in Chicago and San Francisco. **CENTER** During the mid to late 1970s, Dickinson designed hand-carved wood pieces that were painted to look like stone or as if they had stone finishes. **RIGHT** The proportions of this carved-poplar armchair from the mid-seventies suggests a sense of light but sturdy balance with delicate animal legs and feet serving as pedestals minimizing contact with the floor.

OPPOSITE PAGE This galvanized tin table, c. 1975, is signed with a tag, "John Dickinson XLVI." The number 46 in Roman numerals possibly suggests Dickinson's age at the time or the piece number. This table was part of Dickinson's "faux-drapery" line of furniture. Metal was folded to look like fabric. This variation has brass trim along the base to further simulate the appearance of fabric.

ARTHUR ELROD

Few designers have transformed American interiors to the extent Arthur Elrod (1926–1974) did. With his uncanny ability to combine luxurious furnishings and informal lifestyles, Elrod created his own decidedly glamorous—and distinctly American—version of modernism. And one that has stood the test of time. The Hollywood Regency look so popular today—an eclectic mix of the highly decorative tempered with the sobriety of modernism—is something Elrod mastered in the 1950s. Upholstered pieces were plush despite their crisp lines, with fabrics ranging from muted desert hues to Jack Lenor Larsen's bright psychedelics. Highly polished lacquers were used for case goods and, in some instances, for wall treatments and architectural elements. And Elrod designed it all, including the floating cabinetry and pierced room dividers that would remain among his signature touches. "I think Arthur started a whole new approach to interior design through his customization of furniture, and integrating it into the space," said interior designer Marybeth Waterman, who began her career in the Elrod office. "It was appropriate and directly responsive to the architectural space."

Elrod's approach began to transform the field of interior design in 1954, when he opened his first studio in Palm Springs. A native of Atlanta, Elrod studied textile design at Clemson College (now Clemson University) and interior design at Chouinard Art Institute in Los Angeles. Following his schooling, Elrod worked in the interior design department of the W. & J. Sloane department store in San Francisco. His 1954 move to Palm Springs, a popular location for vacation homes, provided Elrod access to the Hollywood celebrities, politicians, and captains of industry who would become his clients (often commissioning projects from Elrod both in Palm Springs and "back home"). Over the years, he designed interiors for Bob Hope, Lucille Ball, Claudette Colbert, Winthrop Rockefeller, and Jack Benny, among many others. Almost immediately, his interiors were published in the *Los Angeles Times* and *Architectural Digest*. In fact, Paige Rense, *Architectural Digest*'s editor-in-chief, noted during her keynote address at an Elrod symposium sponsored by the Palm Springs Art Museum that the frequent publication of Elrod's work was pivotal in establishing the magazine's reputation as a prominent publication of sophisticated interiors.

Although first impressions of Elrod's interiors do not immediately suggest understatement, it was this quality he prized as the "mark of perfection," according to a 1962 story in the *Los Angeles Times* magazine *Home*. Indeed, Elrod is perhaps best known for his generous, unapologetic use of vibrant hues: yellows, oranges, blues, and greens. Yet closer inspection

OPPOSITE PAGE This orange lacquered and faux snakeskin console, c. 1965, was designed for a home in Rancho Mirage, California. The blending of texture and vibrant color is typical of Elrod's style and epitomizes the lifestyle of the groovy sixties as interpreted for laid-back California living.

ABOVE LEFT Arthur Elrod's house in Palm Springs is perched above the town. Elrod's residence, designed by architect John Lautner, has become an icon of modern architecture and design. In the spring 1970 issue, *Architectural Digest* referred to the Elrod house as a "modern palace in the desert." Designed in 1968, the home boasts an open plan ideal for mod-era entertaining. In 1974, Lautner told the *Los Angeles Times* that Elrod was "everything a client should be. He had an understanding of architecture and he was always open to new ideas. He never wanted to do the safe thing." **RIGHT** Elrod and his colleagues at Arthur Elrod Associates designed a number of custom pieces for the interior of his Palm Springs home. To the right of the fireplace is a "floating" sideboard—an Elrod trademark—made especially to match the curvature of the exterior wall. The sofa and low bench (backless, to preserve the views) were also designed by Elrod Associates and made by the Martin Brattrud firm (one of Elrod's trusted manufacturers). The upholstery is a Jack Lenor Larsen stretch fabric.

OPPOSITE PAGE This project was published in the *Los Angeles Times*, September 24, 1961. A single room decorated in two different styles, it was Elrod's version of the "French Touch," although the flokati rug added a definite bohemian look. Elrod could just as easily have created the alternative space, which the *Times* called "Colorfully Contemporary."

reveals judicious restraint. "The pleasure one experiences in beholding an interesting room," Elrod wrote, "must be balanced by an overtone of ease and naturalness." The result was what *Los Angeles Times* writer Dan MacMaster, in his 1974 tribute to Elrod, called "a subtle kind of opulence that avoided the ostentatious." Such "subtle opulence" was revealed not only in Elrod's interiors but also in the wide range of custom furniture and architectural elements he designed for these projects.

Elrod's most successful interiors were those showcasing pieces designed in his own studio. His Palm Springs residence, designed in 1968 by architect John Lautner, is just one example. There, Elrod designed semicircular sofas and upholstered benches that corresponded perfectly to its floor plan of overlapping circles. In such projects, the furnishings and architecture were blended seamlessly, due in part to Elrod's acute sense of scale. "Scale plays such a subtle role in decorating," he wrote in *Home Decorating* magazine, published by the *Los Angeles Times* in 1964, "that its importance often is overlooked. Yet maddening problems develop when it is ignored." By designing his own pieces, Elrod was able to exercise careful control over the scale of the furnishings, an important step in controlling the entire project.

Although there was no recognizable "Elrod look," his trademark attention to detail was evident throughout his body of work. Following the 1972 completion of the interior for Johnson Publishing, Inc. (publishers of *Ebony* and *Jet*), Elrod's partner, William Raiser, told *Interior Design*, "We spent more time on custom design and detailing than any other job in our experience… we shipped by forty-foot trailers and flew many craftsmen from Los Angeles to Chicago." The commission was awarded as a direct result of their prior—and equally successful—interior design for the Johnsons' Chicago high-rise residence, where, according to *Architectural Digest*, every room was "minutely detailed."

The Sigmund Edelstone residence, another Chicago high-rise Elrod designed in close collaboration with Raiser, was, wrote *Architectural Digest*, "one of the most extraordinary interiors of their careers." And again, the success of the design lay in its attention to detail. "The architect is a perfectionist. The interior designers are perfectionists. And, the client is a perfectionist's perfectionist." Elrod himself told *Architectural Digest*, "Mr. Edelstone has a great eye for scale, and is incredibly accurate. He can tell if something is off 1/16 of an inch." However demanding Edelstone was, the Elrod office must have exceeded his expectations. When Edelstone bought a vacation home in Palm Springs, he once again called on Elrod. (Following Elrod's untimely death, the project was undertaken by longtime associate Hal Broderick.)

These details were a result of Elrod's firsthand involvement in each of the projects undertaken by his office. Elrod himself did many of his preliminary sketches, relying on his staff to produce the perspective renderings and scaled detail drawings. He would select the materials, finishes, and colors himself. "He was very hands-on from the inception of the design," said Waterman. It was not unusual for Elrod to specify custom-dyed yarns, for example. "He would take the fabric and actually coordinate it to the room environment and the color palette that he was after." And the color palette itself was an Elrod innovation, according to Michael Calloway,

Elrod's nephew, who, beginning at age twelve, worked periodically in his uncle's office. "He borrowed his palette from the desert landscape in many of his interiors," said Calloway, "which was new at the time."

To be as successful—and prolific—as he was, Elrod relied not only on his own staff, but also on an informal network of expert craftsmen to realize his vision. "We had people who built all our things," said Mari Pasqualetti, who worked in the Elrod office from 1968 to 1970. "Everything was custom built-in—all the case pieces, headboards, whatever." For Elrod, the people involved with his work became family. "He didn't flit around and use a lot of different people to do things," noted Pasqualetti. "He would stay with one group if he loved their work and their work was superb. Everything was absolutely star quality… the highest level you can imagine."

Elrod's commitment to quality gained his firm immediate acclaim. According to Rense, when it came to interior design, "the feeling was they *were* Palm Springs. If you had a house or wanted a house in Palm Springs, there just wasn't anyone else. They were the people to go to." Clients, rarely disappointed, trusted Elrod implicitly, giving his firm carte blanche. Elrod had a reputation for "how beautifully he could combine things," former president of the American Institute of Decorators Adele Faulkner told the *Los Angeles Times* in 1974. "He could do contemporary houses with softness and warmth, and he had a grasp of the facts of living in our time." And, added Faulkner, "he had a great love of people that came out in his work." His relationships with clients were very professional ("He might have worked with a client for ten years, twenty years," but, noted Pasqualetti, "he never addressed women by their first names, *ever*."), Elrod's charm was as legendary as his design talent. "He just made you think that you were the only person in the room," said Pasqualetti. "He just exuded star quality, and it wasn't fake. He was that way with everyone—*everyone*."

Although Elrod demanded only the best, he wasn't afraid to take chances. "Arthur was an innovator—he was not afraid to try anything," recalled Waterman. "When I was working with him, he was laminating fabric—putting resin over fabric and using it as countertops—nobody was doing that. And he was under-lighting sofas—I think he was one of the first people to do that." Calloway said Elrod would "use materials no one else did," gathering inspiration from unlikely sources. "Once, he saw a cracked windshield… went back to the studio and was making designs with cracked glass."

In 1974 Elrod and Raiser were killed in a car crash. Elrod was only forty-eight at the time and at the top of his game. In 1970 Elrod had told the *Los Angeles Times*, "I knew that decorating would be my work forever." In fact, his work—a career spanning only twenty short years—is perhaps more enduring than even Elrod would have imagined. Today, the look he pioneered—with its delicate balance of brightly polished finishes and rich textures—is captivating a new generation. Understatement, it seems—at least as interpreted by Arthur Elrod—is never out of style.

Because Elrod's furniture designs were such an integral part of the interiors for which they were designed, they rarely come up at auction. Nevertheless, pieces attributed to Elrod do sometimes turn up in the many vintage furniture shops in and around Palm Springs—and occasionally in Los Angeles, too. **P. W.**

ABOVE LEFT For the Sigmund Edelstone residence in Chicago (1972), Elrod's partner William Raiser designed the furniture with great attention to detail. The sofa, for example, is upholstered to be seamless. According to an article in *Architectural Digest* where the sofa was published upon completion, "craftsmen from the Prentice Company were flown from Los Angeles to build the sofa in the Chicago apartment." **CENTER** The hanging console and bold yellow color were both signature elements in Elrod interiors; always custom-made, he often used them in a room when case goods were needed. **RIGHT** Arthur Elrod, c. 1970, when he was forty-four years old.

OPPOSITE PAGE TOP For the home of Mr. and Mrs. Roy G. Woods in Oklahoma City (1966), Elrod designed a unique bed finished in a pearlized lacquer that could be raised electronically for television viewing or reading. Its finials match the architectural details and court scenes depicted in the room's Indian-themed wallpaper. **BOTTOM** The "club room" at the Woods residence (Oklahoma City, 1966) was designed to showcase Roy Woods's art collection. Built-in cabinets were custom designed, as were the sofas in Elrod's signature bright citrus palette and all were made by the Prentice Company with whom Elrod frequently worked. Mr. and Mrs. Woods were among Elrod's many clients who commissioned multiple residences. When they purchased a vacation home in Palm Springs, they turned to Elrod for its extensive remodeling and interior design.

WILLIAM HAINES

During the 1930s and early '40s William (Billy) Haines (1900–1973) largely defined the Hollywood Regency decorative style with his sleek combination of custom-made furniture, interiors, and antiques for the homes of the film industry's most successful personalities. Based on a plush, glamorous, and romantic style, Hollywood Regency was independent of a single architectural theme, although it was a neoclassical mix of Georgian, Italianate, and Rococo. Haines distinguished the style by incorporating art and design from China, Japan, and other Asian countries, known as chinoiserie, an aesthetic popularized in eighteenth-century English interiors. Haines used chinoiserie for whimsy and lightness, but it also offered an exotic and unique appeal. As Haines said, "I have often found mixing periods quite normal and often exciting." His innovative use was sometimes referred to as Chinese Chippendale.

The paradox of blending dramatic and contemporary styles contributed to Haines's signature couture interiors. He also acknowledged the influence of fashion, explaining that "dress had to come before furniture design. You see it through the ages, through the open arms of Louis XV chairs to allow panniers [side hoops] of dress, through the lack of arms and rest of Victorian furniture to accommodate the hoop skirt." Commenting years later, "today's dress is long and slinky. We rest on our spines and the base of the neck. That's why we use the overstuffed pieces." For an exclusive clientele not interested in designs that were commercially available, Haines produced specially crafted, elegant, often one-of-a-kind pieces made with the finest materials. Haines, who thought of himself as a decorator and designed furniture throughout his career, did not separate this work from his interiors. Instead, he created an all-encompassing look that integrated architecture, interior, and landscape. He was one of the few decorators at the time to offer full design services with an architect and draftsmen on staff. Although actual construction of furniture pieces was not done at his studio, Haines hired talented local artists, craftsmen, and workshops. In a way, Haines was like a film director, thoughtfully composing furniture and interiors, supervising various people while allowing for creativity (and credit) to help produce his vision for each client.

Haines, a self-taught designer from Staunton, Virginia, was always interested in antiques and furniture, although this was not his first career. Before becoming a preeminent decorator, Haines was a leading man with star status in silent films during the 1920s and early '30s, playing comic and romantic characters under contract at MGM Studios. While still appearing in films, he opened an antique shop on La Brea Avenue in Hollywood near Sunset Boulevard,

OPPOSITE PAGE Haines produced an oversized three-legged coffee table wrapped in leather with hand-tooled detailing along the top edge for the Hollywood screenwriter Nunnally Johnson. The table was a focal point of the commission, which was completed in the mid-1940s. Johnson's coproducer at the time, William Goetz, then hired Haines in 1949 to design the interiors and furniture for his home. A similar table was created for the expansive Goetz house. The Stergis Company produced the designer's leather pieces, including this one, according to Haines's specifications: 17⅝" × 97⅛" × 42⅜".

ABOVE LEFT William Haines in his Brentwood home, c. 1972. He bought the home in 1944 and immediately went to work renovating and decorating it to his standards, especially since he used it as a showcase for his talents by bringing clients and prospective ones there.
RIGHT The Haines Foster Inc. showroom on the Sunset Strip in Los Angeles was also known as the Haines Studio. After opening in 1935, it was the setting for gallery exhibitions of such artists as Cézanne, Van Gogh, Gauguin, Picasso, Renoir, and Hopper. The in situ arrangement of furniture allowed clients to experience Haines's unique blend of art and antiques with custom-designed interiors and furniture.

OPPOSITE PAGE TOP This inviting living room was designed in 1950 for a state-of-the-art home built by Haines and the architect A. Quincy Jones. It featured such innovative details as hidden cabinets that housed film projectors and extra card tables, and the white carpet was recessed into the oak floor. **BOTTOM** The 1941 screening room for the Jack Warner residence in Beverly Hills featured Haines's popular tufted Hostess chairs (also known as the Brentwood chair) in red velvet. The long sofa reappears in 1955 when the Warner's commissioned Haines to design the interiors for their Fifth Avenue penthouse apartment in New York City.

which further established his expertise in antiques and decorative arts. Haines's business partner was Mitchell Foster, who had made the move to Hollywood with Haines from New York City. Foster also served as Haines's film stand-in. Their business, Haines Foster Decorators, specialized in high-quality works. They furnished interiors for many of the homes of Haines's costars and friends. Joan Crawford, also under contract at MGM, was a lifelong friend and Haines's first client in 1929.

By 1934 Haines stopped acting to give his full attention and creativity to interior design. He understood the glamour and excitement of Hollywood and was a part of it, even if he was no longer in front of the camera, commenting, "I've never been quite divorced from show business. Many of my friends are my clients. I feel part of them. I'm still an actor who's hanging some curtains." He also playfully said that he always included custom-made mirrors in clients' bedrooms because film "people like to see how they look even when they are sleeping." Haines's transition to a decorator was immediate, receiving full-scale commissions from many people in the industry, including film director George Cukor, whose home was an early example of Haines's mixture of chinoiserie and antique English furniture. For the estate of studio chief Jack Warner, Haines designed several modernist built-in furniture pieces, such as a sofa with an end table and a bed with an attached bookcase. Concealed shelving was another feature.

Haines was frequently invited by clients to update their primary homes or work on their vacation homes. When he redesigned the Warner house in the 1950s, he placed his Hostess chairs around a custom game table. Haines considered the Warner house "one of the most outstanding jobs we have ever done." The low-back, armless, walnut Hostess chair, with smooth yellow leather upholstery, was later modified with a tufted seat that added to its plush feel. Haines acknowledged the "variation on a theme" as part of his aesthetic, adding "there is nothing original in the world. A sofa is a sofa, a chair is a chair." The Hostess chair became one of Haines's most highly regarded designs. During this era he also introduced his Conference chair, similar to his Round Back chair, with hand-tooled leather that created a rich, subtle detail. Another popular design was the Seniah chair ("Haines" spelled backward), an armchair with walnut legs upholstered with quilted silk canvas. He would also upholster the legs of different chairs and stools with matching fabric.

In 1935 Haines and Foster moved their design studio to Sunset Plaza on Sunset Boulevard in West Hollywood and continued to offer unique objects and ultraluxurious furnishings to an affluent clientele. The studio also hosted gallery exhibitions featuring the works of Cézanne, Van Gogh, Gauguin, Picasso, and Renoir. Other exhibitions included postimpressionist American painters Charles Burchfield, Edward Hoppper, and Henry Lee McFee. Haines's diverse personal preferences later included artists John Singer Sargent and Marino Marini, whose works he had in his own home.

One of the highlights of the Haines Foster design period was their participation in the 1939 Golden Gate International Exposition in San Francisco. For this event they created the Desert Living Room, a modern setting that featured a pair of Haines's saddle-stitched leather game chairs. The use of bamboo at the exhibition was a common thread that naturally fit with

One of the 1954 room settings in the William Haines showroom in Beverly Hills shows off a set of conference chairs upholstered in red hand-tooled leather around a mahogany table decorated with ceramic chinoiserie accents. All are Haines's designs.

ABOVE LEFT A publicity photograph of William Haines was taken in the late twenties when he was under contract with MGM Studios. Haines was a popular actor playing comic romantic leads in dozens of films. By 1934, Haines left his acting career and devoted himself to antiques and interior design. RIGHT Haines was known for incorporating antiques or sculptures into his lamps. The table lamp on the left is cast metal with a Pompeian bronze, the center is a wooden sculpture with a hole drilled into the base to hide the cord, and for the floor lamp on the right Haines used an antique Egyptian mask as its only decoration. The mask lamp sold at Christie's New York in 2006 for $26,400.

Haines's chinoiserie. A couple of years later Haines worked with decorator Tony Duquette for the Asian-themed Mocambo nightclub in Hollywood that also used bamboo. On occasion he made one-of-a-kind lamps for Duquette.

The exposition also included furniture by Wharton Esherick, Josef Frank, Tommi Parzinger, and others. Architect and designer Samuel Marx bought the leather chairs for himself—Haines was one of the few designers whose work Marx placed in his apartment alongside his own. It is possible that over the years Haines may have made additional pieces for Marx. At the time, Marx was in Los Angeles working with architect A. C. Martin on the Streamline Moderne building for the new May Department Store on Wilshire Boulevard and Fairfax Avenue. Haines worked with Marx on the furniture area of the store for its opening in 1940. The room settings and furniture also served as a backdrop for advertisements featuring women's clothing. Marx married into the May Family and was the brother-in-law of Tom May, the head of the department store. It is likely that Marx's appreciation for the detail and originality of Haines's furniture and interiors brought about an introduction to the Mays. Marx and Haines collaborated again in 1952 on the Holmby Hills home of Tom and Anita May in Los Angeles. The modern indoor-outdoor living space was filled with Haines's custom-made contemporary furniture and sophisticated blend of chinoiserie. Haines's close relationship with the Mays resulted in his decorating seven houses for various members of the family. Jean Mathison, who was Haines's assistant for almost twenty years, recalled, "he used to joke that his name should be William May Haines because he did so much work for them."

When Foster retired in 1945, Haines renamed the business William Haines Inc. and eventually moved the studio to South Canon Drive, near Olympic Boulevard in Beverly Hills. He was joined by Ted Graber, the son of a cabinetmaker who made furniture for Haines. Graber learned the craft from his father and became Haines's protégé. Their association lasted almost thirty years, with Haines often attributing much of his success to Graber.

The new Haines studio, completed in 1948, was a showroom for the decorator's contemporary interiors blended with antiques, a combination that Haines became known for creating. For the showroom, he designed a cantilevered corner sofa, a small iron table with a Lucite top mounted to a wall, and tambour doors to hide unsightly metal file cabinets. In the workroom, Haines designed a twelve-foot table with a bleached cork top. Above the table a suspended light box provided storage. For matching colors correctly and viewing materials under different light, the light box could switch between incandescent and fluorescent light.

One of the most notable craftsmen working for Haines was European artist Paul Féher. During Féher's forty years as a freelance draftsman with Haines, he developed most of the detailed sketches and renderings. These were turned over to local craft shops and cabinetmakers who were hired almost exclusively to produce the work. One of the firms they worked with was Eastern Embroidery in Los Angeles, known for making Liberace's beaded capes. For Haines the company hand made quilted upholstery, bedspreads, velvets, and silks. Féher also worked on furniture designs in addition to painting wallpapers, ceilings, and, in earlier days, art deco–style murals. Michael Morrison, another designer who worked with Haines from 1950 to 1960, also contributed to the Haines style by creating many of the complementary accessories and lighting fixtures. Artist Gene Young was employed to paint furniture and perfect colors and finishes.

For many years, the Stergis M. Stergis firm provided leather-covered furniture pieces for Haines. Stergis had gained a reputation as the highest-quality leather company by working on

ABOVE The chairs above, aptly named the Hostess chairs, are from the Warner estate and were designed to surround the card tables in the bar room.

the furniture for the executive offices, dining rooms, and exhibition rooms at the Los Angeles Times building when it opened in 1934. In later years Howard-Robin crafted the sofas and ottomans for Haines, eventually marketing its own line of furniture.

It is difficult to estimate the number of furniture pieces Haines made over his lifetime, because most of the work remains with the original owners. Approximately half of the three thousand renderings, drawings, and illustrations made by the Haines Studio are furniture designs for the more than four hundred homes he worked on. Since there was never a formal "line" of furnishings, Haines created more chair designs, in response to every client who wanted custom-designed chairs for their dining tables, living rooms, and other areas. Mass production was always avoided, as Mathison stated: "if Mr. Haines was approached by a manufacturer to design a line of furniture he would have turned it down because he was strictly a custom-designer, that's why the furniture is so precious today." Haines did not need to promote his practice or style. It was not necessary, especially in the 1950s, when clients paid $50,000 or more to employ his decorative services for a single room.

After Haines's death in 1973, Graber kept the Haines aesthetic active by designing for many significant commissions, most notably the White House décor for President Ronald Reagan and his wife, Nancy. In 1989 Graber turned the firm over to his protégé, decorator Peter Schifando, who with Jean Mathison wrote the book *Class Act: William Haines, Legendary Hollywood Decorator* (2005).

Today Schifando, with his company Lindley Associates in Los Angeles, offers authentic, custom-ordered, signature pieces following the exact specifications and quality defined by Haines. In some cases the original craftspeople or shops that made the furniture during Haines's time continue to craft the pieces and chairs, including the Seniah, Brentwood (Hostess), Conference, and pull up chairs. **J.H.**

PAUL LÁSZLÓ

Paul László (1900–1993) is so closely associated with what has come to be called California modern that it is easy to overlook his European roots. Born at the height of the belle époque, he sidestepped the fading Wiener Werkstatte of his youth, as well as the ascendant Bauhaus style that dominated design during the years he worked in Europe, and remained fairly true to his personal style of elegant modernism, tempered by traditional touches and softened by the bold use of color and texture. Working as an architect and designer in Vienna and Stuttgart before emigrating to Los Angeles, he brought a European sensibility to the land of sunshine and scenery, leaving his imprint on modern design and developing the audience for custom furniture of the highest quality. László had a productive and remarkably long career, stretching close to sixty years.

Furniture was his birthright. László was born to a prosperous and cultured Hungarian family in the small town of Debrecen, and his grandparents were furniture manufacturers. When he was one year old the family moved to Szombathely, near Vienna, where his father opened a large furniture store and manufactory. A German governess watched over Paul and his five siblings, and it was a happy childhood filled with art, music, and refined tastes. In the oral history on file at the University of California, Los Angeles entitled "Designing with Spirit: Paul László," László reports that his mother annually redecorated their home, and that his father always took him along on his business trips to Austria and Budapest.

At age fourteen, László was sent to study in Vienna, where his interest in art was awakened. After a brief stint in the Hungarian army in World War I—he saw action on the Italian front a month before the war ended—László returned to school to study art in Stuttgart at the Staatliche Akademie der Bilden den Künste. Bored and restless after two years, he applied for and miraculously obtained a very junior position with the Cologne-based architectural firm of Fritz August Breuhaus, a large and successful office with commissions throughout Europe. Working fourteen to sixteen hours a day, he managed to acquire enough skills to help on both architectural and interiors projects. He also formed a lifelong commitment to the efficiencies of a small office, convinced that a large firm required client cultivation and person-nel management (at which he claimed to have few skills), leaving little time to actually design.

László next worked for Berlin-based architect Leo Nachtlicht until, young and adventurous and feeling the pinch of Berlin's postwar inflation, he went to Paris, which in his oral history he pronounced "cold, rainy, and unfriendly." Speaking no French and finding no employment,

ABOVE LEFT A portrait of Paul László, c. 1960.
RIGHT The reception room at László, Inc. in Beverly Hills in 1941. László was one of the most unique contributors to California modernism. *Time* magazine profiled him in 1952 dubbing him "The Millionaire's Architect."

OPPOSITE PAGE László's Brentwood home was published in *Town & Country* in 1953. Seen here is a similar armchair as shown on the previous page. Again, László's exemplary design is evident in the sumptuous materials, like the hand-painted mural and wood-veneered ceiling. His layout is ingenious as well; for example, the mural is a sliding screen that opens to enlarge the living area when desired yet the beautiful painted scene remains visible.

he departed for Vienna, where he opened his own office early in 1924. (Austria at the time had only a handful of excellent architects, so the move was not quite as daring as it might have appeared.) Three years later, with a growing client base in Germany, László moved his practice in 1927 to Stuttgart, where his principal clients were the Schildknecht furniture firm, a leather chair manufacturer named Knoll and the Fleischer paper factory, for whom László annually designed new paper napkins, claiming credit for creating the first printed toilet paper. In 1928, underwritten by Schildknecht, László participated in a Dusseldorf competition among an international field of architects. His design of a lady's apartment won an award, and his fame grew, along with his commissions.

During László's Stuttgart years, 1927 to 1936, Bauhaus reached its austere zenith, but he alwaysinsisted that he was not influenced by its work, though the rest of the world was. He considered himself unconnected to movements—"I didn't look left or right"—always following his individual muse. "I don't want to be influenced by anybody," he said. After a lifetime of design, he was proud that his earlier works look as if he might have designed them in his late years.

As he would throughout his career, László almost always designed and controlled every element of his work—the structure and the furnishings, which included furniture, fabrics, lamps, and other decorative accessories, down to the smallest details. Everything was custom-made by a cadre of freelancers who worked regularly for him. László believed that control of every detail was essential to success, and he brought this conviction to America, where it continued to inform all his custom design work.

Among the important projects László designed during his Stuttgart years were the remodeling of the Bleyle and Jeittele homes. For the large residence of Max and Maria Bleyle (1928–29), László covered the entrance hall floor in a custom, hand-woven checkerboard carpeting, for warmth and noise reduction, instead of the usual marble. The walls and ceilings of the garden room and dressing room were covered in eighteen coats of yellow lacquer—a substance László was partial to throughout his career, often using it later to stunning effect on his custom furniture.

The Jeittele home was designed for an excellent amateur musician who conducted musicales at home. László created a distinctive music room with built-in, finely veneered display cabinetry, and walls and ceiling covered, uniquely, in gold-leafed four-inch squares, which served an acoustical as well as artistic purpose.

By the mid-1930s, László's career was thriving, but Europe was rumbling with adumbrations of war. Like so many others who could, László (who was half-Jewish) managed to get a visa and, at age thirty-six, emigrated to the United States. Arriving at New York's elegant Hampshire House hotel sporting fifteen pieces of spiffy new luggage and a green Borsalino hat, he must have cut quite the dapper figure. Ten days later, László and a friend drove across the country, ending up in Los Angeles, which he loved from the first moment.

ABOVE László worked regularly with a group of highly talented and unique artists. The shades pictured (left and right) were handwoven by Maria Kipp. Kipp, a German emigrant, was a well-known textile designer who created most of her pieces by hand. Her work was frequently included in László's interiors or added to individual pieces. She used woven cloth, chenille, wood strips, and Lurex strands, a synthetic fiber with a metallic appearance. F. F. Kern created the lamp bases (on the right and center) in addition to doing sculpted woodwork for László, notably the Dali table. One lamp (right), standing nearly four feet high, has a hand-painted glass-tile base. It is one of the most iconic László pieces and it appeared not only in his home but also in the interiors of several of his most successful projects. Karin and Ernst van Leyden of Botega Karin produced numerous hand-painted tile pieces including the one pictured here. László used their tiles as wall-mounted decorations or they were incorporated into pieces of furniture.

OPPOSITE PAGE This private residence designed by László captures many of the stylistic examples that characterize his body of work. The lamps' handwoven shades mirror the curtains; the sofa and generously sized armchairs—a classic László design—are complemented by an imaginatively shaped coffee table.

Despite speaking no English, he quickly settled in—his reputation was not unknown on American shores—taking an apartment in Beverly Hills and joining a tennis club filled with Hollywood types, from whom he almost immediately got his first commissions: a shoe salon and a jewelry store. He took office space on Wilshire Boulevard, remaining there until he moved his business in 1941 to Rodeo Drive, where he had the opportunity to design the building, landscaping, fabrics, and furnishings. From this elegant showroom, he sold home furnishings and modern art objects, as well as his services as an architect and designer. (It should be noted that László loved the company of Hollywood celebrities and delighted in counting them, and their relatives, among his star-studded client roster.)

Modernism was slower to take root in America than in Europe, but by the mid-1930s it was fashionable in Southern California, and the field was fertile for someone of László's talents and ambition. Never as famous or as sought after as Richard Neutra, László considered himself a more flexible and eclectic designer, less doctrinaire in the application of design tenets. "I believe his style was his personal religion," he said of Neutra. "I was more flexible." While László used a great deal of glass and wood so typical of California design, his take on modern was neither hard-edged nor linear, instead incorporating traces of a softening traditionalism. His furniture was notably comfortable. He often used color boldly, and it is this, as much as the sumptuous textures of lacquer, veneers, marble, brick, flagstone, and gold leaf, not to mention the warm effect of hand-woven fabrics, that gave his homes variety as well as a distinctive character. Of his version of modernism, he said, "It has, I believe, a certain charm, which is missing in some other modern people."

László's emerging American style owed much to Los Angeles's distinctive topography and constant sunshine. His structures accommodated challenging sharp hillsides and irregular lots; vast amounts of glass framed spectacular views; deep roof overhangs provided shade. Houses were oriented backward, away from the street and the narrow lot confines, and toward rear gardens and pools. An open-plan U shape around a central patio pulled the eye toward the interior, and visually integrated the outdoors and the interior.

László worked, as in the past, with a group of skilled craftsmen. For more than forty years, a firm of German artisans made most of his furniture. Standard Cabinet Works fabricated his built-in fixtures and paneling, F. F. Kern created artistic wood carving, and Karin and Ernst van Leyden of Botega Karin produced the modernistic hand-painted glass found in many László projects. He worked with several weavers to create his textiles, including Maria Kipp and one Mrs. Dorothy Liebes in San Francisco. For printed fabrics, he often used firms in Zürich and Stuttgart because they were willing to run small lots. He consistently produced homes, each unique, that were distinctively modern, sumptuous, and comfortable.

When László had his druthers, he controlled every detail of a project, down to the ashtrays. "People would hire him, go to Europe, and come back six or nine months later to find the paintings on the wall, the toilet paper on the roller, and slippers by the bed," said Julius Shulman, the acclaimed architecture photographer, in the 1958 book *Paul László: Interior and Industrial Designer*, published in Zurich by the László firm. László, to the chagrin of some architectural purists, considered decorating as integral to the project as designing.

László's particular skills are evident in the 1940–41 home he built on a difficult lot in Holmby Hills for producer-writer Joan Harrison. The property was both narrow and steep, requiring two retaining walls, but by using his favored U-shape, László provided a vista from every room. As described in the February 1944 issue of *Architectural Forum*, "On opening the entrance door, the entire patio area with its view beyond opens up, and the house, far from seeming constricted, becomes a generous, informally open space, without clear divisions between interior and exterior living areas…. In an open plan such as this the extension of the architect's function [to design all the furniture and accessories] is absolutely essential, since separation of adjoining spaces is frequently achieved solely by introducing an…interior device, the decorating feature being used to define the plan."

After the war—László was in the U.S. Army briefly—he built his own showcase home (1946–47) on Carmelina Avenue in Brentwood, living there for more than thirty years with his wife and two children. For privacy, the five-thousand-square-foot house was set far back on the lot, and because much of the house was thus obscured, he used glass throughout. Seclusion was furthered by twenty-four running feet of a deep protective overhang, and a stone front that blended in with the landscape. The house was centered by a large outdoor living area with a pool and expansive terrace. The September 1956 issue of *Arts & Architecture* magazine described the large living room as charcoal, the textured wood ceiling and the carpet as pearl white, and the furniture partly black and partly white lacquer. The floor and walls of the dining room were all white, and the furniture was bleached white maple. For contrast, the chairs were upholstered in cardinal-red leather.

The ambitious commission László undertook for John and Floreine Hudspeth in 1951–52 in Prineville, Oregon, involved a main residence of over twelve thousand square feet on a seven-thousand-acre ranch with ten bedrooms and spectacular mountain views. More than one hundred custom accessories were made for this home. Hudspeth, who owned lumber mills, originally intended to build what amounted to a small village, which didn't happen, although the shopping center plans were published in the October 1954 *Arts & Architecture* magazine. Among the more distinctive pieces were a fish-shaped table with a top of blue-green seashells; a ten-and-a-half-foot sideboard-buffet of red and black lacquer; a suite of furniture of green lacquer with pink leather; a set of eight dining chairs of light walnut with red patent-leather upholstery; and a number of pieces that utilized Lucite, which interested him as most innovative materials did.

Simultaneous with his home-design projects, László maintained a thriving commercial practice, often producing unusual structures. The 1938 Crenshaw movie theater at 3020 Crenshaw

ABOVE From 1950 to 1952 László was fully occupied with the largest commission of his career: the Hudspeth estate in Oregon. The residence measured over 12,000 square feet and László was involved with all aspects of the design. The Hudspeths also commissioned him to design many of their commercial properties. The final bill totaled $2 million. This sideboard was placed in their dining room and was used as a buffet and to display art. The beauty of the piece is in the details: inlaid corrugated doors with the pattern repeated on the interior and thick Lucite pulls. The base is a deep midnight-blue lacquer. László never hesitated to use strong colors.

OPPOSITE PAGE László's Beverly Hills home was featured in *Architectural Forum* in 1941 and the article stated that the architect's style was "synonymous with California modern." And as seen in these photographs, László's homes were invariably superb venues for presenting his vision as an architect, decorator, and designer of California modern. Shown above are the generous proportions of his living room with a wall in flagstone and screens inlaid with handwoven textiles. Below is his grand office with a view of the plush back patio from his exotic wood-veneered desk.

Opposite page top and bottom: © J. Paul Getty Trust. Used with permission. Julius Shulman Photography Archive. Research Library at the Getty Research Institute.

ABOVE LEFT The large sofa, which was probably made for a specific room and even a specific place in the room, was custom-made with an asymmetrical bulbous form and Lucite legs. **CENTER** Material, color, and form are the defining characteristics of László's approach. The tabletop is inlaid with a mosaic of iridescent aqua-colored seashells, the base is teak and finished with a dark stain and has brass-capped feet, and the table was made for his steadfast clients, the Hudspeths. **RIGHT** The petite dressing chair is on a swiveling Lucite base and was also part of the Hudspeth collection.

OPPOSITE PAGE László's career alternated between commercial projects, such as showrooms and casinos, and high-end residential projects for such celebrities as Cary Grant, Barbara Stanwyck, and Gloria Vanderbilt. With such professional experience it was fitting that László was chosen in 1943 to design the ultraglamorous Beverly Hills Hotel, the preferred Hollywood destination at the time. László not only designed the Rodeo Room but he also did the Polo Lounge and several deluxe bungalows.

Avenue in Los Angeles, now the Kokusai Theater, was undoubtedly one of the few to ever have a port cochère. The 1946 Eddy Harth Building at 9687 Wilshire Boulevard utilized gold filament in the unusually enormous display glass and was the first really modern storefront on Wilshire Boulevard. A major redesign of Bullock's department store in Beverly Hills led to years of design work there and at Bullock's in Pasadena and Palm Springs, as well as work for Saks Fifth Avenue (Beverly Hills), Orbach's (New York), and Robinson's (Newport Beach, California).

Other notable commercial projects included designing Fashion Square shopping mall in Scottsdale, Arizona, and Hall's department stores in Kansas City, Missouri; the Beverly Hills Hotel (including the Rodeo Room and several of the famous bungalows) and the Stardust Hotel dining room in Las Vegas; and the interior offices of the McCulloch Corporation, the Sunbeam Lighting Company, Walston and Company, and the American City Bank Building, all in Los Angeles. He also did work on the clubhouses at the Arizona Country Club in Phoenix, and at the Brentwood Country Club, which he joined in the early fifties and—never one to miss an opportunity—picked up many jobs from members who were movie-industry luminaries.

László seemed to attract oddball assignments. After completing a 1955 home remodeling for John and Frances Hertz in Woodland Hills, he was asked to build the couple a prototype bomb shelter, which before it was finished involved the chairman of the Atomic Energy Commission and Edward Teller, of hydrogen bomb fame, not to mention the efforts of engineers and technicians who installed an elevator, generator, Geiger counter, and who knows what else. In 1950 the magazine *Popular Mechanics* published his design of a futuristic city called "Atomville," a wildly imaginative conjecture about houses under earth mounds, which served as helipads.

Although he is most noted for his designs and labor-intensive custom-made interiors, László for brief periods did some commercial designing of mass-produced pieces, mostly for the Herman Miller firm in New York (1948–52), Brown Saltman (California), Heywood-Wakefield (Boston), and Ficks-Reed (Ohio).

Much of László's work in Europe was destroyed in World War II, but some of his American projects stand as testimonials to an imaginative designer who could build privacy into a structure afflicted with close adjacencies; who could make small spaces look large and large spaces look comfortable; who could, in short, provide a building of comfort and distinction, no matter what its purpose. **R.M.**

SAMUEL MARX

A devotee of American classicism, Samuel A. Marx (1885–1964) was an architect and designer of impeccable standards. While many of his peers working throughout the middle of the twentieth century pursued mass production and affordability with revolutionary zeal, he remained dedicated to the principles of proportion, form, and the highest quality of craftsmanship. And though his works are scarce and less known than those of Mies van der Rohe, an acquaintance whom he admired, or of Charles and Ray Eames, Marx has always attracted the admiration of connoisseurs of deco-inspired modernism.

Based in Chicago from 1910 until 1962, Marx produced much of his work for a coterie of private and corporate clients—among them financiers J. Paul Getty and Arthur Lehman and the actor/art collector Edward G. Robinson—creating highly visible projects, such as the interiors of May Department Store Co. and the Hotel Pierre, along with many magnificent private residences. Marx was especially distinguished for the way he brought together traditional cabinetmaking techniques and sumptuous materials with reductive design forms. A dedicated painter himself, he brilliantly integrated interiors with the artworks they featured. His place in the history of American design has only recently been more widely recognized, in part because so much of his work remained in private hands, but with the publication of more in-depth accounts along with exhibitions of his furniture, the importance of his contribution to an especially refined category of midcentury American design is now receiving its due.

Samuel Marx was born in Natchez, Louisiana, in 1885. His family belonged to a prosperous community of Jewish merchants that flourished in the southern town already famous for its millionaires. His childhood included the usual stepping-stones of privileged southern life, including being sent north to attend preparatory school and then to the Massachusetts Institute of Technology, where he earned his degree in architecture in 1907. He spent the next two formative years studying at the prestigious École des Beaux-Arts in Paris, including an extended grand tour visiting classical sites that provided him with a lifetime of inspiration and admiration for European architecture. And yet he never completely shed his devotion to the American Greek-revival styles so dominant in the south (one of his prized collections was of photographs of antebellum mansions).

At twenty-five, Marx was quite young when he won his first architectural commission to design the Isaac Delgado Museum of Art (the oldest fine arts institution in new Orleans,

ABOVE LEFT Portrait of Marx, c. 1941. **RIGHT** Marx did a handful of large-scale architectural and interior-design projects on the West Coast. The Tudor-revival home of Edward G. Robinson in Los Angeles was filled with modern masterpieces, and Marx's plans honored the importance and placement of the artwork. Adjacent to the house, Marx built a 2,000-square-foot art gallery. The minimalist influence of Ludwig Mies van der Rohe is evident in the dropped ceiling with hidden skylights supported by fossil-stone dividers.

OPPOSITE PAGE In 1937 Marx and his third wife, Florene May Straus, moved into a large apartment on North Astor Street in Chicago. Shortly thereafter the couple started to collect modern art seriously, displaying it prominently throughout their home. They bought major pieces by Braque, Picasso, and Modigliani. In the dining room, here, *Matisse's Variation on Still Life by de Heem* (or *La Desserte*), 1915, hangs over a wall-mounted cabinet in crackle lacquer with a paneled-mirror front. The malachite-green Parsons-style dining room table complements the large sections of drapery in the painting.

Above left: Chicago History Museum. HB-06282 Photographer Hedrich-Blessing. Right: Chicago History Museum. HB-07850 Photographer Hedrich-Blessing. Opposite Page: Chicago History Museum. HB-06194-Z Photographer Hedrich-Blessing.

it is now part of the New Orleans Museum of Art). With its deep portico providing shade and classical colonnade, the museum, completed in 1911, reflected both Beaux-Arts traditions and a sensitivity to vernacular conditions. Marx himself called its style "subtropical Greek," and it revealed an abiding concern for local conditions that continued to influence Marx's work throughout his career.

By the time the museum was built, Marx had already moved to Chicago and set up an architectural office with Fred Lebenbaum (after a brief stint as chief engineer at Shepley, Rutan, and Coolidge, the firm that inherited the practice of H. H. Richardson). His clients—advertising tycoons and executives—were drawn to Marx's ability to create an aura of grandeur without pretension, even for a corporate office. In 1915, when he married Margaret Schaffner, the daughter of a prominent men's clothing manufacturer, he was able to tap into another wealthy client base. The couple moved to the North Shore enclave of Glencoe, and the architect was soon building houses for well-to-do residents in the area. Early projects included the Chicago headquarters for the investment firm A. G. Becker, and a country estate for the industrialist Max Epstein. For the 1933 Century of Progress exhibition in Chicago, Marx designed the first aluminum train car for the Pullman Company. He also furnished the interiors of a home in Manhattan for the investment banker Arthur Lehman, whose family, like Marx's, had roots in the New Orleans cotton business. At the Lehman residence, Marx integrated art and furnishings with a consummate skill that showed off the art without compromising livability and comfort, a skill that became one of his hallmarks.

The Foreman residence in Glencoe, completed in the 1930s, was another fine example of his knack for creating humanely scaled grandeur. Marx designed the architecture as well as all the interiors with many of his signature gestures, such as an ornately carved plaster fireplace with a Victorian blue marble surround set against deep-violet-hued walls to echo the palette of a Renoir painting over the mantelpiece. The room was otherwise devoid of decorative detailing, a look that Liz O'Brien, in her definitive 2007 study *Ultramodern: Samuel Marx, Architect, Designer, Art Collector*, noted was probably influenced by French interiors of the day by Serge Roche and Emilio Terry. The front hallway had ivory and dark brown travertine floors and white walls; the staircase, often an opportunity for a Marxian flourish, had satin-finish chrome newels and a faux-malachite rail; the runner was made of clipped brown fur. In the dining room, the walls were covered in kappa shell, lending an air of pearlescent Orientalism then in vogue, while the woodwork was all silver-leafed. It is not entirely surprising that *Interiors* magazine, in an article from September 1941, referred to the Marx approach as "unctuous ornate modernism."

Marx achieved a high level of quality and stylistic consistency that he maintained throughout a long career. That consistency was due in part to the way he worked. Virtually all the furniture of his own design was produced in one place by the Chicago furniture maker William J. Quigley. Quigley was already an established master craftsman known for reproducing English and American antiques when Marx started working with the company. Quigley was one of a small coterie of high-quality furniture studios serving Chicago's most accomplished residential architects, such as David Adler. Dependent upon recent emigrant craftsmen

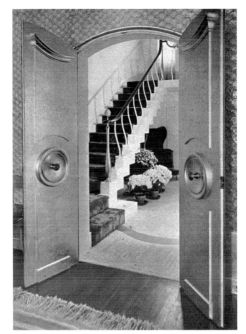

from Europe working in large factory spaces but using the most traditional hands-on techniques, the Quigley company carved woods as well as upholstered sofas, made classical window treatments, and also ornate frames. Local architects would commission entire houses of furniture from the company, resulting in a potentially long wait for orders to be filled. By the fifties, however, it was Marx alone who was keeping Quigley in business, with enough orders to support the entire company. Through collaborations with such talents as Quigley, and also with the noted textile designer Dorothy Liebes, whom he met in 1939, Marx was able to realize his dream of making a unified whole of both the architecture and interiors.

But it was his ability to translate European art trends into classical furniture forms that felt distinctly American that placed him in a unique category among midcentury designers. Always appreciated by collectors and furniture connoisseurs, Marx is now gaining wider admiration from a broader public interested in a level of quality not always associated with design of that period, and that acknowledgment is beginning to be reflected in the high prices at auction and antique dealers. In November 2007, Sotheby's sold a coffee table covered with glass tiles back-painted in silver-leaf from a Chicago apartment that Marx designed in 1949 for $73,000. While Marx would repeat favorite design motifs from project to project, with subtle variations in detail and finish, such furniture pieces were still custom-made for specific residences and have soared in price in recent years.

In the forties, Marx became increasingly known for designing retail and restaurant spaces. He had already redesigned the rotunda at the Hotel Pierre in New York soon after J. Paul Getty acquired the hotel in 1938 (Marx was involved in renovating several public rooms at the hotel through the fifties). In Chicago he attracted considerable attention for his ultrachic remodeling of the Pump Room at the Ambassador East Hotel and of the Tavern Club, with its plaster-cast cactus motif slyly referring to Prohibition. Known for cultivating a debonair persona, Marx was an active member of the famed Arts Club founded in 1916 that exhibited paintings by such modernists as Picasso, Duchamp, and Matisse, whose work Marx would later collect himself. In 1937 he designed the dining room, adding a touch of surrealism with windows decorated in plaster sculpted to look like heavy drapes and an exaggerated fireplace and mantelpiece, also entirely of plaster, that could have been drawn by a Disney animator. Marx even exhibited his own still life and abstract paintings at the Arts Club and even the Art Institute of Chicago, once telling a reporter that "I paint for my own amazement."

Marx was married three times. His first marriage ended in the late 1920s, and his second marriage, to Lora Flanagan, an art student at Cranbrook Academy of Art, lasted only a few years. In 1937 Marx, at age fifty-two, married Florene May Straus, whose father founded the May Department Store chain. This led to many retail and residential commissions, including the May Department Store on Wilshire Boulevard in Los Angeles, on which Marx collaborated with Albert C. Martin.

In terms of both architecture and interiors, the Morton D. May house in Ladue, Missouri, ranks as one of Marx's most forward-thinking projects. Designed for Florene's twenty-six-year-old nephew and the chairman of the May company, the house showed off Marx's talent for integrating International-style architecture, craftsman-level detailing, and local considerations. The low-lying, two-story structure fit easily into its gently rolling landscape, its walls made of concrete, locally quarried Bandera stone, and reclaimed handmade bricks. Ground-floor picture windows and second-floor strip windows lent the house a distinctly modernist flavor. Inside, a sweeping spiral staircase conjured the antebellum stairs of Marx's childhood, rendered as a glossy moderne abstraction. Marx's interest in textures was carried throughout the house, from the English oak–burled sideboard with leather knobs and lacquered pedestal to the oyster-white leatherette folding walls, gunmetal-gray rubber floor tiles, and clear-yellow hand-woven curtains created by the celebrated textile designer Dorothy Liebes.

It would be a mistake, however, to classify Marx's designs as derivative deco or moderne. His silhouettes were at once both more robust and more subtle. The dimensions were, in general, more generous and larger in scale than their European equivalents. In terms of materials, Marx didn't seem interested in the exotic woods and rarified finishes that enamored so many others. He preferred solid American woods, such as oak and burled elm, deployed in matched cuts and with strong grains to show that they too could look opulent and refined. His palette was sophisticated but decidedly neutral, and he opted for luxurious but restrained finishes: silver-leaf, lacquered white parchment, pearly kappa shell, fossil stone, and *cracquelaire* leather (suggesting the glazing on an antique Chinese vase) were some of his favorite treatments for furniture and interior surfaces.

In her thorough study of Marx's complete works, O'Brien devoted the most attention to "Florene and Sam at Home" and it is understandable why. Their apartment on North Astor Street is both home and manifesto, exhibiting a modernist style gentled by a deep appreciation for domestic comfort and a connoisseurship for placing art. Though the buildings Marx designed clearly reflected an awareness of International-style modernism as practiced by such European transplants as Mies van der Rohe, Marx to some degree refuted that influence, calling the style "intellectualized design" and even wasteful, he claimed, for not paying enough attention to climate and local materials. He was quoted in a 1945 profile published in *House Beautiful* saying, with particular foresight, that he preferred the "use of few materials, and those available locally."

The Marx apartment is a fine example of that belief: spaces are free of decorative flourishes, and a few strong materials provide solid counterpoints to an impressive art collection. In one room, Picasso's 1906 masterpiece *A Woman Plaiting Her Hair* hangs over a simple rectilinear mantelpiece made of fossil stone, one of his favorite materials. In the living room, mantelpiece and wainscoting merge to create a continuous stone frieze of rose-colored marble, offsetting the couple's first major acquisition, a large abstract still life by Braque, *Yellow Tablecloth* (1935).

Marx designed most of the furniture, with most of the upholstery by Dorothy Liebes and several light fixtures and chairs by William Haines. To accommodate a growing collection of fine Chinese ceramics, Marx designed several display cases finished in a crackle lacquer that soon became a favorite finish for many of his case goods. The handles were made of Lucite, and the inner panels were covered in gold leaf. Their art collection, including works by Picasso, Matisse, Bonnard, Miró, Giacometti, and others, eventually grew to be so strong that their bequests both to the Metropolitan Museum of Art and the Museum of Modern Art were considered among the most significant donations of modern art ever made to those institutions. In 1986 MoMA named the room where its Matisse paintings were hanging (many donated by Florene after Sam died and she had remarried) the Florene May Schoenborn room.

ABOVE TOP LEFT Marx did not design furniture collections, only individual pieces for specific projects. Here, a silver-leafed verre églomisé coffee table. It holds the record for the most expensive Marx piece sold at auction when it went for $73,000 at Sotheby's in November 2007. **TOP RIGHT** A coffee table with a base wrapped in leather with propeller-like shelves supporting a glass top is an unusually innovative shape for Marx. **BOTTOM LEFT** A pair of simple chests of drawers in ash is given a discreet varnish producing a gentle, otherworldly sheen. **BOTTOM RIGHT** An eight-drawer plinth-base cabinet is shown here with a crackle-lacquer, or craquelaire, finish, a favorite Marx technique.

OPPOSITE PAGE Marx designed the architecture and interiors for several residential projects in Glencoe, an affluent suburb of Chicago. Pictured here is a pair of silver-leafed doors against a kappa-shell wall treatment. The wood banister of the staircase had a faux malachite finish with chrome newels and the runner was made of clipped fur.

Marx designed most of the furnishings himself, without shying away from adapting basic shapes of others to suit his own preferences, as with the Jean-Michel Frank–inspired armchairs covered in a heavy textured tweed or the dining chairs actually designed by Donald Deskey for the Royal Metal Manufacturing Company that, O'Brien points out, Marx had redone, replacing the original perforated metal seats with tufted cushions.

In 1962 Florene and Sam Marx moved to New York in part to help oversee the installation of forty-four of their paintings that were included in *The School of Paris* (Paintings from the Florene May Schoenborn and Samuel A. Marx Collection), a traveling exhibition that opened at the Museum of Modern Art in 1965, a year after Marx died.

Like Tommi Parzinger, Paul László, and T. H. Robsjohn-Gibbings, Samuel Marx looked both to the past and the future in his designs to achieve a modern classicism that was both richly resonant in its materials but also distinctly American in its robustness. He chose to work with a relatively narrow scope of materials and, though refined, they were rarely flashy and served him well in his art-influenced approach, in which the demands of proportion and aesthetic control were always balanced against comfort and livable ease. **J.I.**

ABOVE Marx did several major projects for his wife's relatives. In 1952, he designed this 10,000-square-foot modern monumental home in Holmby Hills, Los Angeles, for Tom May, one of Florene's three brothers. Hollywood decorator William Haines provided most of the furnishings.

OPPOSITE PAGE In 1940 Marx designed an impressive International-style mansion in Ladue, Missouri, for Morton D. May, chairman of the May department store and Florene Marx's nephew. The exterior was radically different from any of the neighboring homes. On the interior, a dramatic swirling staircase, inspired by the antebellum mansions familiar to Marx from his Natchez, Missouri, childhood, brilliantly defined the house's angular and geometric exterior. Sadly, and despite the efforts of preservation groups, the house was demolished in 2005 to make way for a new development.

Opposite page: Chicago History Museum. HB-07051-F Photographer Hedrich-Blessing.

BIBLIOGRAPHY

MASTER BIBLIOGRAPHY

Eidelberg, Martin, ed. *Design, 1935–1965: What Modern Was.* New York: Harry N. Abrams, 1992.

Greenberg, Cara. *Op to Pop: Furniture of the 1960s.* Boston: Little, Brown, 1999.

Jackson, Lesley. *The Sixties: Decade of Design Revolution.* New York: Phaidon Press, 1998.

Marcus, George H. *Design in the Fifties: When Everyone Went Modern.* New York: Prestel, 1998.

Miller, R. Craig. *Modern Design, 1890–1990.* New York: Harry N. Abrams, 1990.

ADDITIONAL SOURCES

Oral History Project, The Art Institute of Chicago

Bancroft Library special collections, University of California, Berkeley

J. B. BLUNK

O'Brien, Gerard, and Mariah Neilson. Interview by Jeffrey Head, January 12, 2008.

MICHAEL COFFEY

Coffey, Michael. Interview by Todd Merrill and Erin Johnson, June 24, 2007. Transcript at Todd Merrill & Assoc., New York.

WENDELL CASTLE

Albrecht, Donald. *AutoPlastic: Wendell Castle, 1968–73.* Exh. cat. New York: R 20th Century Design, 2007.

Brown, Robert, Wendell Castle Oral History Interview, Archives of American Art, Smithsonian Institution, 1981.

Castle, Wendell. Interview by Julie V. Iovine, February 23, 2007.

Iovine, Julie V. "Plastic Fantastic," *The New York Times "T" Magazine,* 1 April 2007.

Newman Helms, Cynthia, ed. *Furniture by Wendell Castle.* Exh. cat. New York: Hudson Hills Press, in assoc. with the Founders Society, Detroit Institute of Arts, 1989.

JOHN DICKINSON

Bethany, Marilyn. "Living in Style." *New York Times,* April 11, 1982, p. SM48.

Brown, Erica. "Design Precision with Playfulness." *New York Times,* July 8, 1979, p. SM14.

———. *Interior Views: Design at Its Best.* New York: Viking Press, 1980.

Crocker, Sam. Interview by Jeffrey Head, February 21, 2008.

Geniesse, Jane. "John Dickinson: Down to bare bones." *New York Times,* May 4, 1978, p. C15.

Goldstein, Doris. "Playing on Furniture." *Art & Antiques* (February 1, 2007).

Green, Lois Wagner. "A Different Vision." *Interior Design* (August 1978): 178–83.

———. "Of Simplicity and Substance." *Interior Design* (August 1979): 198–201.

———. "Savoir-Faire in the Wine Country." *Interior Design* (August 1981): 220–25.

Gueft, Olga. "Jaguar in the Firehouse." *Interiors* (May 1967): 94–95.

Hill, June. "Fun Furnishings." *Chicago Tribune,* May 25, 1975, p. K8.

Los Angeles Times, "Party Performers." February 27, 1966, p. 30.

McKinley, Cameron Curtis. "Furnishings Created by San Francisco Interior Designers." *Architectural Digest* (April 1980): 48, 50, 52.

New York Times (special supplement). "90 Miles of Furniture on Display." October 18, 1965, p. 40.

Obituary of John Dickinson. *New York Times,* March 6, 1982, p. 10.

Safdie, Carlene. Interview by Jeffrey Head, February 18, 2008.

Skurka, Norma. "Pared-down elegance." *New York Times,* October 28, 1973, p. 322.

WHARTON ESHERICK

American Institute of Architects, Public Relations. News release. "AIA Announces Recipient of 1971 Craftsmanship Medal." February 28, 1971. American Craft Council Library, Wharton Esherick archival file.

Bascom, Bob, and Ruth Bascom. Interview by Erin Johnson, December 15, 2007. Transcript at Todd Merrill & Assoc., New York.

Benson, Gertrude. "Wharton Esherick." *Craft Horizons* (January 1959): 33–37.

Castle, Wendell, and Sam Maloof. "Wharton Esherick, 1887–1970." *Craft Horizons* (August 1970): 10–17.

Conroy, Sarah Booth. "Wood craftsman Esherick: holdout in an age of plastic." *Washington Post, Times Herald,* October 10, 1971, p. 161.

Craft Horizons. "The New American Craftsman: First Generation." (June 1966): 15–19.

Fine Woodworking. "Wharton Esherick: Museum Is Sculptor's Masterpiece." (Summer 1977): 45.

Grafly, Dorothy. "Wharton Esherick." *Magazine of Art* (January 1950): 9–11.

———. "Adventure in current design." *Christian Science Monitor* (February 27, 1932): 9.

Hoffman, Marilyn. "Individuality Wins." *Christian Science Monitor* (December 31, 1958): 6.

Interiors, "The Sculptural Environment of Wharton Esherick." (February 1959): 92–95.

Jewell, Edward Alden. "Show of contemporary American sculpture and water-colors opens at Whitney Museum." *New York Times,* Art in Review section, December 5, 1933, p. 30.

Kay, Jane Holtz. "It's crafted by heart, head, hand." *Christian Science Monitor* (January 24, 1969): p. 12.

Kellogg, Cynthia. "Families make sacrifice to aid furniture exhibit." *New York Times,* December 30, 1958, p. 30.

———. "American Design at the Fair." *New York Times,* April 6, 1958, p. SM52.

Keyes, Helen Johnson. "Sixteen New Interiors Assembled at New York's 1940 Fair." *Christian Science Monitor* (July 9, 1940): 6.

Laurer, Robert A., ed. *The Furniture and Sculpture of Wharton Esherick.* New York: Museum of Contemporary Crafts of the American Craftsmen's Council, 1959.

Levins, Hoag. The Wharton Esherick Website. www.levins.com/esherick.html (accessed December 17, 2007).

Metropolitan Museum of Art Bulletin. The Decorative Arts of the Twentieth Century section. Vol. 37, no. 3 (1979).

Miller, Charles. "Wharton Esherick's House and Studio." *Fine Homebuilding* (June/July 1984): 34–43.

New York Times. "Designs and crafts go on display today." March 2, 1954, p. 20.

——— (special supplement). "Wharton Esherick, a sculptor and furniture designer, dies." May 7, 1970.

Pepis, Betty. "To finish a table, add salt, pepper." *New York Times,* May 29, 1954, p. 18.

Philadelphia Museum of Art Bulletin. Contemporary American Crafts section. "Wharton Esherick." Vol. 87, nos. 371/372 (Fall 1991): 9.

Slesin, Suzanne. "Into the woods." *New York Times Magazine,* October 13, 2002. www.jstor.org.

Stone, Michael. "Wharton Esherick: Work of the Hand, the Heart, and the Head." *Fine Woodworking* (November/December 1979): 50–57.

Waltzer, Jim. "Into the Woods: Sculptor Wharton Esherick Thrived Amid Shanty-Chic." *Art & Antiques* (September 1997): 45–48.

Wilson, Janet. "Man of Wood." *Americana* (March/April 1984): 67–70.

Yarnall, Sophia. "Sculptured Wood Creates the Unique Interiors of the Curtis Bok House." *Country Life and the Sportsman* (June 1938): 67–69.

ARTHUR ESPENET CARPENTER

Brown, Robert. Interview by Erin Johnson, November 14, 2007.

Carpenter, Arthur Espenet. Craftsman Portfolio Questionnaire, dated May 9, 1974. American Craft Council, New York.

———. Curriculum vitae, dated December 6, 1982. American Craft Council, New York.

———. Interview by Kathleen Hanna, June 20 and September 4, 2001. Transcript, Archives of American Art Oral History Program, Smithsonian Institution, Washington, D.C.

———. "Reflections on the Chairs of Charles Eames." *Craft Horizons* (April 1973): 20–21ff.

———. "The Rise of Artiture: Woodworking Comes of Age." *Fine Woodworking* (January/February 1983): 98–103.

Carpenter, Tripp. Interview by Erin Johnson, November 17, 2007.

Herman, Lloyd E., ed. *Woodenworks: Furniture Objects by Five Contemporary Craftsmen: George Nakashima, Sam Maloof, Wharton Esherick, Arthur Espenet Carpenter, Wendell Castle.* Exh. cat. St. Paul: Minnesota Museum of Art, 1972.

Jeff Greef Woodworking. "An interview with Art Carpenter: A Career of Experiment in Design." www.jeffgreefwoodworking.com/int/carpenter/index.html (accessed November 15, 2007).

Mastelli, Rick. "Art Carpenter: The Independent Spirit of the Baulines Craftsman's Guild." *Fine Woodworking* (November/December 1982): 62–68.

Obituary of Arthur Espenet Carpenter. *New York Times,* June 5, 2006.

Stone, Michael. *Contemporary American Woodworkers.* Layton, Utah: Gibbs M. Smith, 1986.

———. "Espenet Style." *American Craft* (June/July 1982): 6–9.

PAUL EVANS & PHILLIP LLOYD POWELL

Interiors. Merchandise Cues section. "America House Abets Its Collections of Accessories with New Creative Furniture." (December 1961): 142.

———. "Sparkle and Shine." (January 1971): 42.

Interior Design. "Designer Dialogue Enlivens ASID/Palm Beach Meeting." (December 1975): 28.

———. Market section. "Paul Evans on His Own." (January 1981): 172.

———. "Think Tank Studio." (March 1981): 240–41.

Kellogg, Cynthia. "Exhibit of Crafts Mirrors the Past." *New York Times,* March 4, 1954, p. 31.

Reif, Rita. *New York Times,* May 9, 1957, p. 50.

Reading, Dorsey, and Philip Lloyd Powell. Interview by Todd Merrill and Julie Iovine, July 14, 2007. Transcript at Todd Merrill & Assoc. New York.

T. H. ROBSJOHN-GIBBINGS

Architectural Forum. "Hello There, Mr. Hadrian: Gibbings' Bathroom." (July 1951): 185.

———. "Marshall Field Rooms; Robsjohn-Gibbings Furniture Is Shown in Chicago Department Store House." (January 1948): 13.

———. "New Furniture Line." (January 1947): 116.

———. "Robsjohn-Gibbings and the Tall Bamboo." (October 1948): 54, 56.

Blair, Helen. "Decorator Believes in 'Timeless' Beauty." *Hollywood Citizen News,* February 28, 1938, p. 11.

Flint, Ralph. "Robjsohn-Gibbings: Chair Maitre." *Art News* (June 1942): 22–23, 47–48.

Hill, Barbara. "Streamlining the Past." *Country Life & the Sportsman* (November 1937): 76ff.

Holden, James. "Greek ideas potent now." *New York Sun,* February 18, 1939.

Hope, Henry R. "Black Magic and Modern Art." *College Art Journal* (Winter 1947/48): 116–20. www.jstor.com/.

Hoffman, Marilyn. "Robsjohn-Gibbings Gives Athens Apartment Classical Greece Furniture." *Christian Science Monitor* (June 20, 1962): 4.

House Beautiful. Issues from December 1946; October 1947; October 1948; May 1950; May 1951; May 1952; May 1954; May 1956.

Interiors. "Designers Are Important People." (November 1950): 96–97.

———. "Designs Bathroom of 1960." (July 1951): 14.

———. "Gibbings Circa '51: Designs for Widdicomb Furniture." (April 1951): 146–47.

———. "Mr. Gibbings Rides Again." (May 1952): 122–23.

———. "New Floor Lamp for Widdicomb." (March 1952): 144.

———. "New Gibbings Is Mellower: 55 New Pieces of Furniture, Designed for the Widdicomb Furniture Company." (May 1950): 110–11.

———. "Portrait." (April 1949): 23.

———. "The Elsie de Wolf Award Winners." (March 1962): 10, 201–6

Interior Design. "Glory That Is Greece; Greek Furniture by Robsjohn-Gibbings Designed for Saridis of Athens." (December 1961): 104–7.

———. "Hotel Atlantis." (March 1972): 98–101.

———. "Robsjohn-Gibbings to Design for Greek Firm." (December 1960): 181.

———. "Robsjohn-Gibbings: 25 Years of His Work." (May 1961): 122–31.

———. "Shop in Athens: E. Athiniotakis Jewelry Shop." (April 1966): 212–13.

———. "Viewpoint." (September 1972): 142–43.

Life. "The Color of Spectacle." (September 15, 1961): 78–83.

New York Times Magazine. "Color for Evening by American Design." March 13, 1938, n.p.

Obituary of T. H. Robsjohn-Gibbings. *Interior Design* (December 1976): 206–7.

Patterson, Augusta Owen. "Decoration & the Fine Arts." *Town & Country* (September 1939): 76ff.

Pencil Points. "Perspectives: From Oscar Wilde to Buffalo Bill." (July 1944): 62–63.

Progressive Architecture. "New Furniture Designed by T. H. Robsjohn-Gibbings." (February 1947): 69.

Robsjohn-Gibbings, T. H. "I Want to Be Alone." *House & Garden* (May 1945): 80–81.

———. "Sans Epoque." *Harper's Bazaar* (September 15, 1938): n.p.

Weale, Mary Jo. "Contributions of Designers on Contemporary Furniture Design." Ph.D. diss., Florida State University, Tallahassee, 1968, pp. 847–54.

Metropolitan Museum of Art Bulletin. "Recent Acquisitions." (Autumn 2001): 61.

WILLIAM HAINES

Arco, Hector. "The Style of Hollywood." *Washington Post,* Times Herald, December 28, 1969, p. 43.

California Arts & Architecture (August 1940): Art section.

Fox, Christy. "Decorator is much too busy to retire." *Los Angeles Times,* December 14, 1969, p. G2.

Goodman, Ezra. "Ringing up the curtain on William Haines." *New York Times,* June 5, 1949, p. X5.

Interiors. "Haines' Headquarters." (December 1949): 72–79.

Los Angeles Times. "Don't fence me in! West breeding bigger people, says designer." July 21, 1950, p. A1.

———. "Home shows; space attracts." May 2, 1948, p. 15.

Morgan, Gwen. "New quarters (well, nearly) for U.S. British ambassador." *Chicago Tribune,* October 31, 1969, p. A5.

Peak, Mayme Ober. "Hollywood's bed time stories." *Los Angeles Times,* July 5, 1936, p. 8.

Schifando, Peter, and Jean H. Mathison. *Class Act: William Haines, Legendary Hollywood Decorator.* New York: Pointed Leaf Press, 2005.

Schifando, Peter and Jean H. Mathison. Interview by Jeffrey Head, February 1, 2008.

Scott, John. "Wise stars utilize every spare minute—and at a profit." *Los Angeles Times,* October 30, 1932, p. B15.

———. "Picture actors morons—Yeah?" *Los Angeles Times,* December 6, 1931, p. B11.

Schallert, Edwin. "Stars' doors always open to Bill Haines." *Los Angeles Times,* February 11, 1934, p. A1.

Sullivan, Ed. "Looking at Hollywood." *Chicago Daily Tribune,* July 19, 1938, p. 11.

CHARLES HOLLIS JONES

DuPont. "Teflon, Zytel, Alathon, Lucite: Properties, Characteristics, and Applications at DuPont." Company cat. Ca. 1960.

The Graduate. Film, directed by Mike Nichols (Embassy Pictures Corporation, 1967).

Hollis Jones, Charles. Interview by Ron Fields, July 20, 2007. Los Angeles.

———. Interviews (by telephone and in person) Interviewed by Peter Wolf. January 2005–December 2007.

Hudson, Fred R., and Robert H. Rissman. "Hudson Rissman." Showroom cat. Ca. 1965.

Medill, Robert. "Crystalline Furniture Is Here." *Arts and Decoration* (April 1940): 8–11, 44.

Meikle, Jeffrey L. *Plastic: A Cultural History.* New Brunswick, N.J.: Rutgers University Press, 1995.

Progressive Architecture. "Plastics: The future Has Arrived." (October 1970): 64–109.

Owens, Mitchell. "Grosfeld House." *Elle Décor* (September 2007): 94–95.

ARTHUR ELROD

Architectural Digest. "Publisher's Chicago Contemporary" (November/December 1972): 56–63.

———. "The Quintessential Design for Art" (May/June 1972): 13–23.

———. Personal communication with Michael Calloway, September 13, 2007.

———. "Scale." *Home Magazine Decorating.* Published by the Los Angeles Times (1964): 26–43.

Interior Design. "Johnson Publishing, Co." (October 1972): 130–37.

Interiors. "News" (April 1974): 56–57.

Los Angeles Times. "It's like living in a sculpture." March 15, 1970, pp. M36–39.

MacMasters, Dan. "The life and happy times of Arthur Elrod." *Los Angeles Times,* April 21, 1974, pp. 52, 55.

Pasqualetti, Mari. Interview by Peter Wolf, July 23, 2007.

Rense, Paige. Keynote address for *Design in the Desert: Arthur Elrod.* Symposium sponsored by the Palm Springs Museum Architecture and Design Council, Palm Springs, Calif., February 12, 2005.

Toland, James. "Home Magazine House/1962." *Los Angeles Times,* June 24, 1962, pp. 11–25.

Waterman, Marybeth. Interview by Peter Wolf. September 15, 2007.

HARVEY PROBBER

Gura, Judith, "The Birth of the Modular." *Interior Design* (2003): 176–78.

———. *Harvey Probber: Modernist Furniture, Design and Graphics.* Exh. cat. New York: Sidney Mishkin Gallery, Baruch College/CUNY, 2003.

Interior Design. "An Interview with Harvey Probber: Pioneer in Contemporary Furniture Design." (May 1979): 231–35.

Interiors. "Harvey Probber in the D & D Building." (December 1967): 118–19.

———. "Harvey Probber States His Case." (June 1951): 120–23.

———. "The Probber Chair." (September 1949): 140.

Probber, Harvey. "What Price Fashion?" *Interior Design* (January 1990): 55.

JACK ROGERS HOPKINS

Craft Horizons, "Exhibitions," (December 1973): 45

Hopkins, Esther, Ann Begley, and David Begley. Interview by Jeffrey Head, December 8, 2007.

Interior Design "Market Spotlight," (May 1972): 60.

Landscape Architecture, "Laminated cherrywood sculpted tripod chair-coffee table." (July 1972): 299.

Lauria, Jo, and Suzanne Baizerman. *California Design: The Legacy of West Coast Craft and Style.* San Francisco: Chronicle Books, 2005.

Meilach, Dona Z. *Creating Modern Furniture: Trends, Techniques, Appreciation.* New York: Crown Publishers, 1975.

VLADIMIR KAGAN

Interior Design. "Art & Hear: An Urban Family Apartment." (January 1971): 90–95.

———. "Cooperative Venture." (November 1972): 86–91.

———. "Design—Present and Future." (August 1971): 174, 177.

———. "Finely Crafted Custom Designs from Vladimir Kagan." (June 1979): p. 120.

———. "Kagan: Fashion Institute of Technology, New York, Exhibit." (March 1980): 270–71.

———. "Structural Strategy." (June 1970): 30.

———. "Vladimir Kagan Reshapes Showroom Display." (January 1978): 108.

Interiors. "Kagan Designs for Grosfeld House." (August 1957): 114–16.

———. "Projections: Chemstrand's Exhibit at the D & D Show." (November 1965): 172–73.

———. "Young Man in an Old Tradition." (October 1953): 90–93.

———. "Vladimir Kagan and the Baroque Line." (December 1958): 114–17.

———. "Sensuous Sensibilities in the Space Age." (May 1970): 151, 172.

Kagan, Vladimir. *The Complete Kagan: Vladimir Kagan: A Lifetime of Avant-Garde Design.* New York: Pointed Leaf Press, 2004.

———. Interview by Todd Merrill and Julie Iovine, October 16, 2007. Transcript at Todd Merrill & Assoc. New York.

Saville, Laurel. *Design Secrets: Furniture: 50 Real-Life Projects Uncovered.* Exh. curated by Brooke C. Stoddard. Gloucester, Mass.: Rockport Publishers, 2006.

PAUL LASZLO

Architectural Forum. "Beverly Hills Men's Shop." (May 1948): 119.

———. "Four Houses by the Office of Paul Laszlo." (February 1944): 77–90.

———. "House for A. Rosenfield, Palm Springs." (October 1939): 270–71.

———. "House for a Warm Climate." (November 1945): 134–35.

———. "Hollywood House for H. Schiff." (February 1940): 120–21.

———. "House in Hollywood." (April 1940): 240–41.

———. "House in Beverly Hills for P. Laszlo." (August 1941): 109–11.

———. "House of Pressure-Molded Plastic." (September 1942): 148–49.

———. "Portrait." (May 1948): 26.

Architectural Record. "House Planned for Western Climate." (April 1940): 60–61.

———. "Front of Gold with Dual Meaning: Eddy Harth's, Beverly Hills, California." (May 1947): 102–3.

———. "House in Beverly Hills." (November 1950): 152–54.

Arts & Architecture. "House by Paul Laszlo." (September 1956): 31–33.

———. "Interiors by P. Laszlo." (February 1944): 27–29.

———. "Project for a Postwar House." (November 1944): 30–31.

———. "Shopping Center Designed for a Small Western Town Serves also Social and Civic Need." (October 1954): 26–27.

California Arts & Architecture. "Hillside House Designed by Paul Laszlo." (June 1941): 30–31.

———. "House on a Hillside." (October 1940): 1, 22–23.

———. "House Overlooking a Canyon." (October 1941): 32–33.

———. "Interiors by Laszlo, Inc." (June 1943): 30–31.

———. "Modern Hotel Rooms." (July 1942): 26–27.

———. "Modern Interiors in a Twenty-Two-Year-Old House in Beverly Hills." (May 1942): 27.

———. "My Own Home." (July 1938): 22.

———. "New Interiors: House for D. B. Burnstone." (February 1941): 30–31.

———. "New Shop" (December 1941): 28–29.

———. "Project for a Small House: Experimental House Designed by P. Laszlo." (September 1942): 28–29.

Laszlo, Paul. "Designing with Spirit: Interview with Paul Laszlo." Interview by Marlene L. Laskey, Oral History Program, University of California, Los Angeles, 1986.

———. "Paul Laszlo: Interior and Industrial Designer, Beverly Hills, California." Beverly Hills: Paul Laszlo, printed in Zurich, Switzerland, 1958.

Gueft, Olga. "Subterranean Atomic Suburbia." *Interiors* (February 1953): 70–71.

House & Home. "Every Room in This House Makes High-Style News." (April 1956): 206–7.

Interiors. "Carefree Life in a Steel Frame." (January 1949): 121–23.

———. "Contemporary Domestic Interior." (July 1950): 104–5.

———. "Man-Made Fieldstone Cliff in California." (September 1954): 78–79.

———. "Plexiglas Portals of Laszlo's House." (August 1949): 82.

———. "Ranch House into Poolside Lanai." (February 1956): 106–9.

———. "Spacious, Sculptured Beverly Hill Living Room with a Tropical View." (August 1959): 90.

———. "Specially Designed Components Make a Lush Setting for McCullough." (October 1958): 140–41.

———. "Two Stores with Grillework Accents." (June 1962): 115–17.

Pencil Points. "Small House for the Architect." (June 1940): 367–68.

———. "Small House on a Hillside." (March 1942): 165–67.

Rosas, C. A. "Modern Custom Furniture." *Architectural Digest* (August 1996): 30–32.

Time. "Rich Man's Architect." (August 18, 1952). www.time.com/time/printout/0,8816,816723,00.html (Accessed July 25, 2007).

PHILIP & KELVIN LAVERNE

Franklin, Corinne. "LaVerne: 'Poetry of the Soul.'" *Nashville Banner,* February 12, 1963, p. 8.

Hieronymus, Clara. "LaVerne art represents innovation at Cheekwood." *Nashville Banner,* February 12, 1963, p. 8.

Interiors. "For Your Information." (April 1963): 14.

———. "The Inimitable Lavernes." (March 1968): 118–19.

———. "Treasures, Buried or Not." (August 1972): 134c.

Interior Design. "Market Spotlight" (March 1971): 86.

———. "Market Spotlight" (July 1972): 32.

———. "One-Man Show" (March 1963): 182.

Kellog, Cynthia. "Designers in Loyal Opposition." *New York Times,* May 12, 1957, p. SM27.

Laverne, Kelvin. Interview by Todd Merrill and Julie Iovine, June 7, 2007. Transcript at Todd Merrill & Assoc., New York.

New York Times. "Coffee tables are art also." July 5, 1960, p. 37.

———. "Antiqued bronze without waiting 4,000 years." February 29, 1968, p. 32.

Salkaln, Elaine Mayers. "The Invisibles." *New York Times Magazine,* April 18, 2004. www.nytimes.com/2004/04/18/magazine/18LAVERNE.html?ex=1208664000&en=40cc3c f1aefcb47f&ei=5070 Accessed June 25, 2007.

SAM MALOOF

Adamson, Jeremy. *The Furniture of Sam Maloof.* Exh. cat. Washington, D.C., and New York: Smithsonian American Art Museum in association with W.W. Norton, 2001.

Azar, George Baramki. "Carving Out a Niche in Furniture." *Christian Science Monitor* (March 1995): 11.

Chang, Jade. "The Craft Master." *Metropolis* (April 2007): 224–32.

Defenbacher, Daniel. "Design and the Craftsman." *First Annual Conference of American Craftsmen.* New York: American Craftsmen's Council, 1957.

Doblin, Jay. "The Position of Crafts in America Today." *First Annual Conference of American Craftsmen.* New York: American Craftsmen's Council, 1957.

Dunkel, Tom. "Best Seats in the House." *Smithsonian* (November 2001): 38.

Goode, Stephen. "Maloof Turns Furniture into Art." *Insight on the News.* Volume 18, issue 1. January 2002: p. 36ff. Accessed ebscohost.com on October 2, 2007.

Johnstone, Rob. "Grace and Peace: Sam Maloof and Jimmy Carter." *Woodworker's Journal* (February 2006): 20–22.

Los Angeles Times. "Maloof: the craftsman, completeness without ornamentation." February 12, 1961, p. A18ff.

Maloof, Sam and Wendell Castle. Interview by Edward J. Cook, Charles F.Montgomery, introduced by Dennis Fitzgerald at SOFA, Chicago, October 6, 2001. Transcription at Furniture Society.org. www.furnituresociety.org/frames/fcol/home/shtml (accessed August 5, 2007)

Rozas, Diane. "Velvet Touch." *Art & Antiques.* Volume 30, issue 4. (April 2007): Accessed www.ebsochost.com on October 2, 2007.

Scott, Barrie, and Joanna Werch Takes. "Sam Maloof's Brand New Digs." *Woodworker's Journal* (April 2002): 24.

Silberman, Robert. "Sam Maloof." *American Craft* (April/May 2002): 62–67.

Takes, Joanna Werch. "Class with a Woodworking Legend." *Woodworker's Journal* (December 2000): 46 and ff.

Turner, Tran. "Perfection in Form." *Craft Arts International.* (1998): 92–95.

Walentine, Ellis. "Museums Honor Great Woodworkers." *Woodworker's Journal* (October 2001): 16ff.

Herman, Lloyd E., ed. *Woodenworks.* Exh. cat.

SAMUEL MARX

Architectural Forum. "Department Store for the May Stores, Los Angeles, California." (May 1940): 353–57.

———. "House in Ladue, Missouri." (December 1942): 44–48.

———. "Indoor-Outdoor Living Room." (December 1944): 100–107.

———. "The Pump Room—Samuel A. Marx, Architect." (July 1940): 21–24.

House Beautiful. "Furniture That Starts as Architecture: Grounded in the Past . . . but Appreciative of the Future." (October 1948): 148–51ff.

———. "Meet Samuel Marx." (November 1945): 120.

House & Garden. "Profile of a House." (January 1945): 50–53.

Interior Design & Decoration. "A new impetus for design." (April 1941): 22–25.

Interiors. "Snapshots—Samuel A. Marx." (September 1941): 41–43.

———. "The Year's Work: These Five Interiors . . . Have Been Completed by Leading Designers and Architects." (August 1942): 29–54.

O'Brien, Liz. *Ultramodern: Samuel Marx, Architect, Designer, Art Collector.* New York: Pointed Leaf Press, 2007.

JAMES MONT

Art Digest. "Turkish Designer Produces Modern Décor." (October 15, 1934): 14.

Cartier, Inc. letter to James Mont, July 1, 1966.

Chicago Daily Tribune. "He does everything for stranded pair except marry them." June 3, 1948, p. 1.

———. "Note to husband may be clew to beauty's suicide." April 26, 1937, p. 18.

Contract between James Mont and Ellis K. Orlowitz. Initialed by Mont and signed by Orlowitz, dated February 4, 1963.

Friedland, Gerald. Interview by Todd Merrill and Erin Johnson, July 5, 2007. Transcript at Todd Merrill & Assoc., New York.

Greenfield, June. Interview by Erin Johnson, September 13, 2007.

Karfo, John. Interview by Todd Merrill and Erin Johnson, October 26, 2007. Transcript at Todd Merrill & Assoc., New York.

Los Angeles Times. "Actress suicide and joke party linked by odd quirk of date." April 26, 1937, p. 1.

———. "Actress' death puzzle cleared." May 2, 1937, p.3.

Mont, James. 1937. Design for service bar. US Patent 106,317, filed August 25, 1937, and issued October 5, 1937.

———. 1947. Design for a sofa. US Patent 152,720, filed February 5, 1947, and issued February 15, 1949. (References cited on patent: Montgomery Ward & Co., Catalog No. 131, 1939–1940, sofa on right side of lower cut on p. 477 and davenport in left center of p. 481)

———. Letter to the editor. *New York Times*, March 7, 1936, p. 14.

———. 1953. Portable bar. US Patent 171,856, filed November 3, 1953, and issued March 30, 1954.

———. *The Young Physician's Road Map.* New York: Modern Mode Furniture Co., n.d.

New York Times. "Advertisement." April 17, 1949, p. 42.

———. "Business Records." October 29, 1934, p. 24.

———. "Business Records, Judgments." May 25, 1933, p. 37.

———. "Business Records, Bankruptcy Proceedings." September 26, 1946, p. 51.

———. "Chair to be Auctioned." January 19, 1947, p. 53.

———. "Classifieds." March 28, 1951, p. 39; April 20, 1952, p. W18; June 1, 1952, p. W14.

———. "Court firm on high bail." November 26, 1939, p. 43.

———. "Display advertisement." January 25, 1946, p. 14.

———. "Hostess ends life as 100 guests wait." April 25, 1937, p. 1.

———. "Lans Galleries get Lehne Building." November 19, 1938, p. 30.

———. "Manhattan Mortgages." January 5, 1950, p. 51; September 4, 1952, p. 42.

———. "Manhattan Transfers." March 27, 1952, p. 51; April 4, 1953, p. 19; December 8, 1953, p. 2; November 15, 1956, p. 60.

———. "Oriental motif seen in modern furniture." November 20, 1946, p. 38.

———. "Space-saving devices to expand a tiny apartment." December 24, 1945, p. 12.

Orlowitz, Sheri. Interview by Todd Merrill, August 23, 2007. Transcript at Todd Merrill & Assoc., New York.

Owens, Mitchell. "Call it Auntie Mame chinoiserie." *New York Times*, April 4, 1996. Accessed on www.query.nytimes.com on September 7, 2007.

———. "Furniture a gun moll would have found just swell." *New York Times*, June 15, 1997. www.query.nytimes.com on September 7, 2007.

———. "Godfather of exotic modernism." *New York Times*, October 6, 1996. www.query.nytimes.com on September 7, 2007.

Roche, Mary. "Living-dining room makes available a table with plenty of elbow space." *New York Times*, June 12, 1945, p. 16.

———. "Home, accents, and contrasts." *New York Times*, July 1, 1945, p. 61.

Schneider, Sondra. "Mid-Century Madness." *Ocean Drive* (November 2006): 332–38.

Villinsky, Beth. "James Mont: The Bad Boy of Mid-Century Modern." *Christie's Magazine.* June 10, 1997.

Washington Post. "Bride ends life as 100 guests wait." April 25, 1937, p. 1.

———. "London docks baby assured childhood fit for princess." November 20, 1948, p. 1.

GEORGE NAKASHIMA

Cohen, Edie. "The Nakashima Mystique." *Interior Design* (March 2007): 303–4.

Connors, Thomas. "Woodworking." *Interior Design* (October 2006): 248–55.

Kaufmann, Edgar, Jr. "Nakashima, American Craftsman." *Art in America* (December 1955): 30–33.

Nakashima, George. "A Feeling for Material." *California Arts & Architecture* (November 1941): 30–31.

———. "Actuality." *Perspecta: The Yale Architectural Journal* (1955): 6–33.

Nakashima, Mira. Interview by Todd Merrill and Julie Iovine, July 14, 2007. Transcript at Todd Merrill & Assoc., New York.

———. *Nature, Form & Spirit: The Life and Legacy of George Nakashima.* New York: Harry N. Abrams, 2003.

Herman, Lloyd E., ed. *Woodenworks.* Exh. cat.

TOMMI PARZINGER

Book, Jeff. "Heir of Refinement." www.departures.com/ad/ad_o799_parzinger.html (accessed July/August 1999).

Cameron, Donald, and Nancy Chase. Interview by Todd Merrill and Julie Iovine, June 17, 2007. Transcript, Todd Merrill & Associates, New York, NY.

Connoisseur, The. (October 1939): 203–4.

Interior Design. (September 1972): pp 162–65.

Interiors. (February 1949): pp 104–9.

———. (October 1949): 134.

———. (January 1950): 124.

———. (December 1950): 124–25.

———. (June 1954): 14.

House & Garden. "An Artist's Apartment." (July 1937): 36–37.

———. "Room of the Month." (April 1963): 142

Interior Design. Market section (December 1983): 252.

Kellog, Cynthia. "'Inside out' design is shown in homes." *New York Times*, August 9, 1952, p. 16.

Life. "Silver in Modern Dress: Tommi Parzinger Introduces New Designs to U.S." (1939).

Maggio, Gene. "Four-poster bed returns to fashion." *New York Times*, May 29, 1957, p. 47.

New York Times. "Covered dishes of hammered silver." November 11, 1948, p. 34.

———. "Finished noted in showroom of furniture." September 19, 1957, p. 32.

———. "New candlesticks designed in brass." August 10, 1949, p. 27.

———. "Store adds fabric to ease shopping." November 20, 1959, p. 27.

———. "Treasured chests." January 5, 1958, p. SM41.

Pepis, Betty. "Collection of home furnishings is a one-man show by Parzinger." *New York Times*, November 3, 1950, p. 22.

———. "Design in leather used on furniture." New York Times, April 4, 1950, p. 34.

———. "Hallmarks of designers." *New York Times*, January 22, 1950, p. 164.

———. "Lacquer tones up furniture group." *New York Times*, March 27, 1954, p. 14.

———. "Marble makes the top." *New York Times*, December 10, 1950, p. SM24.

———. "Rattan stressed in new furniture." *New York Times*, October 16, 1952, p. 35.

———. "Redesigned Rattan." *New York Times*, November 25, 1951: p. 229.

———. "Varied, expert use of color adds charm to a development house on Long Island." *New York Times*, May 19, 1954, p. 28.

Reif, Rita. "For an inviting bachelor apartment." *New York Times*, March 10, 1970, p. 46.

Robertson, Nan. "Toyland puts mere reality in dull light." *New York Times*, November 9, 1957, p. 34.

Roche, Mary. "New ideas and inventions." *New York Times*, March 14, 1948, p. SM44.

———. "Modern through the ages." *New York Times*, January 16, 1949, p. SM34.

Storey, Walter Rendell. "Home decoration: Viennese ideas in modern interiors." *New York Times*, December 8, 1940, p. 79.

———. "Modern furniture gains lightness." *New York Times*, August 21, 1938, p. 103.

———. "Modern handicrafts in new vigor and variety." *New York Times*, May 8, 1938, p. 134.

Tommi Parzinger Collection. Cooper-Hewitt Library, National Design Museum, Smithsonian Institution, New York.

SILAS SEANDEL

Chicago Tribune. "Art Note." May 17, 1966, p. B3.

Interior Design. "Art Forms for Interiors." (January 1970): 21.

———. "Architectural Sculpture." (September 1973): 66.

———. "Silas Seandel Milestone." (December 1982): 126–27.

Interiors. "Sculpture for Architecture." (May 1971): 62.

LaJoie, Raymond A. "Welder's Torch with Artist's Touch." *Christian Science Monitor* (February 9, 1968): 19.

New York Times. Display ad. November 14, 1965, p. 27.

Seandel, Silas. Interview by Todd Merrill and Erin Johnson, July 23, 2007. Transcript at Todd Merrill & Assoc., New York.

KARL SPRINGER

Diaz, Jesus. Interview by Erin Johnson, June 19, 2007. Transcript at Todd Merrill & Assoc., New York.

Eckman, Mark. Interview by Todd Merrill and Erin Johnson, August 20, 2007. Transcript at Todd Merrill & Assoc., New York.

Esten, John, and Rose Bennett Gilbert. *Manhattan Style*, pp. 185–87. Boston: Little, Brown, 1990. Images by George Chinsee.

Interior Design. "Gallery of Fine Furnishings." (July 1980): 222–25.

———."The Bristol." (March 1974): 122–33

New York Times. Advertisement. October 31, 1965, p. SMA 73.

———. "Inside Story." January 3, 1971, p. SM32.

———. "The Craft Artists." April 13, 1980, p. SM44.

Plumb, Barbara. "Money isn't everything." *New York Times*, June 25, 1967, p. SM21.

Springer, Karl. 1978. Trademark registration for Karl Springer signature. US Registration no. 1151607, filed September 29, 1978, registered April 21, 1981, and cancelled April 27, 2002.

Springer, Karl. Obituary. *Interior Design* (January 1992): 44.

Thurman, J. "Deco Interpretations: Karl Springer on the Upper East Side." *Architectural Digest* (November 1989): 228–35.

Wetson-Springer, Ilene. Interview by Todd Merrill, July 17, 2007. Transcript at Todd Merrill & Assoc., New York.

Wilkie, Angus. "Everything You Need to Know about Karl Springer." *Elle Décor* (October 2001): 104–10.

Young, May. Interview by Todd Merrill and Erin Johnson, June 20, 2007. Transcript at Todd Merrill & Assoc., New York.

EDWARD WORMLEY

Barter, Judith A., ed. "Shaping the Modern: American Decorative Art at the Art Institute of Chicago, 1917–65." *The Art Institute of Chicago Museum Studies* (2001). www.jstor.com.

Dunbar: Janus Collection. Berne, Ind.: Dunbar Furniture Corp. of Indiana, 1960.

Edward J. Wormley and Edward Crouse Papers, 1831–1991 (bulk 1907–1997). Division of Rare and Manuscript Colls., Cornell University Library.

Gueft, Olga. "Edward J. Wormley: A Portrait; Dunbar Furniture." *Interiors* (November 1956): 92–105.

Gura, Judith. "Rediscovering Wormley." *Interior Design* (February 1997): 22ff.

———. "Three New Showrooms for Dunbar." *Interiors* (March 1952): 122–29.

Gura, Judith, Chris Kennedy, and Larry Weinberg, eds. *Edward Wormley: The Other Face of Modernism.* Exh. cat. New York: DESIGNbase/Lin-Weinberg Gallery, 1997.

Hiesinger, Kathryn B., and George H. Marcus. *Landmarks of Twentieth-Century Design: An Illustrated Handbook.* New York: Abbeville Press, 1993.

House Beautiful. "Meet Edward Wormley." (March 1945): 75.

———. "Edward Wormley." (October 1966): 270–72.

House & Garden. "Active Furniture, New Mobility Gives a Dining Room Two Lives." (October 1945): 81–83.

———. "Room with an About-Face." (April 1945): 60–61.

———. "Wormley: His Work Stems from a Deep Interest in People—How They Live, What They Need." (July 1947): 30–31.

Interior Design. "Dunbar Re-Done." (December 1967): 130–33.

———. "Two Views of Contemporary Living." (September 1962): 140–41.

Interiors. "Art Treasures Framed within the Geometric Clarity of a Collector's Country Home." (July 1960): 70–75.

———. "Cause for Applause: Lightolier's Italian Lamps and Wormley Décor." (November 1950): 130–33ff.

———. "Edward Wormley's Architectural League Proposal." (June 1964): 40ff.

———. "Franklin Harward Fabrics, New York: Edward Wormley's Bright Banners in Massed Array." (December 1958): 90.

———. "How the Seisel Agency Does It: Offices by Wormley." (September 1955): 126–27.

———. "The Elsie De Wolfe Award Winners." (March 1962): 10ff.

———. "Janus House, Wormley's Sentimental Journey for Dunbar." (October 1957): 155–61.

———. "Mansion on the Eleventh Floor: The Mazer Apartment." (January 1963): 66–73.

———. "Name Designers Introduce High Style to Do-It-Yourself." (February 1955): 20.

———. "New Furniture Designs." (March 1950): 123.

———. "Office Furniture: Dunbar distinguishes the executive . . . " (January 1959): 130–33.

———. "Survey of the New Furniture Reveals a New Level of Design, an Old Standard of Workmanship." (March 1949): 136–37.

———. "Well-Lighted Mansion on Wheels." (May 1955): 117–19.

———. "Wormley's Easel, Print Showpiece Designed for Art Society." (January 1956): 12.

———. "Wormley's Way: Residential Furniture for Dunbar." (November 1963): 112–14.

Kaufmann, Edward, Jr. "Edward Wormley: 30 Years of Design." *Interior Design* (March 1961): 190.

———. "What is Modern Industrial Design." *Museum of Modern Art Bulletin.* (Fall 1946). www.jstor.com (accessed November 14, 2007).

Little, Helen. "Wormley: The Eclectic Taste of One of America's Great Furniture Designers." *House Beautiful* (October, 1948): 164–68.

Piña, Leslie, and Nadir Safai, eds. Dunbar: Fine Furniture of the 1950s. Atglen, Pa.: Schiffer Publishing, 2000.

Smith, C. Ray. "Edward Wormley." *Interior Design* (January 1987): 250–53.

Wormley, Edward J. *Everyday Art Quarterly, Walker Art Center, Minneapolis* (1953): 8. www.jstor.com (accessed November 14, 2007).

ACKNOWLEDGMENTS

I would like to thank my grandparents Nathan and Margaret Merrill and my father Duane for instilling in me an early appreciation of American history and the importance of the surviving artifacts that remind us of our great shared American past.

Dung Ngo, my editor at Rizzoli, walked into my shop unknown to me in the spring of 2007. We began a random discussion that quickly lead to the subject of there not being a comprehensive book on the decorative modern furniture of the late twentieth century. I offered my just-completed proposal for such a book and he handed me his card. It is with deep appreciation that I acknowledge his immediate understanding and continued support of this project because of which we have made it to press successfully and miraculously within one year.

I would also like to thank my staff at Todd Merrill Antiques who has endured an extra layer of work throughout the past year. Especially to Erin Johnson who was hired to research and manage this project and ended up contributing text for five chapters. It is with great thanks that I acknowledge the contributions of all those listed below. This book was largely drawn from original sources, as such without the extra effort of many it could not have been completed. Above all, the love and support of my family and wife, Lauren.

—TODD MERRILL

For sheer serendipity, I am thankful for a maintenance man at the *New York Times* who several years ago drew my attention to a large cache of moulding scrapbooks in a forgotten closet, cataloging the design coverage of the *New York Times* magazine and special supplements from the mid-forties through the seventies. I was able to rescue many and have found them to be perfect time capsules—from the articles themselves and their telling style of illustrations to the accompanying advertisements—of the era covered in our book.

I would like also to acknowledge with deep appreciation the objective insights of Deyan Sudjic, the director of the London Design Museum and also the always brilliant perceptions of William L. Hamilton, my former colleague at the *New York Times* and, above all and always, the patient indulgence and love of my sons, Christopher and Cooper.

—JULIE V. IOVINE

INTERVIEWS

Dorsey Reading
Philip Lloyd Powell
Donald Cameron
Nancy Chase
Kelvin LaVerne
Michael Coffey
Mark Eckman
Ilene Wetanson-Springer
June Greenfield
Sheri Orlowitz
Mae Young
Jesus Diaz
Bob and Ruth Bascom
Silas Seandel
Vladimir Kagan
Rina and Norman Indictor
Peter László
Wendell Castle
Mira Nakashima
Charles Hollis Jones
John Karfo
Gerald Friedland
Geoffrey Bradfield
Ron Fields
Mari Pasqualetti
Marybeth Waterman
Esther Hopkins
David Hopkins
Ann Begley
Mariah Nielsen
Gerard O'Brien
Peter Schifando
Jean Mathison
Carlene Safdie
Sam Crocker
Joan and Jory Probber

INSTITUTIONS

Cooper-Hewitt, National Design Museum Smithsonian Institution. Library staff: Steven van Dyk, Elizabeth Broman, Jennifer Cohlman. Images & Reproductions: Jill Bloomer.

Archives of American Art, Smithsonian Institution. Reference Services: Marisa Bourgoin, Wendy Hurlock Baker.

New York Public Library

New-York Historical Society
American Craft Council Library: David Shuford
Museum of Fine Arts, Boston
Chicago History Museum
Huntington Library
Nashville Public Library
The Anna-Maria and Stephen Kellen Archives Center for Parsons the New School. Libraries: Jessica Brieman.
Philadelphia Museum of Art
Wharton Esherick Museum
San Francisco Museum of Modern Art
The Detroit Institute of Arts
The Metropolitan Museum of Art
Los Angles County Museum of Art
The Getty Research Institute
UCLA, Charles E. Young Research Library
Cornell University Division of Rare and Manuscript Collections
Architecture and Environmental Design Library, Arizona State University Libraries

ORIGINAL COMMISSIONED PHOTOGRAPHY FOR TODD MERRILL ANTIQUES

Barron Claiborne
Joe Cernius
Ryan Alosio
David Sullivan
Sheldon Collins

RIZZOLI

Dung Ngo
Ellen Cohen
Charles Miers
Alexandra Tart
Sandy Gilbert-Freidus

MGMT. DESIGN

Alicia Cheng
Asad Pervaiz
Franklin Vandiver

RESEARCHERS / CAPTIONS

Erin Johnson
David Carpenter
Troy Seidman

TODD MERRILL & ASSOCIATES

David Carpenter
Joe Cernius
Gabrielle Auerbach
Jennifer Kaplan
Troy Seidman
David Sullivan
Bruno Kozar
John Marin
Fernando Munoz
Micheal Bruno
Christina Juarez
Marylin White
Eric Chapeau
Pedro AuCapina
Angel Puma
Carolyn Young

AUCTION HOUSES

Christie's: Jason Stein
Sotheby's: James Zemaitis, Blair Hance
Wright: Richard Wright, James Potsch
Sollo/Rago: John Sollo, Anthony Barnes
Bonhams & Butterfields: Frank Maraschiello
LA Modern Auctions: Shannon Loughrey
Treadway/Toomey Auctions: Lisanne Dickson
Phillips de Pury: Marcus Tremonto

DEALERS

PS Modernway: Courtney Newman
Reform Gallery: Gerard O'Brien
Eric Philippe
Moderne Gallery: Bob Aibel
Liz O'Brien
Bill Moore

The antiques trade is built on documentation; it is the foundation by which we evaluate and authenticate. The decorative modern furniture of the late twentieth century represents probably the last relatively undocumented era in furniture making. It is my hope that this book inspires many more. **T. M.**

First published in the United States
of America in 2008 by:

Rizzoli International Publications, Inc.
300 Park Avenue South
New York, NY 10010
www.rizzoliusa.com

ISBN-13: 978-0-8478-3053-4
Library of Congress Control Number: 2008927571

Editors: Dung Ngo, Ellen Cohen
Design: MGMT. design
Production: Maria Pia Gramaglia, Kaija Markoe

Distributed to the U.S. trade
by Random House, New York

Printed and bound in China

2008 2009 2010 2011 2012 / 10 9 8 7 6 5 4 3 2 1

PAGES 2 & 3 A white lacquered, metal studded
Chest-on-Stand by Tommi Parzinger, c. 1950.

PAGE 4 A detail of a Philip Lloyd Powell's hand carved
oak, slate, and silver leaf pedestal table, 1960.